T0377319

Sport, War and Society in Australia and New Zealand

Sport and war have been closely linked in Australian and New Zealand society since the nineteenth century. Sport has, variously, been advocated as appropriate training for war, lambasted as a distraction from the war effort, and resorted to as an escape from wartime trials and tribulations. War has limited the fortunes of some sporting codes – and some individuals – while others have blossomed in the changed circumstances.

The chapters in this book range widely over the broad subject of Australian and New Zealand sport and their relation to the cataclysmic world wars of the first half of the twentieth century. They examine the mythology of the links between sport and war, sporting codes, groups of sporting individuals and individual sportspeople. Revealing complex and often unpredictable effects of total wars upon individuals and social groups which as always, created chaos, and the sporting field offered no exception.

This book was originally published as a special issue of *The International Journal of the History of Sport*.

Martin Crotty has research interests that encompass masculinity, sports history and Australian society at war. He is an Associate Professor and lectures in History at the University of Queensland and is the author or co-editor of a number of books in these fields including *Anzac Legacies: Australians and the Aftermath of War* (2010) and *Turning Points in Australian History* (2009).

Robert Hess has a long-standing interest in the history of Australian Rules football. He is an Associate Professor and lectures in Sport History at Victoria University, Melbourne, and is the current Managing Editor of *The International Journal of the History of Sport*.

Sport in the Global Society: Historical Perspectives

Series Editors: Mark Dyreson and Thierry Terret

Titles in the Series

Sport, War and Society in Australia and New Zealand
Edited by Martin Crotty and Robert Hess

Global Perspectives on Sport and Physical Cultures
Edited by Annette R. Hofmann, Gerald Gems and Maureen Smith

Games and Sporting Events in History
Organisations, performances and impact
Edited by Annette R. Hofmann, Gerald Gems and Maureen Smith

Brazilian Sports History
Edited by Maurício Drumond and Victor Andrade de Melo

A Global History of Doping in Sport
Drugs, Policy, and Politics
Edited by John Gleaves and Thomas Hunt

American National Pastimes – A History
Edited by Mark Dyreson and Jaime Schultz

Delivering Olympic and Elite Sport in a Cross Cultural Context
From Beijing to London
Edited by Fan Hong and Lu Zhouxiang

East Asia, Geopolitics and the 2012 London Games
Edited by J. A. Mangan and Marcus Chu

Encoding the Olympics
The Beijing Olympic Games and the Communication Impact Worldwide
Edited by Luo Qing and Giuseppe Richeri

Gymnastics, a Transatlantic Movement
From Europe to America
Edited by Gertrud Pfister

London, Europe and the Olympic Games
Historical Perspectives
Edited by Thierry Terret

'Manufactured' Masculinity
Making Imperial Manliness, Morality and Militarism
J.A. Mangan

Mapping an Empire of American Sport
Expansion, Assimilation, Adaptation
Edited by Mark Dyreson, J.A. Mangan and Roberta J. Park

Militarism, Hunting, Imperialism
'Blooding' The Martial Male
J.A. Mangan and Callum McKenzie

Olympic Aspirations
Realised and Unrealised
Edited by J.A. Mangan and Mark Dyreson

Post-Beijing 2008: Geopolitics, Sport and the Pacific Rim
Edited by J.A. Mangan and Fan Hong

Representing the Nation
Sport and Spectacle in Post-Revolutionary Mexico
Claire and Keith Brewster

Rule Britannia: Nationalism, Identity and the Modern Olympic Games
Matthew Llewellyn

Soft Power Politics – Football and Baseball in the Western Pacific Rim
Edited by Rob Hess, Peter Horton and J. A. Mangan

Sport and Emancipation of European Women
The Struggle for Self-fulfilment
Edited by Gigliola Gori and J. A. Mangan

Sport and Nationalism in Asia
Power, Politics and Identity
Edited by Fan Hong and Lu Zhouxiang

Sport and Revolutionaries
Reclaiming the Historical Role of Sport in Social and Political Activism
Edited by John Nauright and David K. Wiggins

Sport and Urban Space in Europe
Facilities, Industries, Identities
Edited by Thierry Terret and Sandra Heck

Sport, Bodily Culture and Classical Antiquity in Modern Greece
Edited by Eleni Fournaraki and Zinon Papakonstantinou

Sport in the Cultures of the Ancient World
New Perspectives
Edited by Zinon Papakonstantinou

Sport in the Middle East
Edited by Fan Hong

Sport in the Pacific
Colonial and Postcolonial Consequencies
Edited by C. Richard King

Sport, Literature, Society
Cultural Historical Studies
Edited by Alexis Tadié, J. A. Mangan and Supriya Chaudhuri

Sport, Militarism and the Great War
Martial Manliness and Armageddon
Edited by Thierry Terret and J. A. Mangan

Sport Past and Present in South Africa
(Trans)forming the Nation
Edited by Scarlet Cornelissen and Albert Grundlingh

The 1984 Los Angeles Olympic Games
Assessing the 30-Year Legacy
Edited by Matthew Llewellyn, John Gleaves and Wayne Wilson

The Asian Games: Modern Metaphor for 'The Middle Kingdom' Reborn
Political Statement, Cultural Assertion, Social Symbol
Edited by J. A. Mangan, Marcus P. Chu and Dong Jinxia

The Balkan Games and Balkan Politics in the Interwar Years 1929–1939
Politicians in Pursuit of Peace
Penelope Kissoudi

The Beijing Olympics: Promoting China
Soft and Hard Power in Global Politics
Edited by Kevin Caffrey

The History of Motor Sport
A Case Study Analysis
Edited by David Hassan

The New Geopolitics of Sport in East Asia
Edited by William Kelly and J.A. Mangan

The Politicisation of Sport in Modern China
Communists and Champions
Fan Hong and Lu Zhouxiang

The Politics of the Male Body in Sport
The Danish Involvement
Hans Bonde

The Rise of Stadiums in the Modern United States
Cathedrals of Sport
Edited by Mark Dyreson and Robert Trumpbour

The Triple Asian Olympics
Asia Rising – the Pursuit of National Identity, International Recognition and Global Esteem
Edited by J.A. Mangan, Sandra Collins and Gwang Ok

The Triple Asian Olympics – Asia Ascendant
Media, Politics and Geopolitics
Edited by J. A. Mangan, Luo Qing and Sandra Collins

The Visual in Sport
Edited by Mike Huggins and Mike O'Mahony

What is the Future of Sport History in Academia?
Edited by Duncan Stone, John Hughson and Rob Ellis

Women, Sport, Society
Further Reflections, Reaffirming Mary Wollstonecraft
Edited by Roberta Park and Patricia Vertinsky

Sport, War and Society in Australia and New Zealand

Edited by
Martin Crotty and Robert Hess

LONDON AND NEW YORK

First published 2016
by Routledge
2 Park Square, Milton Park, Abingdon, Oxon, OX14 4RN, UK

and by Routledge
711 Third Avenue, New York, NY 10017, USA

Routledge is an imprint of the Taylor & Francis Group, an informa business

© 2016 Taylor & Francis

All rights reserved. No part of this book may be reprinted or reproduced
or utilised in any form or by any electronic, mechanical, or other means,
now known or hereafter invented, including photocopying and recording,
or in any information storage or retrieval system, without permission in
writing from the publishers.

Trademark notice: Product or corporate names may be trademarks or
registered trademarks, and are used only for identification and
explanation without intent to infringe.

British Library Cataloguing in Publication Data
A catalogue record for this book is available from the British Library

ISBN 13: 978-1-138-67706-7

Typeset in Times New Roman
by RefineCatch Limited, Bungay, Suffolk

Publisher's Note
The publisher accepts responsibility for any inconsistencies that may have
arisen during the conversion of this book from journal articles to book chapters,
namely the possible inclusion of journal terminology.

Disclaimer
Every effort has been made to contact copyright holders for their permission to
reprint material in this book. The publishers would be grateful to hear from any
copyright holder who is not here acknowledged and will undertake to rectify
any errors or omissions in future editions of this book.

Contents

Series Editors' Foreword	ix
Citation Information	xi
Notes on Contributors	xiii

1. Introduction: Sport, War and Society in Australia and New Zealand   1
   Martin Crotty and Rob Hess

2. Exploding the Myths of Sport and the Great War: A First Salvo   3
   Wray Vamplew

3. Australasia's 1912 Olympians and the Great War   19
   Bruce Coe

4. Missing in Action? New Perspectives on the Origins and Diffusion
   of Women's Football in Australia during the Great War   32
   Rob Hess

5. Fronting Up: Australian Soccer and the First World War   51
   Ian Syson

6. The Role of Sport for Australian POWs of the Turks during the
   First World War   68
   Kate Ariotti and Martin Crotty

7. Men Who Defaulted in the Greatest Game of All: Sport, Conscientious
   Objectors and Military Defaulters in New Zealand 1916–1923   81
   Greg Ryan

8. 'Carry On': The Response of the Victorian Football League to the
   Challenges of World War II   94
   Bruce Kennedy

9. W. N. 'Bill' Carson: Double All Black, Military Cross Recipient   111
   Lynn Charles McConnell

10. The Controversial Cec Pepper and the Australian Services Cricket Team:
    The Test Career That Never Was   119
    Peter Crossing

Index	135

Series Editors' Foreword

On January 1, 2010 *Sport in the Global Society*, created by Professor J.A. Mangan in 1997, was divided into two parts: *Historical Perspectives* and *Contemporary Perspectives*. These new categories involve predominant rather than exclusive emphases. The past is part of the present and the present is part of the past. The Editors of *Historical Perspectives* are Mark Dyreson and Thierry Terret.

The reasons for the division are straightforward. *SGS* has expanded rapidly since its creation with over one hundred publications in some twelve years. Its editorial teams will now benefit from sectional specialist interests and expertise. *Historical Perspectives* draws on *The International Journal of the History of Sport* monograph reviews, themed collections and conference/workshop collections. It is, of course, international in content.

Historical Perspectives continues the tradition established by the original incarnation of *Sport in the Global Society* by promoting the academic study of one of the most significant and dynamic forces in shaping the historical landscapes of human cultures. Sport spans the contemporary globe. It captivates vast audiences. It defines, alters, and reinforces identities for individuals, communities, nations, empires, and the world. Sport organises memories and perceptions, arouses passions and tensions, and reveals harmonies and cleavages. It builds and blurs social boundaries, animating discourses about class, gender, race, and ethnicity. Sport opens new vistas on the history of human cultures, intersecting with politics and economics, ideologies and theologies. It reveals aesthetic tastes and energises consumer markets.

By the end of the twentieth century a critical mass of scholars recognised the importance of sport in their analyses of human experiences and *Sport in the Global Society* emerged to provide an international outlet for the world's leading investigators of the subject. As Professor Mangan contended in the original series foreword: "The story of modern sport is the story of the modern world—in microcosm; a modern global tapestry permanently being woven. Furthermore, nationalist and imperialist, philosopher and politician, radical and conservative have all sought in sport a manifestation of national identity, status and superiority. Finally for countless millions sport is the personal pursuit of ambition, assertion, well-being and enjoyment."

Sport in the Global Society: Historical Perspectives continues the project, building on previous work in the series and excavating new terrain. It remains a consistent and coherent response to the attention the academic community demands for the serious study of sport.

Mark Dyreson
Thierry Terret

Citation Information

The chapters in this book were originally published in *The International Journal of the History of Sport*, volume 31, issue 18 (December 2014). When citing this material, please use the original page numbering for each article, as follows:

Chapter 1
Introduction: Sport, War and Society in Australia and New Zealand
Martin Crotty and Rob Hess
The International Journal of the History of Sport, volume 31, issue 18 (December 2014) pp. 2295–2296

Chapter 2
Exploding the Myths of Sport and the Great War: A First Salvo
Wray Vamplew
The International Journal of the History of Sport, volume 31, issue 18 (December 2014) pp. 2297–2312

Chapter 3
Australasia's 1912 Olympians and the Great War
Bruce Coe
The International Journal of the History of Sport, volume 31, issue 18 (December 2014) pp. 2313–2325

Chapter 4
Missing in Action? New Perspectives on the Origins and Diffusion of Women's Football in Australia during the Great War
Rob Hess
The International Journal of the History of Sport, volume 31, issue 18 (December 2014) pp. 2326–2344

Chapter 5
Fronting Up: Australian Soccer and the First World War
Ian Syson
The International Journal of the History of Sport, volume 31, issue 18 (December 2014) pp. 2345–2361

CITATION INFORMATION

Chapter 6

The Role of Sport for Australian POWs of the Turks during the First World War
Kate Ariotti and Martin Crotty
The International Journal of the History of Sport, volume 31, issue 18 (December 2014) pp. 2362–2374

Chapter 7

Men Who Defaulted in the Greatest Game of All: Sport, Conscientious Objectors and Military Defaulters in New Zealand 1916–1923
Greg Ryan
The International Journal of the History of Sport, volume 31, issue 18 (December 2014) pp. 2375–2387

Chapter 8

'Carry On': The Response of the Victorian Football League to the Challenges of World War II
Bruce Kennedy
The International Journal of the History of Sport, volume 31, issue 18 (December 2014) pp. 2388–2404

Chapter 9

W. N. 'Bill' Carson: Double All Black, Military Cross Recipient
Lynn Charles McConnell
The International Journal of the History of Sport, volume 31, issue 18 (December 2014) pp. 2405–2412

Chapter 10

The Controversial Cec Pepper and the Australian Services Cricket Team: The Test Career That Never Was
Peter Crossing
The International Journal of the History of Sport, volume 31, issue 18 (December 2014) pp. 2413–2428

For any permission-related enquiries please visit:
http://www.tandfonline.com/page/help/permissions

Notes on Contributors

Martin Crotty teaches History at the University of Queensland, Australia. He has written in the fields of sports history, masculinity studies and the experiences of Australians during and in the aftermath of World War I.

Robert Hess is an Associate Professor in Sport History with the Institute of Sport, Exercise and Active Living in the College of Sport and Exercise Science at Victoria University, Melbourne, Australia.

Wray Vamplew is Emeritus Professor of Sports History at the University of Stirling and Visiting Research Professor at the International Football Institute, University of Central Lancashire, UK. He has been Managing Editor of *The International Journal of the History of Sport* since 2010. His current research is focused on a history of the British sports club.

Bruce Coe is an Australian private scholar and Olympic historian who is a member of the Australian Society for Sports History and the International Society of Olympic Historians.

Ian Syson is a Senior Lecturer in Literary Studies at Victoria University, Melbourne, Australia. He is writing a cultural history of soccer in Australia.

Kate Ariotti is a Lecturer in Australian History at the University of Newcastle, Australia. Her work focuses on the impact of wartime imprisonment on Australians during the First World War, specifically how those affected by captivity in Turkey coped with the unique challenges it posed.

Greg Ryan is Dean of the Faculty of Environment, Society and Design at Lincoln University, New Zealand. He has authored or edited five books and written numerous articles on the history of sport in New Zealand with a particular emphasis on cricket and rugby.

Bruce Kennedy is a retired Australian civil servant, and has recently become a published historian and statistician in Australian Rules football. He is currently researching and writing another book relating to the Victorian Football League and the two world wars. His other historical and statistical studies include cricket.

Lynn Charles McConnell is a writer/editor in New Zealand who is studying History as a mature student at Massey University. He has written 18 books and is the compiler of the *Encyclopedia of New Zealand Cricket*. During an award-winning career in newspaper

NOTES ON CONTRIBUTORS

and online journalism, he has specialised in sports but also has an interest in military history.

Peter Crossing is a secondary school chemistry teacher and cricket coach. He has had many years' involvement as a player, coach, committeeman and President of Prospect District Cricket Club, Adelaide, South Australia. He has had numerous book reviews published in the *Canberra Times*.

Introduction: Sport, War and Society in Australia and New Zealand

Martin Crotty[a] and Rob Hess[b]

[a]School of History, Philosophy, Religion and Classics, The University of Queensland, Brisbane, Australia; [b]College of Sport and Exercise Science, Victoria University, Melbourne, Australia

The papers in this special collection had their genesis at 'Sporting Traditions XIX', the biennial conference of the Australian Society for Sports History (ASSH). Held in Canberra over three days and four nights in July 2013, the event was ambulatory in that each day of the conference was held at a different location in the nation's capital. On Thursday, July 4, the proceedings were hosted by *The International Journal of the History of Sport* as part of its commitment to regional workshop/conferences designed to foster new scholarship in the discipline. The theme for this day of the conference was 'Sport, War and Society in Australia and New Zealand', and, fittingly, all papers were delivered within the confines of the iconic Australian War Memorial (AWM). Dr Brendan Nelson, Director of the AWM, was on hand to welcome delegates and he officially opened the programme by offering a reflection not only on his leadership role at the Memorial but also on his own experiences as the former Minister for Defence (2006–2007) in the Australian federal government. This address set the scene for the keynote lecture of Professor Wray Vamplew, and the varied range of papers that followed.

Part of the impetus for the day was the fact that the conference was being held on the eve of commemorations associated with the centenary of the Great War, hence the title of 'Anzac Centennial' for this collection of papers. However, even though the first units of the Australian Imperial Force were raised in August 1914, it has been the grouping together of the Australian and New Zealand Army Corps (Anzacs) in Egypt prior to the landing at Gallipoli in April 1915, and their subsequent involvement in the conflict at Anzac Cove and more broadly on the Western Front, that has attracted ongoing attention from writers and historians. While a growing band of scholars have taken an interest in the sporting and recreational activities of Australian and New Zealand military personnel (either behind the lines or in prisoner-of-war camps), and there have been some significant explorations of the impact of war on sport in the domestic sphere (especially in terms of the recruitment of athletes and the backlash against the continuance of organised sporting competitions), no collection of academic essays has ever been dedicated to gathering together the latest work on these topics from an antipodean perspective.

In this context, it is important to note that the papers are not narrowly restricted to themes and issues associated with sport and the Great War. True to our original brief as editors, this collection encompasses the gamut of inter-connections between sport, war and society in Australia and New Zealand across time, hence the inclusion of relevant organisational histories and biographical material related to World War II.

To conclude, it is appropriate to thank all those delegates who attended the Canberra conference of ASSH and provided feedback to the presenters. We also extend our gratitude not only to the contributors but also to those colleagues who spent considerable time and energy in providing detailed critiques of all the submissions. Finally, we thank Routledge for their generous support of the conference and the publication of this assembly of papers.

Exploding the Myths of Sport and the Great War: A First Salvo

Wray Vamplew

School of Sport, University of Stirling, Stirling, UK

> This article examines the connection between sport and the First World War. It challenges the conventional wisdom that the athleticism associated with a public school education made a significant contribution to the British war effort. Additionally it argues that athleticism had a negligible influence on elementary school pupils who comprised the bulk of the military forces. It also suggests that while army authorities eventually accepted that sport had a positive role to play and made it a compulsory element of military training, it also existed as an escape from hostilities rather than just preparation for them.

> Serious sport has nothing to do with fair play. It is bound up with hatred, jealousy, boastfulness, disregard of all rules and sadistic pleasure in witnessing violence: in other words it is war minus the shooting.

George Orwell, 'The Sporting Spirit,' *Tribune*, December 14, 1945.

Sport and War: Fact, Myth and Conventional Wisdom

The theme of this paper is a questioning of the veracity of existing work on the subject of sport and the First World War; essentially it asks 'why should we accept what has been said?'. It concentrates on the research findings – and the evidence used – of those who have established the current conventional wisdom on the topic. The metaphorical title of the article is not intended to be disrespectful to previous critics, several of whom are cited in this article, but merely to indicate that they sniped at specific individual targets whereas this salvo is intended to present a broader critique.

Two sporting images of British troops have become part of Britain's collective memory of the First World War: a Christmas Day football match in 1914 between British and German troops and, more generally, men advancing into battle kicking a football ahead of them. There is an element of truth in each belief but the research of Iain Adams has demonstrated that neither holds up fully to scrutiny. Certainly British and German troops fraternised during the Christmas 1914 period over perhaps 20 miles of the British lines, but a detailed search for (and of) evidence suggests that 'it is improbable that a "proper" football match occurred', though 'it would seem highly likely that football was played in a true playful manner in many places'.[1] Moreover the 'football charges' were limited to 10 months between late September 1915 and early July 1916, involved few military units and indeed possibly occurred only twice.[2] Neither story is totally false and that is a danger with myths: the element of truth around which they are based offers a degree of protection from common-sense rejection. Unless historians undertake serious and comprehensive research, such myths can distort the true picture and allow misinformed conventional wisdom to go unchallenged. The 'Christmas football match' and the 'football charge' are what might be termed micro-level 'myths'. However, there are possibly myths at the macro-level which also need to be investigated.

A recent special issue of this journal focused on sport and the First World War.[3] It suggested several new(ish) research findings including that the presence of British and American forces helped spread the playing of football and basketball throughout France, and that German troops who watched prisoners of war playing sport began to prefer such sporting activities to their traditional Turnen gymnastics, with their officers actually encouraging such playing in the later years of the war to improve morale and reduce the risk of desertion.[4] However, much of the volume invoked an old tenet that:

> in the Anglo-Saxon world at least, sport had for some time been a way of preparing soldiers for war.[5]

This conventional view echoed that in Mason and Riedi's major study of sport in the armed services:

> The belief that sport and war were in some sense the same, that sport was 'mimic war' and war only the 'greater game', was certainly firmly held in the late Victorian and Edwardian public schools.[6]

And only last year, in an academic article on cricket and the First World War, John stated:

> public schoolboys in England were conditioned to believe that the values, skills and abilities which permitted one to excel in sport were analogous to those which were required to prevail in warfare.[7]

Public School Sport and Preparation for War: The Evidence?

This perceived relationship between public school sport and warfare was epitomised in the famous poem *Vitaï Lampada* by Henry Newbolt, a late Victorian lawyer, novelist and poet. Verse one suggests that public school sport – or at least cricket – was a character-forming activity.

> There's a breathless hush in the Close to-night
> Ten to make and the match to win
> A bumping pitch and a blinding light,
> An hour to play and the last man in.
> And it's not for the sake of a ribboned coat,
> Or the selfish hope of a season's fame,
> But his Captain's hand on his shoulder smote
> 'Play up! play up! and play the game!'.

And a subsequent verse maintains that this character served the nation well in times of need on the battlefields of the Empire.

> The sand of the desert is sodden red,
> Red with the wreck of a square that broke;
> The Gatling's jammed and the Colonel dead,
> And the regiment blind with dust and smoke.
> The river of death has brimmed his banks,
> And England's far, and Honour a name,

But the voice of a schoolboy rallies the ranks:
'Play up! play up! and play the game!'.[8]

Newbolt thus postulated a link between sport in the so-called public schools (in reality private institutions for the privileged) and preparation for war. Military men such as General Sir Horace Smith-Dorran concurred. In a speech at Harrow in 1917 he claimed that 'the best material for leading troops came from those who had public school training of which such an important part consists of games and sports'.[9]

This idea was later taken up by academics. One of the first was physical educator McIntosh who in 1968 declared that 'by the end of the [nineteenth] century it was not the public school system in general but the playing fields that were associated with the imperial battlefields'.[10] Historian Best also identified a close link between public school sport and militarism:

> There was a clear relationship between militarism and sport in the British public schools. Sport concerned the military in two ways: firstly, as the straight road to physical health and strength indispensable to the good soldier; secondly, because of the special value attributed to team games in training the essential qualities of the officer and leader.[11]

But the major proponent has been Mangan who, building on the idea of 'athleticism' – a concept which he placed at the heart of public school culture – saw 'the public school embrace of the Games Cult as military preparation' and maintained 'English playing fields were recognised training grounds for imperial battlefields'.[12] His path-breaking book *Athleticism in the Victorian and Edwardian Public School: The Emergence of an Educational Ideology*, published in 1981, has become the seminal reference on education and athleticism. In it he postulated that

> physical exercise taken considerably and compulsorily, in the sincere belief of many, however romantic, misplaced or myopic, that it was a highly effective means of inculcating valuable instrumental and impressive educational goals: physical and moral courage, loyalty and co-operation, the capacity to act fairly and take defeat well, the ability to command and obey.[13]

His later research has been dominated by his 'foremost scholastic preoccupation, interest and indeed fascination – the makings of masculinity through the medium of the playing field'.[14] A major aspect of this work has been to consolidate the link between athleticism and militarism.

His basic contention is that a form of social engineering took place in the mid-nineteenth century that civilised the public schools.[15] This was based on the introduction of compulsory team games, notably cricket and rugby, and specifically to the value system around how they should be played. Upright conduct was expected as part of the fair play code that ensured controlled manliness rather than brutality.[16] Moreover, public schoolboys in Britain were conditioned to believe that the values, skills and abilities which permitted them to excel in sport were analogous with those which were required to prevail in warfare. As Mangan puts it, 'the games field and the battlefield became closely intertwined in the period leading up to the First World War and it was team games like rugby and cricket that were supposed to give Englishmen an inherent superiority when it came to the supreme sacrifice in battle'.[17] It was 'on the sacred playing field – the public school *sanctus sanctorum* – [that] courage, determination and endurance for battle were honed'.[18] Mangan cites the headmaster of Sherbourne who maintained that the vital characteristics of a military officer were 'self-control, self-discipline, hardiness and perseverance' and then quotes himself as saying it is a truism that 'the most effective means of acquiring those qualities was the school playing field'.[19]

The nub of the argument that has become conventional wisdom is that Britain's educational institutions for the upper and middle classes used sport in a way that its practitioners could easily and effectively adopt for military purposes. The logical chain runs as follows: public schools played sport in a particular way; this way of playing encouraged certain characteristics that could be transferable into warfare; many military officers attended public school; ergo public school sport was helpful to the war effort.[20] However, I would argue that this view has become conventional wisdom without being appropriately tested. It has been recycled not researched. Where is the real evidence that this occurred? That many army officers attended public school and that games were played at those schools is a correlation but not a proof.

To my mind Mangan conflates two aspects of the public school: school life in general and school sport in which 'the ferocity of keenly-contested house matches helped create a hardened imperial officer class'.[21] Begging the question of how we know they were ferocious, should not more emphasis be placed on school life more generally which was, to quote Mangan himself, 'frequently a physical and psychological struggle for survival against hunger, cold and callousness in one form or another'.[22] Public schools taught their pupils the life skills to survive 'bullies, beatings, battles and bruises' in a micro-world that was 'hard, harsh and brutal'.[23] The boys may have played sport often but school life was there constantly so which might have the greatest socialisation influence?

One line of evidence that Mangan utilises is contemporary poetry. Mangan sees the link between playing sport and preparing for war as not just the aggression of the playing fields or even the qualities that were engendered there, but also the martial rhetoric in the exhortations of visiting speakers, headmasters' addresses, and chaplains' sermons and heroic poetry. He states that the relationship between sport and war 'became a significant feature of the schools well before the great war and was expressed extensively in verse' and that 'highly influential agents of indoctrination into militarism, however difficult it may be to measure their influence with any precision, were the prose, "poetry" and paintings that enveloped the public schoolboy at school and at home'.[24]

I have reservations with poetry as a line of evidence. The engagement mentioned in the second verse of *Vitaï Lampada* (quoted above) is the Battle of Abu Klea in Sudan in January 1885. As a note of historical accuracy it was not a Gatling that jammed but a Gardner machine gun: how much of the rest of the poem is also subject to poetic license?[25] Poetic metaphor is no substitute for hard empirical evidence. Nevertheless Mangan is less concerned with historical accuracy and more with how the poetry reflected emotions and attitudes. He sees the poetry as being used to promote militarism in the schools and also to reflect the views of the boys themselves. He accepts that much of the writing was second-rate, but argues that this did not detract from the emotion or meaning of the verses which were intended not merely to stir the boys but to 'instruct ... and persuade'.[26] There is a presumption that the influence of the poets was positive but, as Mangan rightly accepts, 'it is impossible to assess with certainty the influence of the rhetoric' though, against all statistical reasoning, he then maintains 'it may have been, and probably was, deeply influential'.[27] Elsewhere, despite noting that the impact of the poets 'cannot be measured with any precision', he claims their influence was 'extraordinary and extensive'.[28]

Mangan's work is more literate than numerate. Occasionally he uses broad quantified terminology – as when he claims that games fanaticism at Marlborough involved the 'majority' of the boys[29] – but generally he prefers to rely on the subtlety of language rather than the precision of numbers to persuade readers of the plausibility of his arguments. He writes well but even the finest prose cannot disguise the fact that statistically we do not know what proportion of public schools adopted an educational policy formally encouraging the development of athleticism with its compulsory games and associated character-building or what proportion of military officers were educated at public schools. The answers may be 'the vast majority' but this needs to be shown not assumed.

Even if we look less quantitatively, there are still unanswered questions. As partially closed communities public schools were in a position to impose athleticism on their students, but we do not know whether the boys actually accepted the ramifications of the code. To what extent did they merely pay lip service and then get on with trying to win however they could? Was it compliance rather than commitment? Mangan acknowledges that in the main the boys played games for enjoyment not for their moral attributes.[30] Were they indoctrinated by osmosis? Did playing sport automatically endow the boys with military capabilities? Or did they accept the tenets of athleticism at all? What I am asking is whether there were more Flashmans than Tom Browns? We just do not know. Certainly there were boys who opposed athleticism; Mangan himself notes the factions at Marlborough.[31] Too many academics have simply bought into the athleticism story without considering whether the substance matched the rhetoric.

In a scholarly case study of Old Wykehamists (those who had studied at Winchester), Mangan demonstrates the variation in the perceived experiences of students at that school.[32] This, however, must weaken the general thrust of the athleticism as successful training for war. That not all the boys would be gung-ho for sport infers that they might not have shared the martial doctrines purportedly underlying the playing of games. He also notes the downgrading of games at Shrewsbury.[33] It should also be noted that it was not just the athletes who fought courageously during the First World War.[34] The more we accept differences between schools, between houses, between headmasters and housemasters and between pupils, the weaker any generalisation must become. Mangan himself accepts that 'complexity was a feature of the public school embrace of the Games Cult as military preparation'.[35] Indeed 'complexity was a feature of middle-class athleticism and its associated constellations, patterns and trends'.[36]

There is also a definitional problem. Despite Mangan's basic definition of athleticism remaining unchanged in his later publications, its application as a concept by himself and his followers has become so broad, so subtle and so complex as to encompass almost anything the user wishes it to include. Once it is argued, as done by an acolyte of Mangan, that 'athleticism was an ideology that was always individually interpreted and utilised', you are on a slippery slope to rendering the definition meaningless for analytical purposes.[37]

Sporting Ability, Military Skills and Transferability

Some of the team games played at public schools also featured in officer sport. Certainly football and the army had long-standing connections. In January 1851 a team representing the 93rd Sutherland Highlanders beat one from Edinburgh University in a football match.[38] The Royal Engineers won the Football Association (FA) Cup in 1875 and an Army Football Association was formed in 1881. Yet the skills of football and cricket (to use the sport that featured in *Vitaï Lampada*) were not in themselves military assets.

Other sports, however, offered skills that could be readily transferable to martial requirements. There was a public schools shooting tournament – the Ashburton Shield – but, even though it was team competition, it does not appear to be highlighted as character-building in the athleticism literature. The shooting butts at the schools were probably associated with the cadet corps of the schools, though Mangan's study of Winchester suggests that many boys did not take the defence corps seriously.[39] This reinforces Best's earlier view that at least before 1900 the corps do not seem 'to have given any significant military enthusiasm and expertise' though, as he notes, there were 'immense differences between schools'.[40] There thus may or equally, based on the evidence, may not have been a spillover from this particular public-school sport to martial skills.

However, it would seem that at officer level the emphasis was not on games but on equestrianism. Indeed 'officers spent an extraordinary large proportion of their time hunting' and, although the glory days of the military steeplechase had gone by the end of the nineteenth century, racing too remained a popular officer activity.[41] Add to these sports the polo and pig-sticking practiced abroad and equestrian sport can be seen as central to an officer's sporting life.

All were considered by some military men to assist the human capital formation of the army officer. Lt. Col. E.A.H. Alderson considered hunting took up 'the fighting education of the young Officer just where the barrack-square and the drill-field can go no further'; Baden-Powell, the hero of Mafeking, thought pig-sticking and polo 'an exceptionally practical school for the development of horsemanship and of hardiness in the use of arms while mounted'; Major General Knox maintained that nobody had 'done so much as has the fox and foxhound to foster the cult of character, quick decision, and nerve so necessary for leadership in war'; and Lt. Col. E.D. Miller thought 'the same qualities which bring a man to the front at polo are required by anyone who aspires to lead men'.[42] Additionally a writer in *Bell's Life* argued that senior officers encouraged their juniors to ride in steeplechases 'because it excites that courage, presence of mind and skill in horsemanship without which their glorious achievements of Balaclava and Inkerman would never have been recorded'.[43] Vamplew and Kay have argued that horseracing, where the rider was always just one fall away from paralysis, demanded more courage than football and rugby, especially after hacking was prohibited in those sports, or cricket with its pads and a bat with which to protect one's person.[44] Some jump meetings organised for military riders often had a course deliberately more severe than at conventional steeplechases.[45] Lowerson has noted that, after the failures of the Boer War, the general discussion on occupational competency, a result of Britain's struggle in international economic competition, was widened to include the instrumentality of sport in military training.[46] However, efforts by some military reformers to restrict equestrian sport for officers proved futile and in 1911 the Army Council declared that hunting had 'special military value' and polo possessed 'distinct military advantages'.[47]

Hunting, steeplechasing, polo and pig-sticking accustomed men to the taking of physical risks. Certainly these activities needed horsemanship and courage on horseback (rather than on the playing field). None of these sports were part of the public schools' extracurricular programme. Despite Arnold's proscription of field sports at Rugby – a stance also taken by some other public school headmasters – such sports continued, albeit in a more rationalised and organised form, at Eton and elsewhere. However, these were not the courage-promoting activities of riding to hounds and racing over fences, but the less dangerous pursuits of foot beagling and angling.[48] The necessity to own horses for their equestrian activities forced officers to have substantial private incomes and restricted entry to the regiments to those who could afford an officer lifestyle. They may well thus have been class-based activities as field sports 'largely defined the rural upper-classes in Britain'.[49] Many of the younger members of this group would have attended public school but the link is with their social class not necessarily their school life.

There was one sport that was virtually exclusive to the military. Although now shorn of its martial connections, when the modern pentathlon was introduced to the Olympics in 1912, it had distinctive military attributes. Indeed the invented tradition – used to seal its place in the Olympics – is that its five components of riding, shooting, fencing, swimming and running were based on the 'adventures of a liaison officer whose horse is brought down in enemy territory; having defended himself with his pistol and sword he swims across a raging river and delivers the message on foot'.[50] Certainly, as Heck, the scholarly authority on the event, points out, the early modern pentathlete was strongly connected to military service and military officers dominated the entries at the first Olympic event.[51] It may be of significance that at its Olympic debut the target for the shooting was not a conventional circle but the outline of a soldier.[52] Not till 1952 did a civilian win the Olympic gold medal as 'previously the sport had almost exclusively been practised by military officers'.[53]

It is not clear whether the modern pentathlon was officially supported by the British army, though a recent history of the sport suggests that at least two of the three British Olympic entrants in 1912 – Ralph Cliverd, Douglas Godfree and Hugh Durant – were military officers as it states that Cliverd had to ride a horse provided by the host nation because, unlike his compatriots, he lacked full military honours.[54] Both of these officers also competed in other Olympic events, Godfree in fencing and Durant in shooting.

Yet there are unanswered questions. The link between being good at the modern pentathlon and being a good military leader has never been clarified, nor has anyone ever assessed whether pentathletes were better military officers than those who pursued other leisure activities.

The mechanism of sport aiding war was not necessarily the sports in themselves. It was the way in which they were played that was regarded by Mangan and others as teaching 'the psychological and physical tools necessary for war'.[55] There is no doubt that some public-school educated officers accepted that sport made the warrior and some 'certainly took into the services the belief that war was only another form of sport, the "greater game"'.[56]

There is, however, some incoherence in the asserted links. If the ideas were inculcated, were they all good for military purposes? Although probably sincerely held by its adherents, Riedi and Mason conclude that 'public school beliefs regarding the interrelationship between playing field and battlefield were largely specious'.[57] The 'athleticism' view that winning might be important but that the manner of securing victory is even more important may not be good military policy. According to Mangan, two of 'the famous ingredients of character training which the public schools considered their pride and prerogative' were 'the capacity to act fairly and take defeat well'. It can be questioned whether this really was good military training.[58] Playing fair is not always the best way to ensure victory. It is salutary to note that after the Boer War even Newbolt was forced to admit: 'You may get from the playing fields the moral qualities such as leadership and endurance and fair play which are indispensable for war, but you cannot get the scientific training which is also indispensable'.[59]

Sport and the Other Ranks

The public schools were at one side of the educational spectrum, along with the preparatory schools providing private sector schooling for those upper-class and middle-class families willing and able to pay for their services. On the other were the state schools of elementary, higher elementary, and state-owned or state-subsidised grammar schools. Mangan makes a plausible case that many grammar schools adopted the cult of athleticism in emulation of the public schools, what he terms 'deferential absorption'.[60] He produces evidence that several (perhaps many) grammar schools attempted to emulate the public schools, including the development of a games culture, though this was sometimes hampered by a necessity also to concentrate on examination results.

Yet it was the elementary schools 'from which the armed services drew most of their recruits'.[61] In this context Mangan and Hickey have argued that the London teacher training colleges followed the public schools and ancient universities in eventually adopting athleticism as part of their educational ideology and that 'by the end of the first decade of the twentieth century athleticism was firmly entrenched in the London colleges'.[62] They then argue that the products of these colleges, 'imbued with a sense of the moral value of team games ... took this moral conviction into the elementary school'.[63] Yet an article that began with them claiming that this had 'some impact' ends with the more dubious assertion that ' ... the diffusion, assimilation and reproduction of athleticism ... was responsible for gradually promoting new masculinity, a masculinity of the games field, in the elementary schools and among the elementary schoolboys of England, Britain and the Empire'.[64] While admitting that 'the ideology [of athleticism] faced many difficulties in these [elementary] schools, and that it is unlikely that it had the same powerful impact as in the public schools', Mangan and Hickey emphasise that 'the point is that the ideology existed, was promulgated and was absorbed in the schools'.[65]

Yet how was the ideology passed on? Most physical education in the elementary schools consisted of drill rather than sport. Mangan accepts that elementary school pupils had 'mostly physical exercises (drills, military drill, calisthenics and gymnastics) for physical health and social obedience'.[66] Military drill had received a boost in 1891 when state school fees (paid by all but the children of the very poor) were abolished in schools that taught military drill. It was boosted again by the rejection on fitness grounds of the vast majority of volunteers for the South African War.[67] However, this was not taught by the athleticism adherents from the training colleges as such work was deemed of too low a status and was left to peripatetic non-commissioned officers.[68]

Nor was athleticism passed on via sport in school hours as this was not even mentioned in the national curriculum until 1906 and, even then, it was 'allowed' rather than prescribed and no funds were made available to support it.[69] Mangan himself notes that the 1909 physical education curriculum did not include the 'team games that were so popular in the private sector. This was presumably due to lack of space and cost and to the enduring conviction of some that games were for the middle classes and drill for the masses'.[70]

The other avenue put forward by Mangan for a link between athleticism and the elementary schools is the extra-curricula matches organised out of school hours by college-educated teachers who had themselves been imbued with the culture of athleticism. Hickey, in an overconfident assertion of accomplishment, believes he has 'demonstrated beyond question that athleticism was an established feature of elementary schools in the late Victorian and Edwardian eras' and offers 'compelling evidence that it was widespread'.[71] A response from Kerrigan provides a cautious and more balanced view. Whereas Hickey sees athleticism as almost the default position for any provision of school sport, Kerrigan, drawing on a wider range of primary sources, argues that other motivations were also applicable, such as the promotion of health and fitness, the passing on of skills, the improvement of pupil-teacher relations and simply having fun. He concludes that 'many schools and districts involved in elementary-school football showed no signs of the influence of athleticism'.[72]

Mangan and Hickey ask 'how is it possible to find out how athleticism was received by the children themselves?' but they never answer the question.[73] Perhaps it cannot be answered but it should not be assumed that the children accepted its precepts. Mangan and Hickey rely on information in the log books of two London schools, neither of which specifically show that fair play and moral conduct were central to boys' football, contrariwise any emphasis seems to be on winning. They argue that W.J. Wilson and J.

G. Timms, respectively, headmasters of Oldridge Road Board School, Balham, and Rosendale Road Board School, Lambeth, instilled 'in the boys a belief that games were rewarding both physically and morally' without producing any supportive evidence: that fair play was a feature of elementary school football is assumed rather than demonstrated.[74] Moreover, they reproduce a poem from the magazine of Bellenden Road Board School produced by the boys themselves whose unequivocal theme is how to beat an opponent by artful means and win useful prizes.[75] One critic also notes that several pioneers of elementary school football had a pronounced desire to win, scarcely the mind-set of those promulgating athleticism.[76] The very fact that the schools participated in competitive leagues seems to go against the grain of athleticism.

Kerrigan has been criticised by Hickey for not presenting a formal definition of athleticism, but Hickey goes to the opposite extreme by taking Mangan's definition and adding to it the following: 'a subscription to team games as vehicles for the inculcation of physical and moral courage, loyalty, obedience, co-operation, self-sacrifice and duty in school, college and university'[77] Yet he never clarifies how many clauses of this definition need to be met before athleticism can be said to have featured. He uses the analogy of athleticism being an á la carte menu and argues that because the elementary schools could not consume all the ingredients it does not mean that they did not digest some. He fails to state how many courses have to be eaten from his pick and mix menu for it to be classified as a meal, though ultimately he notes that the essence of athleticism 'was organised games for the inculcation of character, and it was these games that were the defining element of athleticism in elementary schools'.[78] However, his evidence of 'practical athleticism' and 'athleticism in action' simply shows that organised sport was being played.[79]

It is being argued here that if sport was played in the elementary schools it did not necessarily mean that athleticism was at work, but it must also be considered whether much sport was played anyway. Although Mangan accepts that until 1900 games were 'denied by the state to the elementary school (and afterwards not greatly encouraged there)', Mangan and Hickey argue that 'the absence of games (in elementary schools) has been exaggerated both prior to and after 1900'.[80] This may be true, but they do not demonstrate that they existed on any scale even after schools were permitted to introduce them into the curriculum after 1906. Although there were a few schools sport associations formed in some large cities, there is no evidence of widespread diffusion of team games to the state schools before the outbreak of the war. Extra-curricula sport was *voluntary* (in itself a difference from the *compulsory* nature of sport under the athleticism code) which would limit the number of participants. We need to know how many children played sport and whether the experiences of the two London schools dealt with in detail by Mangan and Hickey were typical of those not only in the capital but elsewhere in Britain.

For the working class, the role of sport and war through the volunteer rifle brigades requires more examination. Jackson argues that, although the initial aim was to recruit middle-class volunteers, working-class men unexpectedly became the mainstay of the force. Although founded primarily as a defence organisation, certainly for rural workers they also served as sporting outlets. Jackson suggests that many of the Volunteer Rifle Corps, instituted in 1859 as a means of encouraging national defence, also effectively acted as sports clubs for many of their rural members by providing opportunities for competitive shooting with prizes for the best shots. Some went further and organised teams for sports unconnected with defending the homeland. Members of the Argyllshire Volunteers, for example, played cricket, football and shinty.[81] One such Volunteer team, Third Lanarkshire Rifle Volunteers, transmogrified into Third Lanark FC, a major Scottish football team at the turn of the century.

When the products of the elementary schools came to play sport in the army, there is no evidence that they were influenced by athleticism, except in the sense perhaps that those who advocated army sport were themselves guided by the public school view of sport. Riedi and Mason cite Major R.B. Campbell of the Army Gymnastics staff, asking 'what qualities prevail in games? Physical fitness, executive action and confidence – the three essential qualities for war' and quote a training pamphlet of October 1917 that prohibited money prizes as 'they kill good sport, encourage selfishness, and destroy the spirit of individual sacrifice which games are intended to foster'.[82] However, much of their other 'evidence' is drawn from public school sources rather than army spokesmen.[83] Nevertheless, although Riedi and Mason accept that athleticism 'certainly influenced the middle-class men who designed the army's sports programme', they pointedly add the rider 'if not necessarily the soldiers who encountered it'.[84] French, in his study of the regimental system, suggests that as far as other ranks were concerned their attitudes to sport were probably much like those of civilian working-class males; to them sportsmanship, fairness and good manners were less important than winning.[85] As Osborne notes, for private soldiers sport was 'male' not 'manly'.[86]

It has been insufficiently appreciated that by 1914 sport for regular soldiers was a well-established feature of army life. In the 1913/1914 season, for example, the annual Army Football Cup attracted more than 90 entries, and almost every battalion had at least one football team.[87] Campbell claims that army sport 'flourished' in the 1870s and that by the end of that decade regimental sport was a 'fixture', but his examples do not suggest that it was widespread at that time.[88] However, although perhaps the chronology and intensity of the development need to be determined, there is no doubt that on the eve of the First World War a wide range of sports was played, by which time 'it was widely accepted within the army that sport could have a number of practical benefits: that it could increase fitness, decrease drunkenness, help build regimental identity, enhance relations between officers and other ranks, and between the army and civil society, and improve morale'.[89]

Participation in sport continued when the troops went overseas on a war footing, at first improvised and informally organised at battalion level, but by early 1915 with some competitions to play in.[90] Yet it should be emphasised that playing sport was generally voluntary and largely a 'grassroots and unofficial movement'.[91] Active participation in sport remained a matter of choice, except perhaps when a particularly enthusiastic officer might 'request' his troops to play. The only compulsory sports were individual not team ones: the boxing, swimming, fencing and cross-country running that were attached to the mainly gymnastic physical training. However, by the end of the conflict it had become compulsory and an 'official part of the army system'.[92] Sport 'both as a leisure pursuit and as recreational training ... had become part of military training' as the authorities formally recognised that it could contribute to military efficiency. This required a change in attitude on the part of the military establishment. Although in 1919 Field-Marshall Haig praised team games for promoting 'decision and character on the part of leaders, discipline and unselfishness among the led, and initiative and self-sacrifice on the part of all', some years earlier he had been less enthusiastic, blaming football for men being tired when on night sentry duty.[93] It might be argued that the military authorities had effectively conceded that the ordinary soldier's loyalty was less to any high principles of 'king and country', and more to his immediate comrades, something that could be fostered by playing and watching sport together.[94] Previously watching sport had been regarded often with hostility and at best lukewarm acceptance, but now a partisan, civilian spectator culture was being utilised to develop esprit de corps in a conscripted, mass army.[95]

A fruitful line of enquiry, as suggested by Mason and Riedi, would be into looking at sport as a way of relieving both the tedium and the danger of service life.[96] Even in total war there is time for leisure. Fuller has reckoned that some 60% of an infantryman's service on the Western Front was spent behind the lines.[97] Surprisingly there is very little mention of troops' recreational activities in Holmes' magisterial study of British soldiers on the Western Front.[98] Yet we know that many of them played sport. To bring in a personal note, my grandfather, a farmer by preference, was a bombardier in the Royal Artillery during the First World War. His job was to run the mule trains delivering ammunition to the front. It was a dangerous and dreadful occupation. He rarely talked about the horror of his experiences. After the war he never left the village except on fishing trips organised by the local workingmen's club. He said he had seen the world and he did not like it. Once I asked him 'Grandad, how did you get through the war?' His answer was succinct. 'Rum', he said 'and football'. Sport for him was an escape from the hostilities not a preparation for them.

Evidence and Actuality

It is not being argued that Mangan and those who have adopted his view on public school sport and preparation for war are necessarily wrong. It is that the evidence they have produced so far may be indicative but is neither conclusive nor compelling. There is too much supposition and assertion and not enough demonstration. Well-crafted prose can communicate an historical argument but an eloquent case still needs evidential backup. To draw on a Scottish legal term, the verdict at the moment is 'not proven'. Although some officers continued to play rugby and cricket after they left public school, for most officers equestrian sports were their dominant sporting activity. This was a reflection of class rather than schooling. Whether these activities made them better officers in a changing warfare environment is a moot point.

For the men that they commanded sport became recognised as a means of promoting fitness and esprit de corps by playing together but also in raising morale by watching comrades participate in competitive matches. Mangan has argued that 'games were utilitarian. They were practical instruments for creating morale, enthusiasm and good will'.[99] This was as true for the other ranks in the forces as it was for the pupils in public schools.

Where Mangan and his followers are in error is in trying to transplant the concept of athleticism into state elementary education before the First World War. Here the argument is unconvincing and the evidence in support weak and selective. There is no way in which sport – as distinct from physical education – can be said to have prepared the rank and file for war. Most state and church schools did not do sport. Any military link with physical exercise in the elementary schools lay with drill not sport. If athleticism is to embrace non-competitive, non-team-oriented drill, the major component of elementary school education, and non-compulsory, team sport in which winning was the dominant motivation of the players, it is clearly, as Mangan recognises, not the same concept as the athleticism of both the public and grammar schools.[100] It has to be questioned whether it was even similar or if it existed at all.

Acknowledgements

This article began life as a keynote address at the XIXth Sporting Traditions Conference in Canberra, July 2013. I am grateful for comments from the audience. Although the author was Managing Editor of this journal at the time the above article was written subject to anonymous refereeing organised by the editors of this issue.

Notes

1. Adams and Petney, "Germany 3-Scotland 2," 39.
2. Adams, "Over the Top." Although Veitch, "'Play Up! Play Up! And Win the War'," 376, claims there were at least five other incidents, Adams found no collaborative evidence of any other alleged instance.
3. Terret and Mangan, *Militarism, Sport, Masculinity*.
4. Terret, "Prologue," 324–325.
5. Ibid., 324.
6. Mason and Riedi, *Sport and the Military*, 3.
7. John, "'A Different Kind'," 24.
8. Newbolt, *Poems*, 78–9.
9. Quoted in Birley, "Sportsmen," 306.
10. McIntosh, *Physical Education*, 70.
11. Best, "Militarism," 141.
12. Mangan, "Tragic Symbiosis," 435, 439.
13. Mangan, *Athleticism*, 9.
14. Mangan, "Swansong," 9.
15. Mangan, "From Hooligans to Heroes," 99.
16. Fair play was thus virtually an 'invented tradition' which had utilitarian roots but evolved into an ideology.
17. Mangan, "Games Field," 141.
18. Mangan, "Tragic Symbiosis," 448–9.
19. Ibid., 438.
20. Many of Mangan's followers have documented the spread of the public school ethos, with its cult of athleticism, throughout Britain's formal and informal empire. Yet few have suggested that this led to the creation of a militaristic officer class elsewhere.
21. Mangan, *Athleticism*, 138.
22. Mangan, "Social Darwinism," 92.
23. Mangan, "'Bullies, Beatings, Battles and Bruises'," 30; Mangan, "'Muscular, Militaristic and Manly'," 31.
24. Mangan, "Tragic Symbiosis," 441; Mangan, "Duty," 130–131.
25. http://www.britishbattles.com/egypt-1882/abu-klea.htm. In passing it is noted that poets portrayed their version of the game, an idyllic one in which there was no cheating, and umpires' decisions were accepted. A neglected area of research is the extent to which the rhetoric of fair play as espoused in such poetry was actually transmitted to the playing fields.
26. Mangan, "Moralists," 185.
27. Mangan, "Games Field," 150.
28. Mangan, "'Muscular, Militaristic and Manly'," 45.
29. Mangan, "Athleticism," 74.
30. Ibid., 69.
31. Ibid., 72.
32. Mangan, "Happy Warriors."
33. Mangan, "'The Grit of Our Forefathers'," 341.
34. Hands, "Preface," 432.
35. Mangan, "Tragic Symbiosis," 435.
36. Ibid., 449.
37. Hickey, "'A Potent and Pervasive Ideology'," 1860.
38. The Highlanders were presented with a medallion by their opponents which is probably the oldest existing trophy in world football. McBrearty, "Curator of the Scottish Football Museum."
39. Mangan, "Happy Warriors," 475.
40. Best, "Militarism," 134.

SPORT, WAR AND SOCIETY IN AUSTRALIA AND NEW ZEALAND

41. Mason and Riedi, *Sport and the Military*, 52.
42. For Alderson, Baden-Powell, Knox, see Mason and Riedi, *Sport and the Military*, 68; For Miller see Campbell, "'Training for Sport is Training for War'," 26. See also Stein, "Soldiering."
43. Quoted in Seth-Smith, *The History of Steeplechasing*, 42.
44. Vamplew and Kay, "Captains Courageous," 375.
45. Ibid., 376.
46. Lowerson, *Sport and the English Middle Classes*, 285.
47. Mason and Riedi, *Sport and the Military*, 76–7.
48. Mangan and McKenzie, "The Other Side."
49. Campbell, "'Training for Sport is Training for War'," 22.
50. Heck, "Modern Pentathlon at the London 2012 Olympics," 724.
51. Heck, "When Workmen Shoot," 8.
52. Heck, "Modern Pentathlon and the First World War," 415.
53. Heck, "Modern Pentathlon at the London 2012 Olympics," 725.
54. Archibald, *Modern Pentathlon*, 24.
55. Mangan, *Athleticism*, 5.
56. Mason and Riedi, *Sport and the Military*, 43.
57. Riedi and Mason, "'Leather'," 487.
58. Mangan, *Athleticism*, 9.
59. Newbolt, *The Book of the Happy Warrior*, 222, quoted in Mangan, "Duty Unto Death," 134–5. Newbolt also penned '*He Fell Among Thieves*', an heroic poem in honour of Lieutenant George W. Hayward, a soldier actually killed after falling asleep when guarding his camp, hardly a role model for military-minded schoolboys. Mangan, "Games Field," 142.
60. Mangan, "Imitating Their Betters," 251.
61. Riedi and Mason, "'Leather'," 489.
62. Mangan and Hickey, "Athleticism," 112, 135.
63. Mangan and Hickey, "English Elementary Education Revisited and Revised," 72.
64. Mangan and Hickey, "Athleticism," 113, 136.
65. Mangan and Hickey, "English Elementary Education Revisited and Revised," 73
66. Mangan and Galligan, "Militarism," 572.
67. Ibid., 571.
68. Mangan and Hickey, "Missing Middle-Class Dimensions," 82–3.
69. Ibid., 83–4.
70. Mangan and Galligan, "Militarism," 594.
71. Hickey, "'A Potent and Pervasive Ideology'," 1879, 1868.
72. Kerrigan, "'Sweet Analytics'," 2523.
73. Mangan and Hickey, "English Elementary Education Revisited and Revised," 73.
74. Ibid., 76–80, quote cited on page 80.
75. Ibid., 83–4.
76. Kerrigan, "'Sweet Analytics'," 2503.
77. Hickey "'A Potent and Pervasive Ideology'," 1856.
78. Ibid., 1859.
79. Ibid., 1863.
80. Mangan, "Imitating Their Betters," 251; Mangan and Hickey, "English Elementary Education Revisited and Revised," 67.
81. Jackson, "Patriotism or Pleasure."
82. Riedi and Mason, "'Leather'," 509–10; Campbell quoted in Osborne, "Sport, Soldiers," 18.
83. Reidi and Mason, "'Leather'," 496.
84. Mason and Riedi, *Sport and the Military*, 89–90. Despite their possible allegiance to athleticism, the officer class frowned on their subordinates when they insisted on kicking ball ahead of them when going into battle and, worse still, fraternised with the enemy in the famous Christmas Day football encounter. Adams and Petney, "Germany 3-Scotland 2," 39; Adams, "Over the Top," 817.
85. French, *Military Identities*, 238–9.
86. Osborne, "Sport, Soldiers," 20.
87. Riedi and Mason, "'Leather'," 490.
88. Campbell, "'Training for Sport is Training for War'," 31.

89. Riedi and Mason, "'Leather'," 496.
90. Ibid., 493.
91. Ibid, 495.
92. Ibid., 508.
93. Ibid., 494.
94. Roberts, "'The Best Football Team, The Best Platoon'," 34, 37.
95. Ibid., 29.
96. Mason and Riedi, *Sport and the Military,* 514.
97. Fuller, *Troop Morale,* 6.
98. Holmes, *Tommy.*
99. Mangan, "Imitating Their Betters," 249.
100. Mangan and Hickey, "English Elementary Education Revisited and Revised," 88.

References

Adams, Iain. "Over the Top: 'A Foul; a Blurry Foul!'." *The International Journal of the History of Sport* 29, no. 6 (2012): 813–831.

Adams, Iain, and Trevor Petney. "Germany 3-Scotland 2, No Man's Land, 25th December, 1914: Fact or Fiction?" In *The Bountiful Game? Football Identities and Finances*, edited by Jonathan Magee, Alan Bairner, and Alan Tomlinson, 21–41. Oxford: Meyer & Meyer Sport, 2005.

Archibald, Andy. *Modern Pentathlon: A Centenary History 1912–2012*. London: Grosvenor House, 2012.

Best, Geoffrey. "Militarism and the Victorian Public School." In *The Victorian Public School*, edited by Brian Simon and Ian Bradley, 129–146. Dublin: Gill and Macmillan, 1975.

Birley, Derek. "Sportsmen and the Deadly Game." *British Journal of Sports History* 3, no. 3 (1986): 288–310.

Campbell, J. D. "'Training for Sport is Training for War': Sport and the Transformation of the British Army." *The International Journal of the History of Sport* 17, no. 4 (2000): 21–58.

French, David. *Military Identities: The Regimental System, the British Army and the British People, c.1870–2000*. Oxford: Oxford University Press, 2005.

Fuller, J. G. *Troop Morale and Popular Culture in the British and Dominion Armies 1914–1918*. Oxford: Clarendon, 1990.

Hands, Robert. "Preface: They Also Served – Re-evaluating and Reconsidering the Neglected." *The International Journal of the History of Sport* 28, nos 3–4 (2011): 429–434.

Heck, Sandra. "Modern Pentathlon and the First World War – When Athletes and Soldiers Met to Practise Martial Manliness." *The International Journal of the History of Sport* 28, nos 3–4 (2011): 410–428.

Heck, Sandra. "Modern Pentathlon at the London 2012 Olympics: Between Traditional Heritage and Modern Changes for Survival." *The International Journal of the History of Sport* 30, no. 7 (2013): 719–735.

Heck, Sandra. "When Workmen Shoot, Ride and Fence – Modern Pentathlon and the Promise of Social Integration at the Beginning of the 20th Century." *Stadion* 37 (2010): 1–13.

Hickey, Colm. "'A Potent and Pervasive Ideology': Athleticism and the English Elementary School." *The International Journal of the History of Sport* 28, no. 13 (2011): 1852–1890.

Holmes, Richard. *Tommy: The British Soldier on the Western Front 1914–1918*. London: HarperCollins, 2004.

Jackson, Lorna. "Patriotism or Pleasure? The Nineteenth Century Volunteer Force as a Vehicle for Rural Working-Class Male Sport." *Sports Historian* 19, no. 1 (1999): 125–139.

John, Simon. "'A Different Kind of Test Match': Cricket, English Society and the First World War." *Sport in History* 33, no. 1 (2013): 19–48.

Kerrigan, Colm. "'Sweet analytics': Athleticism and Elementary-School Football Associations." *The International Journal of the History of Sport* 29, no. 18 (2012): 2500–2531.

Lowerson, John. *Sport and the English Middle Classes 1870–1914*. Manchester: Manchester University Press, 1993.

Mangan, J. A. "Athleticism: A Case Study of the Evolution of an Educational Ideology." *The International Journal of the History of Sport* 27, nos 1–2 (2010): 60–77.

Mangan, J. A. *Athleticism in the Victorian and Edwardian Public School: The Emergence of an Educational Ideology*. Cambridge: Cambridge University Press, 1981.

Mangan, J. A. "'Bullies, Beatings, Battles and Bruises:' Great Days and Jolly Days' at One Mid-Victorian Public School." *The International Journal of the History of Sport* 27, nos 1–2 (2010): 30–59.

Mangan, J. A. "Duty Unto Death: English Masculinity and Militarism in the Age of the New Imperialism." *The International Journal of the History of Sport* 27, nos 1–2 (2010): 124–149.

Mangan, J. A. "From Hooligans to Heroes and from Ferocity to Fair Play: Some English Historical Origins of Modern World Sport." *The International Journal of the History of Sport* 27, nos 1–2 (2010): 98–103.

Mangan, J. A. "Games Field and Battlefield: A Romantic Alliance in Verse and the Creation of Militaristic Masculinity." In *Making Men: Rugby and Masculine Identity*, edited by John Nauright and Timothy Chandler, 140–157. London: Cass, 1996.

Mangan, J. A. "'The Grit of Our Forefathers': Invented Traditions, Propaganda and Imperialism." *The International Journal of the History of Sport* 27, nos 1–2 (2010): 337–361.

Mangan, J. A. "Happy Warriors in Waiting? Wykehamists and the Great War – Stereotypes, Complexities and Contradictions." *The International Journal of the History of Sport* 28, nos 3–4 (2011): 458–491.

Mangan, J. A. "Imitating Their Betters and Disassociating from Their Inferiors: Grammar Schools and the Games Ethic in the Late Nineteenth and Early Twentieth Centuries." *The International Journal of the History of Sport* 27, nos 1–2 (2010): 228–261.

Mangan, J. A. "Moralists, Metaphysicians and Mythologists: The 'Signifiers' of a Victorian Sub-Culture." *The International Journal of the History of Sport* 27, nos 1–2 (2010): 169–189.

Mangan, J. A. "'Muscular, Militaristic and Manly': The Middle-Class Hero as Moral Messenger." *The International Journal of the History of Sport* 13, no. 1 (1996): 28–47.

Mangan, J. A. "Social Darwinism and Upper-Class Education in Late Victorian and Edwardian England." *The International Journal of the History of Sport* 27, nos 1–2 (2010): 78–97.

Mangan, J. A. "Swansong." *The International Journal of the History of Sport* 27, nos 1–2 (2010): 9–20.

Mangan, J. A. "Tragic Symbiosis: Distinctive 'Anglo-Saxon' Visions and Voices." *The International Journal of the History of Sport* 28, nos 3–4 (2011): 435–457.

Mangan, J. A., and Frank Galligan. "Militarism, Drill and Elementary Education: Birmingham Nonconformist Responses to Conformist Responses to the Teutonic Threat Prior to the Great War." *The International Journal of the History of Sport* 28, nos 3–4 (2011): 568–603.

Mangan, J. A., and Colm Hickey. "Athleticism in the Service of the Proletariat: Preparation for the English Elementary School and the Extension of Middle-Class Manliness." *European Sports History Review* 2 (2000): 112–139.

Mangan, J. A., and Colm Hickey. "English Elementary Education Revisited and Revised: Drill and Athleticism in Tandem." In *Sport in Europe: Politics, Class, Gender*, edited by J. A. Mangan, 63–91. London: Cass, 1999.

Mangan, J. A., and Colm Hickey. "Missing Middle-Class Dimensions: Elementary Schools, Imperialism and Athleticism." *European Sports History Review* 4 (2002): 73–90.

Mangan, J. A., and Callum McKenzie. "The Other Side of the Coin: Victorian Masculinity, Field Sports and English Elite Education." *European Sports History Review* 2 (2000): 62–85.

Mason, Tony, and Eliza Riedi. *Sport and the Military*. Cambridge: Cambridge University Press, 2010.

McBrearty, Richard. "Curator of the Scottish Football Museum." *Herald Magazine*, March 23, 2013, 21.

McIntosh, Peter. *Physical Education in England Since 1800*. London: G. Bell, 1968.

Newbolt, Henry. *Poems Old and New*. London: Murray, 1898.

Osborne, John M. "Sport, Soldiers and the Great War." *British Society of Sports History Bulletin* 11 (1991): 17–34.

Riedi, Eliza, and Tony Mason. "'Leather' and the Fighting Spirit: Sport in the British Army in World War 1." *Canadian Journal of History* XLI (2006): 485–516.

Roberts, James. "'The Best Football Team, The Best Platoon'; The Role of Football in the Proletarianization of the British Expeditionary Force, 1914–1918." *Sport in History* 26, no. 1 (2006): 26–46.

Seth-Smith, Michael. *The History of Steeplechasing*. London: Michael Joseph, 1969.

Stein, C. "Soldiering and Sport." *Baily's Magazine* LXXIV (1900): 235–240.

Terret, Thierry. "Prologue: Making Men, Destroying Bodies: Sport, Masculinity and the Great War Experience." *The International Journal of the History of Sport* 28, nos 3–4 (2011): 323–328.

Terret, Thierry, and J. A. Mangan, eds. *Militarism, Sport, Masculinity: Martial Manliness and Armageddon 1914–1918,* special issue in *The International Journal of the History of Sport* 28, nos 3–4. Abingdon: Routledge, 2011.

Vamplew, Wray, and Joyce Kay. "Captains Courageous: Gentlemen Riders in British Horseracing, 1866–1914." *Sport in History* 26, no. 3 (2006): 370–385.

Veitch, Colin. "'Play Up! Play Up! And Win the War': Football, the Nation and the First World War 1914–15." *Journal of Contemporary History* 20, no. 3 (1985): 363–378.

Australasia's 1912 Olympians and the Great War

Bruce Coe

Private Scholar, Canberra, Australia

> In 1912, two women and 26 men comprised the Australasian team at the 1912 Olympic Games in Stockholm, Sweden. Over the following years during World War I, 77% of the male members of the team volunteered to serve the British Empire. Four made the supreme sacrifice, one of whom was the great, highly respected swimmer Cecil Healy. Many were wounded and a sizeable number were highly decorated for their war service. This article examines the contribution of the 1912 Australasian Olympians to the Great War, and the participation of a number in the post-hostilities Inter-Allied sporting competitions.

On April 23, 1912, a journalist from the *Daily News* of Perth, Australia, wrote a piece about the Australasian team en route to the upcoming Olympic Games in Stockholm.[1] He had journeyed down to the port city of Fremantle to meet the RMS *Osterley* that was briefly stopping over before setting out across the Indian Ocean and on to Tilbury, England. On board he was to meet a cross-section of young amateur sportsmen from different social, religious and political backgrounds. In London, the various members of the team were due to meet up with a number of England-based athletes and to then make their respective ways to the Swedish capital in time for the opening ceremony of the Games of the Vth Olympiad on July 6, 1912.

In the article titled 'Thin Bronzed Line of Muscular Australia',[2] the unknown writer reflected on the thoughts of Charles Burgess Fry on Australians on sporting fields. Fry, the multi-talented English, Corinthian sportsman in the fields of cricket, football and athletics (he once equalled the world record for the long jump),[3] thought that Australians were 'hard bitten' and they 'permeated' the world of sport. If he had been aboard the *Osterley* that day, speculated the writer, he would have seen in the swimmers, rowers and track athletes 'the sharpness of profile, the alert attitude, and the hard squareness of the jaw lines which somehow betokens age, even though the eyes are beaconing the fire of youth'. He would have noted 'the easy erectness of the Olympic oarsmen'. The writer himself then observed swimmers Cecil Healy as 'bronzed and as pleasant looking as of yore', Billy Longworth as having 'the schoolboy face, and the strong man's figure' and Harold Hardwick as 'gigantic'.[4]

In concluding, the journalist noted that this touring party was well organised, as opposed to previous trips of Australasians (men only) to the Olympic Games, which had had been rather *ad hoc* ventures, and 'probably never before has Australia stood in the position of getting such an advertisement as will be supplied by the visit to Sweden of this great team of athletes'.[5]

SPORT, WAR AND SOCIETY IN AUSTRALIA AND NEW ZEALAND

Once in England, and before travelling to Stockholm, the rowers established their international rowing *bona fides* at the Royal Henley Regatta. In a closely fought race for the Grand Challenge Cup, the Australians, competing under the banner of the Sydney Rowing Club (even though two Victorians were on board), defeated the highly fancied local crew from the historic Leander Club. A member of the victorious crew was Sydney 'Syd' Middleton, who was already an Olympic gold medallist as a member of the champion Wallabies team in London in 1908. Commenting on the race, Frederick Septimus Kelly, the Australian-born champion oarsman who had won a gold medal at London 1908 in a Great Britain eight, said of the Australians: 'The general impression was that they were good and fast. I was glad they won as I liked them personally, especially their modesty.'[6]

In his diary entry for June 18, 1908, Kelly had written about the casual attitude taken to competing in the early Olympic Games of the modern era. He said that he had received an invitation from a fellow rower, Raymond Etherington-Smith, to try out for a British crew entered to row in the Olympic regatta in six weeks' time:

> I received a telegram before breakfast from Etherington-Smith, asking me to row in the Olympic crew this afternoon and after breakfast, thinking perhaps someone had failed, I telegraphed to say I would. At 10.30am Etherington-Smith turned up himself and explained that they had no satisfactory man for 2 and asked me whether I would come and be tried. I told him I did not want to as I had a great deal to do, but said I would row if they were really in a hole.[7]

Stockholm Olympic Games

By the opening ceremony of the Olympic Games, in the newly-constructed Stockholm stadium, the team members from the *Osterley* had been joined by the England-based Theodore 'Theo' Tartakover (swimming), Allan Stewart (athletics) and Hugh Ward (rowing), as well as two women swimmers, Sarah 'Fanny' Durack and Wilhelmina 'Mina' Wylie (see Table 1). Durack and Wylie had belatedly set off for Sweden after a selection imbroglio over Australian women swimmers competing at the Olympic Games had been played out in their native Sydney.[8] Tartakover had landed in England in mid-1907, and had become a travelling companion of the multi-talented Reginald 'Snowy' Baker who had arrived a few months earlier.[9] Both had competed at London 1908, Baker in swimming, diving and boxing, where he won a silver medal in the middleweight division,

Table 1. Australasian team.

Athletics	Rowing	Swimming	Tennis
George Hill (NZ)	Stuart Amess	Leslie Boardman	Anthony Wilding (NZ)
William Murray	E. Roy Barker	Malcolm Champion (NZ)	
Stuart Poulter	Roger Fitzhardinge	Sarah 'Fanny' Durack	
Claude Ross	Simon Fraser	Harold Hardwick	
W. Allan Stewart	Henry 'Harry' Hauenstein	Cecil Healy	
	Keith Heritage	William 'Billy' Longworth	
	Cecil McVilly	Frank Schryver	
	Sydney 'Syd' Middleton	Theodore 'Theo' Tartakover	
	Thomas Parker	Wilhelmina 'Mina' Wylie	
	Harry Ross-Soden		
	John Ryrie		
	Robert Waley		
	Hugh Ward		

SPORT, WAR AND SOCIETY IN AUSTRALIA AND NEW ZEALAND

and Tartakover in swimming. In 1912, Tartakover was employed with the New South Wales (NSW) Agent-General in London. Ward, the 1911 Rhodes Scholar from NSW,[10] was studying at Oxford University and, like many Australian rowers at English universities at the time, was a candidate for competing for Australasia or Great Britain at the Olympic Games. Australasia had first choice. Indeed, two other Australian students at Oxford University, Charles Littlejohn[11] and Beaufort Burdekin, were to row for Great Britain at Stockholm. Tasmanian-born, Melbourne-educated, William Allan Stewart was of Scottish stock and when he entered the London Hospital Medical College in 1908 he was the fourth generation of his family to enter that institution.[12] He was the current 100 and 220 yards champion of Scotland and was another who could have competed for either Australasia or Great Britain.

By the opening ceremony, Australasia had already won a bronze medal through the great New Zealand (NZ) tennis player Anthony Wilding.[13] Wilding had played in the covered courts tennis tournament, held in May, which was the first event of the Olympic festivities.[14] An Olympic outdoor tournament was held in late June to early July, but by then Wilding had departed Stockholm and was competing at Wimbledon where he won the gentlemen's singles tournament, his third victory there in a four consecutive-year run of triumphs (1910–1913).

Once competitions began, at the main stadium Stewart was the highest achiever of the Australasians by winning his heats in the 100 and 200 metres, before bowing out in the semi-finals. Murray, who had set world-leading times in walking before setting off for Stockholm, unfortunately fell foul of the international walking judges and was disqualified in his event.

With one change of personnel in the Australasian eight after the victory in the Grand Challenge Cup, Hugh Ward in for Keith Heritage, the combination entered the Olympic regatta with high hopes of a medal, possibly gold. Alas, a less-than-advantageous station on the not-so-straight rowing course saw the crew somewhat surprisingly defeated by Leander, now representing Great Britain, in a quarter-final. James Merrick of Canada, a future member of the International Olympic Committee, wrote to Sydney's *Referee* sporting newspaper with his version of the race, opining that the Australians would have won had they not been disadvantaged by their station. He did not believe that the change in the crew affected the result.[15] Great Britain progressed through the succeeding rounds to claim the gold medal. Merrick concluded his letter to the *Referee* by saying that he believed that the Australians were the best crew at the Henley and Stockholm regattas, due to 'perfect' blade work and 'admirable' crew work.[16] Littlejohn and Burdekin, the fellow Australian rowers at Oxford University with Ward, rowed in the second Great Britain eight at Stockholm that won the silver medal behind the Leander crew.[17] Cecil McVilly, the sculler in the team, had steering problems in his event and although he was first across the line in his heat he was subsequently disqualified for colliding with his German opponent. In the Diamond Challenge Sculls at Royal Henley he had similar navigational difficulties and was eliminated early in the regatta.

It was in the swimming pool that the Australasians shone. Fanny Durack and Mina Wylie finished first and second in the women's 100 metres freestyle. They both won their heats and semi-finals, with the former setting a new world record in her heat. The official report of the Olympic Games said of Durack's successive victories that she 'won without difficulty', 'won as she liked' and, in the final, 'led from start to finish'.[18] The pair tried unsuccessfully to be permitted to swim two legs each in the women's team race (4 × 100 metres) which on their times in the individual event they might very well have won.[19] Durack and Wylie were the first of Australia's long line of women Olympic medallists.

Six Americans, five Australians (Tartakover, Leslie Boardman, Healy, Longworth and Hardwick) and five Germans were amongst the 36 entries in the first round heats of the men's 100 metres freestyle.[20] At the completion of the second-round heats, Healy and Longworth had qualified for the semi-finals along with three Americans and two Germans. The Americans thought that all seven swimmers would progress straight through to the final, hence, not unreasonably, believed that semi-finals were not required. However, semi-finals were swum, without the Americans, with Healy and the ailing Longworth finishing first and third, respectively, in one, and a German winning by a walkover in the other. Upon realising their error, the American officials pleaded their case for the non-appearances of their swimmers for the semi-finals and their subsequent disqualification from the event. Twenty years later, Ernest Samuel (E.S.) Marks, the long-time administrator of multi-farious amateur sports, who had accompanied the Australasian team on its Olympic odyssey, gave to a Sydney newspaper his version of what happened next. He said that the English and German members of the International Jury for swimming (of which he was a member) wanted strict adherence to the rules of competition and thus were not in favour of a proposal allowing the Americans to swim in a special race in an attempt to qualify for the final.[21] If the winner of that race swam faster than Longworth's semi-final time then the first two placegetters would be permitted to advance to the final.[22] Then, according to Marks: 'Cecil Healy and Billy Longworth told ... [me] that they would not participate in the final if the Americans were not conceded that favour. That settled the opposition.'[23] Based on the two Australians' approach, Marks was able to convince his fellow jury members to permit the swimming of the special race. The race was swum with Duke Paoa Kahanamoku eclipsing Longworth's time, thus he and the runner-up, fellow American Kenneth Huszagh, qualified for the final. Kahanamoku went on to win the gold medal race from Healy and Huszagh. Longworth's rapidly declining health precluded him from contesting the medals. Healy's sportsmanship had cost him becoming an individual Olympic champion but his action received much acclaim throughout the host city.[24] Marks's role in the matter remained hidden until a newspaper article in the early 1930s. In 1916, Healy had told the story to the quarterly *Lone Hand* but he had only said that the member of the international jury had been an Australian, and not E.S. Marks:

> Healy strongly urged the Australian representative to insist on the Americans being given an opportunity to compete in the final, insisting that it would be unsportsmanlike to bar their entry. Finally, mainly owing to the Australian's attitude, and in spite of opposition from the Germans, the Americans were allowed to compete in a special semi-final.[25]

Five days later, Healy collected that seemingly elusive Olympic gold medal when he was the lead-off swimmer for the victorious Australasian team in the 4×200 metres freestyle relay which set a new world record in the process.[26] His fellow team members were Boardman, Hardwick and the New Zealander Malcolm Champion. Hardwick also won bronze medals in the 400 metres and 1500 metres freestyle.

1913 and 1914

At the conclusion of the Olympic Games, Healy continued travelling and swimming in Europe, especially winning hearts in France with his charm and good-natured approach to his sport, before returning to his native Sydney. Stewart completed his medical studies in London where, in the following year, he qualified as a physician and surgeon and immediately commenced employment at the London Hospital. He also started to concentrate on rugby, and in four Tests for the country of his forefathers, Scotland, scoring eight tries, including three in his debut match, against France, and four in his third, against Ireland.[27] Ward also returned to his studies, at Oxford University, and rowed in the winning crew in the 1913 Boat Race. Tartakover continued working for the NSW government in London. Durack and Wylie continued in their record-breaking ways in Australia. Likewise, a healthy Longworth returned to form, winning multiple state and national swimming titles. Middleton stepped back from competing and turned his attention to the administrative side of both rugby and rowing. In 1913, McVilly again attempted the Diamond Challenge Sculls at Royal Henley and this time, with all his steering ills eradicated, became the first Australian-based sculler to win the famous race. Hardwick started winding down his swimming but concentrating more on boxing, easily winning the NSW amateur heavyweight title in 1914 and turning professional in early 1915. Buoyed by the successes of their fellow athletes at Stockholm, the eyes of all hopeful Olympians from Australasia were turned to Games of the VIth Olympiad, in Berlin in 1916. Olympic participation funds were set up to send the largest-ever Australasian team to the German capital. E.S. Marks, a noted champion of amateurism and the Olympic movement, enunciated his ideas in the Sydney press on the size of such a team, and the attendant costs. If £12,000 was raised, Marks believed Australasia could send a team of 70, to compete in 14 sports in Berlin.[28]

Healy and Hardwick were also prolific writers about sport, and in 1913 the latter wrote about the preparations of teams from the various European countries in the lead up to Berlin 1916, and the merits of Australia hosting an Olympic Games, as soon as 1920.[29] Perhaps the most portentous of Healy's many articles was in Sydney's *Sunday Times* in February 1913, titled 'The Peace of Europe',[30] when he warned about a possible future world war with Germany, based on what he had seen while travelling around Europe during a number of successful swimming tours, including after Stockholm. He had noticed Germany's preparations for war, its militarism within and without the sporting bodies, including the importance being placed on the teaching of swimming during military instruction. He even speculated that German sailors, because they had been taught to swim, had higher chances of survival if their ships were sunk. Healy questioned whether the Olympic Games in Berlin would eventuate.

Olympians at War

As Healy had feared, the clouds of war that had been mustering over Europe for a number of years began to break in July 1914. Late on August 4, 1914, England and Germany went to war. As a result, as part of the British Empire, this nation was also at war. Throughout Australia, young men hastened to join the colours. Sportsmen, and particularly those in the amateur ranks, were part of the rush. As Healy had speculated, the Olympic Games scheduled for Berlin were cancelled in March 1915.[31] Based on that 1912 description of the fit and active Australasian team as they sailed through Perth en route to the Olympic Games, it is little wonder that over the next four years 77% of the male members (four athletes, nine rowers, six swimmers and the one tennis player) of the squad at Stockholm volunteered to serve in the bloody turmoil at Gallipoli, the Middle East and Western Europe that was World War I.

The rate of enlistment by the 1912 Olympians was starkly different from that of the 1908–09 (First) Wallabies, of which Middleton was a member. In his 1939 book, *Viewless Winds*, Herbert' Paddy' Moran, the captain of the team, commented on the unwillingness of the majority of his squad to play in the 'greater game':

SPORT, WAR AND SOCIETY IN AUSTRALIA AND NEW ZEALAND

> When the war broke out those thirty-one men [the touring squad] were still in the flower of their physical vigour, yet only seven took part in the war. There is surely food for refection in all this.[32]

Subsequent to the release of *Viewless Winds*, research has revealed that the rate of enlistment in the war of the First Wallabies was not quite as low as Moran had indicated. Ten, including Moran, joined the colours and at least another endeavoured to sign up but was rejected on medical grounds.[33] There may have been others who had been deemed unfit for war service on medical or other grounds who did not make this fact known publicly. In the book, Moran offered a possible reason for the dearth of enlistments. He believed that the less-than-welcoming reception that his team had received in England in 1908, particularly from the press, could have soured the patriotic thoughts many of his players had towards the Mother Country, England.[34] A number of the non-volunteers were of Irish stock, and particularly after the 1916 Easter Uprising in Ireland their feelings towards England would have been rapidly ebbing. Another factor could have been that a considerable number of the tourists had turned to Rugby League once back in Australia and had begun to be paid handsomely for their endeavours on the field of play. Going off to the front would have reduced their incomes. This was the fear of many of the proponents for the cancelling of professional sport during the war.

The war took its grim toll on the 1912 Australasian Olympians. Claude Ross, Keith Heritage, Cecil Healy and Anthony Wilding were all killed in action. Many others were wounded, some multiple times. Although not a 1912 Olympian, Frederick Septimus Kelly, who had commented so favourably on the Australians at Royal Henley, was killed along with two fellow members of his Great Britain crew. He was awarded the Distinguished Service Cross, for gallantry at the Gallipoli peninsula, while serving with the Hood Battalion of the Royal Naval Division.[35] His brother, William, the member for Wentworth in the House of Representatives in the Australian Federal Parliament, was a minister in Joseph Cook's government at the declaration of war.

The Victorian, Claude Murray Ross, had not been a standout runner in Australia before leaving for the Olympic Games. He financed his own trip to Stockholm with the hope of gaining further athletics experience. He was eliminated after the heats of the 400 metres. Within days of war being declared in August 1914, he enlisted in the Field Artillery Brigade of the 1st Division, Australian Imperial Force (AIF).[36] In 1915, he was at both the landing (April) and evacuation of Gallipoli (December). In early 1917, he gained his commission in the Royal Flying Corps and in August died in the skies over France.[37] His name is on the Arras Flying Services Memorial. In a sad sequel, his brother Roderick, also a World War I aviator, fathered a son who he named Claude Murray Ross. Claude Murray Ross II died in a flying accident in Canada in February 1941 while training for his 'wings' in the Royal Australian Air Force.[38]

Keith Heritage, from Tasmania via Sydney, was the crew member replaced by Hugh Ward in the rowing eight between the winning of the Grand Challenge Cup at Royal Henley and the Olympic regatta. Heritage had rowed in winning crews in Australia's inter-state eights regattas in 1906 and 1909 (for Tasmania) and 1911 (for NSW). Like Ross, Heritage wasted no time in enlisting, being accepted in the Naval and Military Expeditionary Forces on August 18, 1914. In early 1915, he joined the 19th Battalion, 2nd Division, of the AIF, often called the Sportsmen's Battalion. Other Olympians in that battalion at various times throughout the war were Healy and Middleton. Heritage and Middleton landed at Gallipoli in August 1915, and left the peninsula during the evacuation the following December, with the former one of the last to leave.[39] In June 1916, he was awarded a Military Cross (MC) for leading a successful raid on enemy trenches near

Armentières. A month later, on July 26, Captain Keith Heritage was killed in action at Pozieres. He is buried at Pozieres British Cemetery.[40]

The brilliant Anthony Wilding, originally from Christchurch, a much-admired man on the tennis court and by his friends and colleagues in life and war, was a Captain in the Royal Marines when he died on May 9, 1915, from shellfire near Neuve Chappelle in Northern France.[41] His grave is at Rue-des-Berceaux Military Cemetery, Richebourg-L'Avoue. A few days before his death Wilding penned a prophetic letter to his commanding officer:

> For really the first time in seven and a half months I have a job on hand [leading a gun crew] which is likely to end in gun, I, and the whole outfit being blown to hell. However, it is a sporting chance, and if we succeed we will help our infantry no end. I know the job exactly, and the objects in view from my study of them – it is the only way to play business or war.[42]

In July, a report appeared in the Melbourne *Argus* speaking about recruiting appeals for amateur sportsmen.[43] It spoke of how the combined amateur sporting bodies of Victoria had appealed for funds for Australia to be 'efficiently' represented at the Olympic Games in Berlin. Now, they were appealing to amateur sportsmen to band together to go to Berlin as soldiers rather than athletes. Part of that clarion call for more volunteers to enlist was a poem that mentioned the death of Anthony Wilding:

> The Wilding-Fairbairn heroes,
> Who met death with a dauntless face,
> Have bequeathed a great example,
> To the sons of a lion race.
>
> From spirit land they call us,
> Who died for their country's fame,
> To lay aside out playthings,
> And play the 'greater game'.[44]

It is not surprising that Cecil Healy, world-class swimmer, swimming educator, advocate of healthy living, hero in the surf, champion of the surf club movement and highly respected gentleman, volunteered to serve his country.[45] He enlisted in the 19th Battalion on September 15, 1915. The newly appointed (May 1918) Lieutenant Healy almost survived the carnage but on August 29, 1918, at Mont St Quentin, near Péronne, on the Somme, bravely, as could be expected, he died leading his men into battle, 74 days before the end of the war.[46] A few weeks before his death, he wrote to a friend harking back to his 1913 *Sunday Times* article.[47] His grave is in the New British Cemetery, Assevillers.

Many tributes were written for Healy. His good friend, and at times his commanding officer, Syd Middleton, wrote to *Le Journal* in Paris advising of Healy's death. The battle-weary Middleton[48] succinctly summed up what hundreds of Healy's many friends, fellow competitors and soldier colleagues would have been thinking: 'By Healy's death the world loses one of its greatest champions, one of its best men. Today in the four years I have been at the Front, I wept for the first time.'[49] Healy's international renown was emphasised when, in addition to *Le Journal*, the *New York Times* published news of his death.[50] Within weeks of Healy being killed in action, a memorial book *Cecil Healy: In Memoriam* was produced. It contained a number of the articles that he had written for the press and many of the tributes, letters of condolence and obituaries written upon his death. The profits from the sale of the publication were invested in War Loan Bonds, with the interest providing prizes for junior swimmers in NSW.[51] Healy's standing within the Australian community had been emphasised when a lantern slide of him in army uniform was used as part of the recruitment campaign to encourage sportsmen to volunteer for war service.[52] Another well-known and highly respected Australian sportsman, the cricketer Albert 'Tibby' (often

SPORT, WAR AND SOCIETY IN AUSTRALIA AND NEW ZEALAND

spelt 'Tibbie') Cotter, was also featured on a lantern slide (in his cricket creams and Australian cap) as part of the recruitment campaign.[53] Cotter, like Healy, did not survive the war. He was killed at Beersheba.

Allan Stewart's photo album of Stockholm 1912, held in the *Royal London Hospital Archives,* contains a photograph of Healy with the inscription: 'Cecil Healy, Australian swimming champion at the Olympic Games, Sweden 1912. Killed in France on the Somme 1918. RIP. A great athlete.'[54] Stewart resigned his position at the London Hospital on August 3, 1914, to enlist for war, and by the end of the month was commissioned temporary Lieutenant in the Royal Army Medical Corps.[55] He was soon amidst the battlefield carnage in France. In June 1915 he was wounded[56] and the following December he returned to the London Hospital to resume his medical career.[57]

Syd Middleton enlisted in the 19th Battalion on May 5, 1915. His sporting prowess and readiness to join the colours saw much mention of his wartime exploits in the *Sport* newspaper, the official organ of the Sportsmen's Unit,[58] which had the policy of upholding 'all that is manly, all that is British and Australian, and all that is worth while in the interests of sport'.[59] After four years at war, at Gallipoli and on the Western Front, Middleton had risen to the rank of major (at times, temporary lieutenant-colonel), and had been Mentioned in Despatches (MID) and awarded the Distinguished Service Order (DSO).[60]

The two Australians, Littlejohn and Burdekin,[61] who rowed for Great Britain at Stockholm, also went to war. Littlejohn joined the Royal Army Medical Corps in August 1914, and two months later had the distinction of tending to a mortally wounded Prince Maximillian of Hesse-Kassel, a nephew of Kaiser Wilhelm II, at Caestre in northern France.[62] Littlejohn received an MC for 'great gallantry and initiative' at Ypres in late 1918.[63] Rowers, both from Australia and England, and particularly from the universities, were major contributors to the war effort. Of the 18 young men who comprised the crews in the 1914 Oxford–Cambridge Boat Race, all enlisted and five were killed in action.[64]

Post-War Sport

Middleton emerged from the carnage in the Middle East and the Western Front relatively unscathed. Within weeks of the Armistice, he became the organising secretary of the AIF Sports Control Board. The board was created 'to entertain several hundred thousand soldiers whose job had been completed – in so far as the fighting part of them was concerned' while they were waiting in England before sailing home to Australia, and demobilisation.[65] In the foreword to *Soldiers and Sportsmen*, the book of the AIF Sports Control Board, Brigadier-General Jess, Commandant, AIF Headquarters in London wrote of Middleton:

> the Board possessed as Organising Secretary Major Middleton, D.S.O., an International athlete, whose wide experience and knowledge of sport has been of incalculable value. To his untiring energy, sound judgement, tact and strong personality may be attributed the organisation and capable management which so materially affected the magnificent successes of the Australian soldier sportsmen chronicled on the succeeding pages.[66]

Not only did Middleton organise the sports for the AIF Sports Control Board, he also found the time to coach one of the AIF rowing crews at a time when it was without a mentor. Roger Fitzhardinge, the stroke of the Olympic crew, had been considered for the coaching role but he was still in Australia.[67] Middleton eventually rowed in the six seat of the principal AIF crew at the Royal Henley Peace Regatta.[68] That combination, with another Olympian, Harry Hauenstein, Military Medal (MM),[69] rowing at number five,

26

duly won the premier eight-oar event at the regatta and received the winner's cup from King George V.[70] A reserve for the crew, Harry Ross-Soden (he had been replaced in the line-up at the last minute[71]), had also rowed at Stockholm. Besides competing, Hauenstein and Ross-Soden assisted with the administration of the rowing component of the Sports Control Board. Over the next two decades, three of Middleton's crewmates spoke glowingly about his involvement in the winning of the King's Cup. Captain H. Clive Disher, the stroke, said:[72]

> Behind all the upsets [in the preparation of the crew] one man stood firm. Even he felt the strain but he held the men together, pressed the authorities for their comfort, met every difficulty, and in the end was himself a member of the winning crew ... 'It was Sid [sic] Middleton's crew. He made it his: in the boat and out of it. He was our stronghold in all times of trouble.'[73]

Sergeant Albert Smedley, the coxswain, said that 'he was an inspiration ... a grand oarsman, one of the finest I have ever seen, and the English critics recognised his worth'.[74] And Gunner George Mettam, who rowed in the seven seat, said that Middleton's 'encouragement in times of stress and oarsmanship were big factors in the success of the crew'.[75]

In December 1919, Sydney Albert Middleton was appointed Officer of the Most Excellent Order of the British Empire (OBE), to add to his DSO, 'in recognition of valuable services rendered in connection with the war'. In March 1945, with the end of World War II in sight, the NSW Rugby Union contacted a number of England-based Australians who had been involved with the sport to 'inaugurate services football for repatriated prisoners and all sections of the armed forces in or returning through England'.[76] Middleton was one of those to be contacted. He died in London on September 2, 1945,[77] as one of the unsung champions of Australian sport, from both the competition and administration points of view.

Another significant contributor to AIF Sports Control Board events, as an organiser and a competitor, was Lieutenant Billy Longworth. William Murray was at times a member of the AIF athletics team and the 'gigantic' Harold Hardwick, a sapper in the army in Egypt, was at times a member of the AIF swimming and boxing squads. In April 1919, he travelled to Aldershot, England to contest the Inter-Theatre of War boxing tournament, where he won the heavyweight championship and was subsequently voted by his fellow competitors as the Ideal Sportsman of the Empire. The criteria for winning that accolade were: playing the game for the game's sake, being selfless at play, being able to accept winning and losing in equal measure, readily accepting the umpire's judgement, accepting winning with humility, being ready to assist others in their pursuit of sport, and having a cheerful disposition.[78] Those criteria spoke volumes about Hardwick the man and Hardwick the sportsman.

At the invitation of General John Pershing, Commander-in-Chief, American Expeditionary Forces, Australia was one of 18 Allied nations (29 were invited) to send a team to the Inter-Allied Games, conducted in Paris in June–July 1919.[79] The Australian contingent, ready to compete in many sports, was assembled under the auspices of the AIF Sports Control Board. Hardwick competing as a swimmer, not as a boxer, finished second in the 1500 metres and third in the 800 metres. Longworth was runner-up in both the 400 and 800 metres. The pair teamed with Ivan Stedman (who became an Australian medallist at the next two Olympic Games, Antwerp 1920 and Paris 1924) and Jack Dexter to win the 4×200 metres relay.[80] In rowing, the AIF crew that had been successful at the Royal Henley Peace Regatta, but was now without Middleton and Hauenstein, finished second behind a combination from Cambridge University.

Prior to the opening ceremony of the 1920 Olympic Games in Antwerp, Belgium, Cardinal Mercier conducted a solemn service in the Antwerp Cathedral in honour of those Olympians who had died during the war.[81] The vanquished nations from the war – Germany, Austria, Bulgaria, Hungary and Turkey – were not invited to send teams to Antwerp, nor to Paris in 1924. The 13-strong team Australian team[82] (NZ was now competing as a separate country) that led the parade of nations at the opening ceremony proudly marched behind the flag that had been carried at the similar event at Stockholm (and London 1908).[83] At least half of the 12 men on the team were war veterans. It was not until London 1948 that Australia sent a team of 70, as suggested by E.S. Marks for Berlin 1916, to an Olympic Games.[84]

Conclusion

In summary, from that gathering of young men on the RMS *Osterley*[85] in April 1912 with 'the sharpness of profile, the alert attitude, and the hard squareness of the jaw lines'[86] it is not surprising that by the end of the decade they had garnered manifold bravery decorations at war, including one DSO (to Middleton), three MCs (to Heritage, Ward[87] and McVilly[88]), one Distinguished Conduct Medal (to swimmer Frank Schryver),[89] two MMs (to Hauenstein and Schryver) and a number of MIDs.

Furthermore, it is interesting to note that of the 26 young men from various social, religious and political backgrounds who comprised the Australasian Olympic team at Stockholm 1912, 77% enlisted to fight in the Great War. At the time when many were enlisting, the full grim reality of what lay ahead at Gallipoli and the Western Front was not apparent, yet they still proceeded. Others had heard about the carnage in Turkey and the early days of European battles yet volunteered to serve their King. At their joining the colours, only two, Hauenstein (rowing) and Hardwick (boxing), had become professional sportsmen; the balance of the team had remained amateurs. Further studies could be undertaken into comparing the rates of enlistment for World War I of the professional and amateur sportsmen of Australasia.

Acknowledgements

I thank Barbara Coe for her editorial advice during the preparation of this paper.

Notes

1. In 1912, as in 1908, Australia and New Zealand sent a composite team to the Olympic Games.
2. *Daily News* (Perth), April 23, 1912, 2.
3. Arlott, *Oxford Companion to Sports*, 356–7.
4. *Daily News*, April 23, 1912, 2.
5. Ibid.
6. Radic, *Race Against Time*, 263–4. Kelly was a champion rower, having thrice won the Diamond Challenge Sculls at the Royal Henley Regatta (1902, 1903, and 1905).
7. Ibid., 106.
8. Gordon, *Australia and the Olympic Games*, 79–81.
9. Growden, *Snowy Baker Story*, 66–73.
10. *Referee* (Sydney), December 8, 1915, 13.

11. *Western Argus* (Kalgoorlie), June 18, 1912, 31; *Argus*, June 24, 1912, 9. Littlejohn was born in New Zealand, completed his secondary education at Scotch College, Melbourne and commenced his tertiary studies at the University of Melbourne. He was Victoria's 1909 Rhodes Scholar and proceeded to Oxford University. *Argus*, March 13, 1909, 16.

12. *London Hospital Medical College Register of Students, 1904–1908*, 895–6.

13. Wilding had teamed with the Melburnian, Norman Brookes, to win the Davis Cup for Australasia in 1907–1909. They were to win again in 1914 (Trengove, *The Story of the Davis Cup*, 309–13).

14. Wallechinsky and Loucky, *The Complete Book of the Olympics*, 1141.

15. *Referee*, April 23, 1913, 9.

16. Ibid.

17. Wallechinsky and Loucky, *The Complete Book of the Olympics*, 890.

18. Begvall, *The Official Report*, 957.

19. Gordon, *Australia and the Olympic Games*, 85.

20. Begvall, *The Official Report*, 716–7.

21. Coe, "ES Marks," 67–8.

22. Begvall, *The Official Report*, 717–8.

23. 'Australian Sportsmanship', unidentified news clipping, n.d. (c. 1932). Contained E.S. Marks Sporting Collection held at the Mitchell Library, Sydney.

24. *Sydney Morning Herald* (*SMH*), August 21, 1912, 9.

25. *Lone Hand* (Sydney), March 1, 1916, 216.

26. Begvall, *The Official Report*, 725.

27. Clark, Mason, and Samuelson, *Test Rugby Lists*, 386.

28. *SMH*, March 14, 1913, 8. E.S. Marks's proposed team: 2 military riders, 12 riflemen, 15 soccer footballers, 12 rowers, 2 gymnasts, 5 men and 5 women swimmers, 1 diver, 2 golfers, 2 tennis players, 1 road and 1 track cyclists, 3 general athletes, 2 boxers, 2 wrestlers, one yacht with a crew of 6.

29. *Saturday Referee and The Arrow* (Sydney), November 22, 1913, 3; *Referee*, February 12, 1913, 9.

30. *Sunday Times* (Sydney), February 2, 1913, 19.

31. *Argus* (Melbourne), March 11, 1915, 7.

32. Moran, *Viewless Winds*, 70.

33. National Archives of Australia (NAA): B2455, DALY HF (Item barcode 3484859); NAA: B2455, HAMMOND C A (Item barcode 4256468); NAA: B2455, HICKEY J J 2676 (Item barcode 5457337); NAA: B2455, MCMURTRIE C (Item barcode 1956954); NAA: B2455, RICHARDS THOMAS JAMES (Item barcode 8012773); NAA: B2455, STEVENSON JOSEPH MASON (Item barcode 8089552); *Referee*, September 12, 1917, 12; *Referee*, November 13, 1918, 9; *Referee*, July 9, 1919, 1.

34. Moran, *Viewless Winds*, 69.

35. Radic, *Race Against Time*, 386.

36. *Weekly Times* (Melbourne), May 8, 1915, 21; NAA: B2455, ROSS CLAUDE MURRAY (Item barcode 8038093).

37. *Argus*, February 1, 1917, 3; *Argus*, October 20, 1917, 13.

38. NAA: A705, 53/1/880 (Item barcode 1054280); NAA: B2455, ROSS RODERICK (Item barcode 8038405).

39. Matthews and Wilson, *Fighting Nineteenth*, 53.

40. NAA: B2455, HERITAGE K CAPTAIN (Item barcode 5476366).

41. Myers, *Captain Anthony Wilding*, 292.

42. Ibid., 286.

43. *Argus*, July 14, 1915, 10.

44. 'Fairbairn' was G. Eric Fairbairn, a Victorian oarsman and part of the Fairbairn rowing dynasty, who was studying and rowing at Cambridge University prior to the war and was killed in action France (June 21, 1915) while serving with the Durham Light Infantry (*Leader*, July 3, 1915, 20.). He had won a silver medal at London 1908 in a coxless pair representing Great Britain.

45. Rodwell and Ramsland, "Cecil Healy," 6–10.

46. NAA: B2455, HEALY C LIEUTENANT/2 (Item barcode 4749469).

47. Healy, *Cecil Healy*, 42.

48. Growden, *Wallaby Warrior*, 145–7.
49. 'Famous Swimmer Killed in Action', unidentified news clipping, September 13, 1918. Found in Healy, *Cecil Healy*, contained in the Davis Sporting Collection held at the Mitchell Library, Sydney.
50. 'Lieut. Healy Killed' (*New York Times*, September 13, 1918, 4).
51. Healy, *Cecil Healy*, 3.
52. http://www.awm.gov.au/collection/P04366.007, accessed March 23, 2014.
53. http://www.awm.gov.au/exhibitions/fiftyaustralians/12.asp, accessed March 23, 2014.
54. PP/STE/1 1902–1919, Royal London Hospital Archives and Museum.
55. *Times* (London), August 29, 1914, 4.
56. *Flemington Spectator* (Melbourne), October 14, 1915, 3.
57. *London Hospital Medical College Register of Students, 1904–1908*, 895–6.
58. Also called The Sportsmen's Recruiting Committee.
59. *Sport* (Sydney), July 26, 1917, 1; Phillips, "Australian Sport," 142–3, "Sport, War and Gender Images," 87–9.
60. NAA: B2455, MIDDLETON SYDNEY ALBERT (Item barcode 8012773).
61. *SMH*, June 1, 1915, 8.
62. *Examiner* (Launceston), February 27, 1919, 3.
63. *Supplement to the London Gazette*, July 30, 1919, 9750.
64. http://www.independent.co.uk/news/world/world-history/history-of-the-first-world-war-in-100-moments/a-history-of-the-first-world-war-in-100-moments-the-tragic-fate-of-the-1914-boat-race-crews-revealed-9241149.html, accessed April 11, 2014.
65. Goddard, *Soldiers and Sportsmen*, 9.
66. Ibid., 3.
67. *Referee*, March 19, 1919, 9.
68. *Referee*, March 19, 1919, 86–7; *Argus* July 3, 1919, 8.
69. NAA: B2455, HAUENSTEIN H (Item barcode 4768919).
70. The King's Cup eventually became the trophy for competition by the eight-oared crews at the annual Australian inter-state rowing championships.
71. *Referee*, July 9, 1919, 7.
72. Helms World Trophies (Helms Awards). After World War II, at the request of the California-based Helms Athletic Foundation, a committee of prominent Australian sporting 'experts'(administrators, ex-competitors and journalists) produced a list of Australasia's foremost amateur athletes for each year, excluding war years, back to 1896. For his contribution to the winning of the King's Cup in 1919, Clive Disher was thus retrospectively awarded the Helms World Trophy for Australasia for that year. Stockholm Olympians to be similarly honoured were Anthony Wilding (1909), Harold Hardwick (1911), Cecil Healy (1912), Cecil McVilly (1913), Billy Longworth (1914) and Fanny Durack (1915). *Advertiser* (Adelaide), August 25, 1950, 10.
73. *Sporting Globe* (Melbourne), May 8, 1935, 12.
74. *SMH*, May 14, 1935, 16.
75. *Sunday Times*, May 19, 1935, 24.
76. *SMH*, March 27, 1945, 6.
77. *Times* (London), September 6, 1945, 7.
78. Goddard, *Soldiers and Sportsmen*, 35–6.
79. Mallon & Bijkerk, *The 1920 Olympic Games*, 380–1.
80. *Referee*, July 9, 1919, 11.
81. Mallon & Bijkerk, *The 1920 Olympic Games*, 361; *Referee*, September 29, 1920, 15; *The Tablet*, August 28, 1920, 287–8.
82. Australian Olympic Committee, *The Compendium*, 19–20.
83. *Referee*, May 19, 1920, 10.
84. Australian Olympic Committee, *The Compendium*, 28–33.
85. The RMS *Osterley* saw action during World War I, transporting many Australian troops to and from battlefronts. Unlike many other passenger ships during the war, it was not commandeered as an official troopship but continued to sail under the RMS *Osterley* name. It was scrapped in 1930, but not before it had completed 59 round trips between England and Australia over 20 years of service. http://www.aif.adfa.edu.au:8888/Transports.html, accessed July 1, 2013; *SMH*, April 2, 1930, 12.

86. *Daily News*, April 23, 1912, 2.
87. *Referee*, October 18, 1916, 16.
88. *Argus*, June 16, 1953, 2.
89. NAA: B884, W243654 (Item barcode 6498602).

References

Arlott, John, ed. *The Oxford Companion to Sports and Games*. St Albans: Paladin, 1977.
Australian Olympic Committee (comp.). *The Compendium: Official Australian Olympic Statistics 1896–2002*. Brisbane: University of Queensland Press, 2003.
Begvall, E. (ed.), and Adams-Ray, E. (trans.). *The Official Report of the Olympic Games of Stockholm 1912*. Stockholm: Wahlström & Widstrand, 1913.
Clark, David, Ray Mason, and Stephen Samuelson. *Test Rugby Lists*. Melbourne: Five Mile Press, 1999.
Coe, Bruce Stephen. "ES Marks and His Contribution to Australian Sport." PhD diss., Faculty of Health, University of Canberra, 2011.
Goddard, G. H. *Soldiers and Sportsmen*. London: AIF Sports Control Board, 1919.
Gordon, Harry. *Australia and the Olympic Games*. Brisbane: University of Queensland Press, 1994.
Growden, Greg. *The Snowy Baker Story*. Sydney: Random House Australia, 2003.
Growden, Greg, ed. *Wallaby Warrior: The World War I Diaries of Australia's only British Lion, Tom Richards*. Sydney: Allen & Unwin, 2013.
Healy, H (comp.). *Cecil Healy: In Memoriam*. Sydney: Publisher unknown, 1919.
Mallon, Bill, and Anthony Th. Bijkerk. *The 1920 Olympic Games: Results of All Competitions in All Events, with Commentary*. Jefferson, NC: McFarland, 2003.
Matthews, Wayne, and David Wilson. *Fighting Nineteenth: History of the 19th Infantry Battalion, AIF, 1915–1918*. Sydney: Australian Military History, 2011.
Moran, H. M. *Viewless Winds: Being the Recollections and Digressions of an Australian Surgeon*. London: Peter Davies, 1939.
Myers, A. Wallis. *Captain Anthony Wilding*. London: Hodder and Stoughton, 1916.
Phillips, Murray George. "Australian Sport and World War One." PhD diss., School of Human Movement Studies, University of Queensland, 1991.
Phillips, Murray G. "Sport, War and Gender Images: The Australian Sportsmen's Battalions and the First World War." *The International Journal of the History of Sport* 14, no. 1 (Apr. 1997): 78–96.
Radic, T., ed. *Race Against Time: The Diaries of F.S. Kelly*. Canberra: National Library of Australia, 2004.
Rodwell, Grant, and John Ramsland. "Cecil Healy: A Soldier of the Surf." *Sporting Traditions* 16, no. 2 (2000): 3–16.
Trengove, A. *The Story of the Davis Cup*. London: Stanley Paul, 1985.
Wallechinsky, David, and Jaime Loucky. *The Complete Book of the Olympics: 2012 Edition*. London: Aurum Press, 2008.

Missing in Action? New Perspectives on the Origins and Diffusion of Women's Football in Australia during the Great War

Rob Hess

College of Sport and Exercise Science, Victoria University, Melbourne, Australia

Previous work on female participation in Australian Rules football has highlighted the seemingly discontinuous character of the women's game as it spread from Western Australia to Victoria during the period of the Great War. In this paper, an overview of the current literature on the topic is provided, and there is a focus on hitherto 'missing links' in the existing sequence of events – the knowledge of which has the potential to create a more integrated narrative of the code. In particular, the photographic, filmic and textual evidence for matches of women's football played in South Australia during the Great War is discussed. These games, with proceeds directed to such charities as the 'Workers' Memorial Fund' as well as 'comforts for the Anzacs', attracted sizeable crowds and were sometimes played under the patronage of the governor of the state, the mayor of Adelaide and senior military officers. The paper concludes with a reflection on how the availability (or unavailability) of particular digitised sources, and the serendipitous nature of research itself, can have a problematic influence on investigations associated with marginalised sports such as women's football.

Recent literature associated with the commemoration of the centenary of the Great War has contributed to an ever-widening diversity of perspectives on this seminal global conflict.[1] In many cases, these new investigations have been based on the latest digitisation of a varied array of sources and documents, leading to studies that are more sophisticated and comprehensive, such as Jay Winter's multi-volume collection that provides a 'transnational' exploration of World War I.[2] Australia's contribution to the Great War has attracted ongoing interest from writers and historians ever since the Australian and New Zealand Army Corps (Anzacs) were grouped together in Egypt prior to the landing at Gallipoli in April 1915.[3] Numerous explorations into the Australian experience of war have been published, with studies ranging from well-regarded works by eminent academics, such as L.L. Robson,[4] Bill Gammage[5] and Michael McKernan,[6] to best-selling, more populist volumes by Patsy Adam-Smith and Les Carlyon.[7] Importantly, a key aspect of the last two decades of scholarship has been a more critical emphasis on the mythos surrounding the so-called 'Anzac legend', and deeper deliberations on memories of loss and grief associated with the Great War on the domestic front.[8] These significant themes are invoked in the titles of several works, including *An Anzac Muster: War and Society in Australia and New Zealand,*[9] *The Gates of Memory: Australian People's Experiences and Memories of Loss and the Great War*[10] and *Broken Nation: Australians in the Great War.*[11] Several anthologies have also taken a more explicitly critical stance, with noteworthy examples including *Australia's War, 1914-18*,[12] *Gender and War: Australians at War in the Twentieth Century*[13] and the controversial *What's Wrong With Anzac?: The Militarisation of Australian History*.[14]

While much of the recent public attention has been driven by the forthcoming centenary of the sacrifices of antipodean troops at Gallipoli, and a concomitant debate on the meaning and national significance of Anzac Day,[15] the remembrance of Australasian involvement on the Western Front, where the remains of dozens of long-lost soldiers have lately been unearthed, has also contributed to a broadening of the focus beyond the ill-fated, but much feted, campaign at what later became known as Anzac Cove in Turkey.[16] Academic research has also been driven by a number of Australian Research Council funded projects, including such studies as 'Anzac Day at Home and Abroad: A Centenary History of Australia's National Day', 'Revisiting Australia's War: International Perspectives on Australian and New Zealand Anzac Journeys – Pilgrimages to the Cemeteries, Sites and Battlefields of World War Two' and 'A Land Fit for Heroes: A Social, Cultural and Environmental History of Soldier Settlement in NSW, 1916–1939'.[17]

In addition, there has been a small but steady stream of international studies on female involvement in the war, and, aside from those women who directly participated as nurses, the experiences, reactions and responses of females on the 'home front' during the Great War are beginning to be explored in more depth. For example, Yvonne Klein has edited a collection of 19 illuminating first-hand accounts of the war years written by women from a number of nations,[18] and Kate Adie has recently published a substantive volume on the legacy of British women on the home front during the war.[19] As the website of the British National Archives succinctly explains,

> The response of women to the outbreak of war in August 1914 was mixed. A small number adopted a staunch anti-war position and later worked with the conscientious objectors' movement. A much larger minority threw their patriotic weight behind the Allied cause.

However, in general, the majority of British women '... fell somewhere between these two extremes, viewing the war as an inevitability for which they now had to make sacrifices'.[20]

While some material has focussed on the experiences of Australian women, particularly in terms of their changing role in the workforce or in volunteer organisations such as the Red Cross Society,[21] there are very few published works that contemplate the sporting practices of women in Australian during the period of the Great War.[22] This is partly due to the perception that most sport during the war years was curtailed, with many male teams decimated by the large number of young men who voluntarily enlisted, or entire competitions ultimately closed down by patriotic sports administrators who were keen to demonstrate their moral support for the war effort.[23] However, it was precisely these circumstances that helped to create opportunities for women to participate as players in a football code that they had supported as spectators and auxiliaries in disproportionately large numbers.[24]

Women's Football in Western Australia and Victoria during the Great War

It is not the purpose of this paper to detail either the broad experiences associated with Australian sport during the Great War or the distinctive background to women's overall involvement in Australian Rules football. However, it is worth noting that while general overviews of Australian sport usually echo the orthodox perspective that the nation's character was forged in battle during the course of a war fought in aid of the motherland, there are a handful of studies that look specifically, and critically, at aspects of sport in the context of World War I,[25] and there are also several biographical works that highlight the stories of individual sportsmen from this period.[26] In addition, the work of Murray Phillips in examining the role of gender images in the recruitment of the so-called 'Sportsmen's Battalions' during World War I is salient.[27] Phillips contends that sport at this time was 'a popular vehicle to inculcate masculinity, manliness and manhood', and was part of the dissemination of a 'complex web of ideals to the wider British Empire'.[28] It is this consideration then which helps to explain 'the vitriolic debate over the continuation of male sporting activities and the absence of consternation over female sport'.[29] Significantly, while Phillips admits that the Sportsmen's Battalions were based around popular notions of Australian masculinity, he also recognises that 'women's sense of identity was also constructed around the recruiting movement and the impact of battle was just as relevant to non-combatants as combatants'.[30] In particular, Phillips notes that while some women were thrust into conflicting positions, especially concerning the divisive issue of conscription, their prohibition from active military service meant that they had little choice but to take on orthodox 'feminine' compassionate roles. Thus, they assembled themselves into organisations such as the Red Cross Society and the Australian Comforts Fund.[31]

Previous work on female participation in Australian Rules football during the Great War has highlighted the lack of knowledge surrounding the diffusion of the women's game as it spread from its supposed point of origin in Western Australia in 1915 to Victoria in 1918.[32] As noted in the relatively sparse literature on this topic, the history of women's football in Australia can be characterised as fragmentary and discontinuous in nature.[33] Teams are formed and games are played, only for the groups of participants to soon dissolve, sometimes after a single match or a season or two, with the games and the players lost to memory until years later when completely different groups of women, often ignorant about the previous manifestations of the game, become enthused about the code and the same cycle begins again. In essence, the early development of the women's game in Australia has remained hidden from view, and has rarely featured in mainstream histories of the code.

The reasons for this current state of play are multifaceted, and relate to the contours of historiography, methodology and epistemology surrounding this topic. In short, previous work has highlighted the belief that women first played a match of Australian Rules football in Perth in 1915, just a few months after Australian troops participated in the campaign at Gallipoli. As Peter Burke explains, and as noted above, this contentious period in Australian history was marked by significant pressure on sporting organisations in general and football clubs in particular to cease their activities so that the war effort could be fully supported.[34] Burke explores the emergence of women's football in Perth at this time against a backdrop of class tensions created by conscription debates, and in the general context of the development of workplace sport, particularly football teams. He notes that there were points of distinction with the British wartime economy, claiming that 'in Australia there was no sudden influx of women into the industrial workforce or non-traditional workplace roles'.[35] This observation is important because, as discussed below, virtually all of the women's teams that played football in Perth and nearby localities during the course of the Great War appear to be associated with specific workplaces. Moreover, Burke is cognisant that employers almost invariably sided with imperialists in British military conflicts, and he claims it was not long before business owners 'were joining the rising patriotic chorus', and becoming closely aligned with recruitment drives.[36] He explains that, throughout 1915, many of the usual annual, informal and friendly workplace football matches continued, but the government and most employers were united against the continuation of professional forms of sport.[37] As the war dragged on, however, suspending various forms of workplace sport became an additional and tangible means for employers to mark their forceful support for the war, and many workplace teams and competitions were disbanded.[38] There were, though, situations where employers encouraged football as a means of building patriotism, and some games continued on the agreement that if an admittance fee was charged, then it had to be donated to a wartime or patriotic cause. In short, 'Workplace football matches, held in conjunction with fundraising efforts, thus became one way that companies could display their patriotism'.[39]

Patriotic fervour, the need to provide socially acceptable forms of entertainment for an increasingly war-conscious society, and amenable employers supportive of the benefits of workplace sport, therefore underpinned the beginnings of women's football in Perth.[40] Burke devotes considerable attention to the phenomenon of women's workplace football games in Perth during the war, but despite the recent digitisation of a significant number of newspaper archives (through the auspices of the National Library of Australia),[41] and the efforts of those who have gleaned basic particulars from digitised press items,[42] many of the actual details of games are still sketchy and poorly contextualised.[43] Nonetheless, it is important to note the defining characteristics of the original teams involved. In the two known matches that took place in 1915, the opposing teams consisted of shop assistants and factory employees from a large retailing firm, Foy and Gibson. Subsequent photographic evidence and oral testimony indicates that the women played in long skirts and caps, and were coached by men, with not insignificant sums raised for various charities.[44] In summary, Burke claims that 'most of the large Western Australian retailing firms followed this example and organised football teams comprising woman employees'. He continues by succinctly explaining that 'In 1916, other Perth stores such as Boans, Economic and Bon Marche, as well as the retail trade in the port town of Fremantle, were represented in the competition', and notes that there was a further expansion in 1917 when a country team organised by retailers from the town of Kalgoorlie challenged Foy and Gibson, the most successful team and unofficial premier of the Perth competition.[45]

While it is not the intention of this essay to explore the circumstances of all these matches, it is clear from the rather limited evidence that these games were relatively well attended and achieved their aim of raising funds for a number of war-related charitable organisations. Moreover, since Burke and others have completed their initial studies based on what might be considered 'traditional' archive sources (such as microfilmed and hard copies of newspapers, along with carefully chosen interviews), it has become apparent that even though easily accessible digital newspaper archives have recently become available (and are somewhat in vogue for research purposes), there are still considerable gaps in knowledge and often misleading 'disconnections' between the different types of archives and the methods used to select and access the material. For example, digital archives are not yet able to confirm the details of all the women's games in Western Australia, partly because not all newspapers for the period of the Great War are digitised for that state, partly because not all games would have been reported in the press, and partly because some relevant supporting documents have either been ignored or used selectively. For instance, one image of the Foy and Gibson women's team from 1917 appears not to have been published in the contemporary press, but is available for online viewing from the website of the State Library of Western Australia.[46] However, as the catalogue entry reveals, the names of the women (and the single male in the photograph) are handwritten on the back of the image. The listing of identities by name is not yet digitised and thus not readily accessible to online researchers, leading to the situation where these particular women continue to remain virtually anonymous, despite the fact that the image has been published in various books.[47]

As noted elsewhere,[48] the participation of employees of the Boan Brothers department store in some of the above women's matches is instructive. The firm's founder, Henry 'Harry' Boan, who arrived in Perth in 1895, was strictly anti-unionist, and his firm soon became synonymous with the employment of women.[49] He was also a generous corporate citizen, had close business links with Britain, gave generously to the Patriotic Fund and other charities and was an active supporter of the conscription campaigns of 1916 and 1917.[50] In a period of political turbulence and department store rivalry, Boan encouraged the women in his store to participate in football matches for ostensibly charitable purposes. However, it seems apparent that female teams, in general, and the Boans' team, in particular, were perhaps also used as weapons in the public debate over the continuation of male sport, and were, deliberately or not, associated with support of the conscription referenda. In this context, the scattered press reports of the matches are revealing. In October 1917, the *Western Mail* featured a photograph of 'The winners of the ladies' fancy dress football match played on the Subiaco oval on Saturday last' (see Figure 1). The image shows 20 women in three rows in an outdoor setting, with the umpire, Harry Crapp, standing to the side. The accompanying text indicates that 'The game was arranged by the employees of Boan Bros. to forward the interests of Miss G. Howlett's candidature in the

Figure 1. Employees of Henry Boan's department store played a number of football matches to raise money for charities during the period of the Great War. Image and caption from the *Western Mail*, October 5, 1917.

popular lady competition in aid of the Children's Home'. Boan, elected unopposed as a Member of Parliament just a few months earlier, is recorded as having 'set the ball in motion' in front of 'a good attendance', and although the reporter considered that 'As a game of football it was a failure', it was admitted that the majority of players, who were 'picturesquely attired', participated 'with vigour'.[51]

The reference to striking apparel is worthy of comment, because even though the contest was promoted as a 'fancy dress' football match, it seems that the women's uniform consisted of caps, scarves, long dresses, stockings and presumably boots. Although, as mentioned below, football (and cricket) games where both male and female participants dressed in a range of different theatrical costumes were played in the late-nineteenth century, and continued to feature as novelty events well into the twentieth century, it seems that many female footballers in Australia during the time of the Great War wore similar garb to the original Foy and Gibson teams of 1915. Thus, even though described as 'fancy dress' football, the wartime games were quite distinct from other burlesque contests where varied costumes were often meant to be grotesque or to parody fictional or historical characters. In this sense, the identical long dresses and other accoutrements worn by the women, restrictive though they must have been for any form of sport, signified that their contests were perhaps more legitimate than those played by participants in clown costumes or animal masks (as discussed below).

Boan's background and status are also important because of the possibility that he was a link-person in the diffusion of women's football to the eastern states. Victoria's capital city, Melbourne, is the acknowledged point of origin for the code itself, and hence it had a more well-developed football culture than other Australian cities.[52] While it is likely that women (or men, possibly dressed as women) may have participated in carnivalesque-type matches in Victoria during the late 1880s and 1890s,[53] and there is a newspaper report from the seaside town of Williamstown 1886 which has an intriguing report of a women's match featuring players with 'skirts tucked up', drop-kicking and marking 'the sphere' (observed by an office boy 'while out on an errand'),[54] the first well-documented evidence of a match between two female teams in Victoria relates to a contest between the 'Lucas Girls' and the 'Khaki Girls' in Ballarat on September 28, 1918.

As explained in a previous publication,[55] this game was similar to the matches in Perth, in that it was played between two workplace teams for patriotic charity purposes. In this instance, the 'Khaki Girls' from the Commonwealth Clothing Factory in South Melbourne and the 'Lucas Girls' from a textile and clothing company in Ballarat played an exhibition game in front of several thousand spectators in order to raise funds for the building of an Arch of Victory, with money from the day's afternoon tea set aside for the Ballarat East Red Cross and the Trenches' Fund (see Figure 2). Ballarat, one of Victoria's major rural towns, was renowned for its support of the war effort, and in May 1917 Mrs W.D. 'Tillie' Thompson, a director of E. Lucas & Company, began implementing the idea that trees should be planted in honour of each Ballarat citizen who had enlisted in the Australian Imperial Force (AIF). This suggestion was enthusiastically taken up by the employees of the company, and within a month approximately 500 staff, who became known locally as the 'Lucas Girls' (or 'Lucas' Girls'), began to plant trees along an avenue leading into the town.[56]

The task of understanding the background and motivations of the Lucas Girls has been helped by the fact that an elegant history of the Lucas company was published in 1964. The founder of the firm was Eleanor Lucas (born 1848, died 1923), a widow with four young children who set up a backroom workshop in Ballarat in 1888. Described as having 'an unwavering Christian faith' and a member of the local Church of Christ, the company

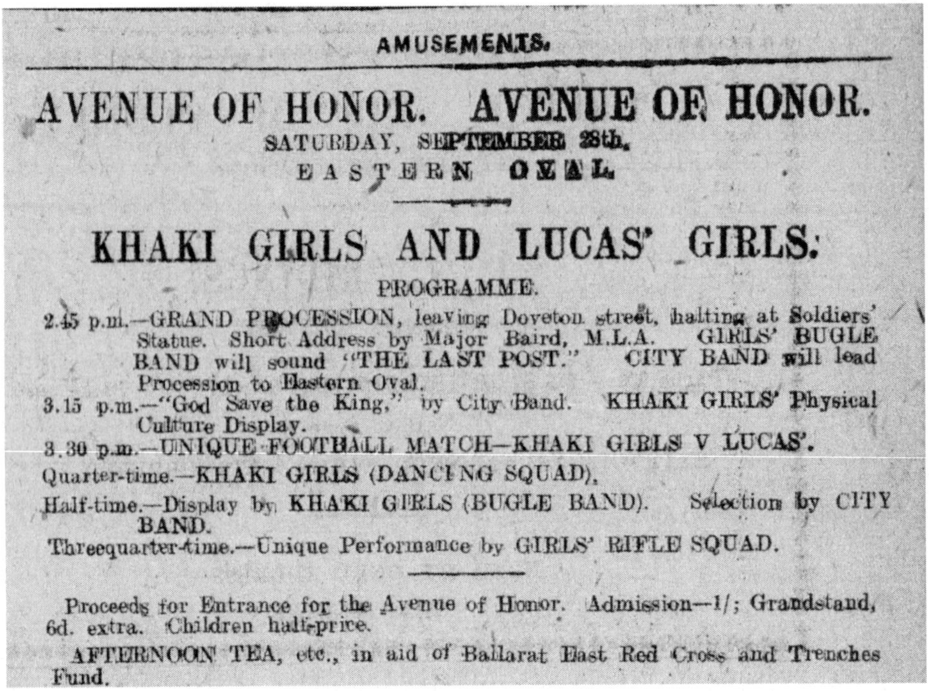

SPORT, WAR AND SOCIETY IN AUSTRALIA AND NEW ZEALAND

AMUSEMENTS.

AVENUE OF HONOR. AVENUE OF HONOR.

SATURDAY, SEPTEMBER 28th.

EASTERN OVAL

KHAKI GIRLS AND LUCAS' GIRLS.

PROGRAMME.

2.45 p.m.—GRAND PROCESSION, leaving Doveton street, halting at Soldiers' Statue. Short Address by Major Baird, M.L.A. GIRLS' BUGLE BAND will sound "THE LAST POST." CITY BAND will lead Procession to Eastern Oval.

3.15 p.m.—"God Save the King," by City Band. KHAKI GIRLS' Physical Culture Display.

3.30 p.m.—UNIQUE FOOTBALL MATCH—KHAKI GIRLS V LUCAS'.

Quarter-time.—KHAKI GIRLS (DANCING SQUAD).

Half-time.—Display by KHAKI GIRLS (BUGLE BAND). Selection by CITY BAND.

Threequarter-time.—Unique Performance by GIRLS' RIFLE SQUAD.

Proceeds for Entrance for the Avenue of Honor. Admission—1/; Grandstand, 6d. extra. Children half-price.

AFTERNOON TEA, etc., in aid of Ballarat East Red Cross and Trenches Fund.

Figure 2. Employees of the Lucas Company and the visiting Commonwealth Clothing Factory played a football match to raise money for Ballarat's Arch of Victory. Advertisement from the *Ballarat Star*, September 27, 1918.

history makes it clear that, in a business eventually employing many hundreds of young girls, 'comradeship in work and shared belief in community service' were the formula that ensured sound relations between management and labour.[57] Thus, the Lucas employees were not only instrumental in fund-raising for the Arch and the Avenue, but also allowed to leave their machines, for instance, to welcome and farewell Anzac troops, distributing gifts and singing choruses at the local train station.[58] As labour historian Raelene Frances notes, the purpose of such sanctioned activities was not just to encourage patriotism in the Lucas Girls, but also to encourage loyalty to the firm and its values, thus providing a bulwark against any potential industrial action on the factory floor.[59]

Importantly, the Lucas company history reveals that some of the like-minded paternalistic customers of the firm included Harry Boan (who was born near Dunnolly, not far from Ballarat, in 1860), as well as other businessmen involved in promoting women's football in Perth during this period. It is therefore not unreasonable to surmise, as indeed Burke does, that the match in Ballarat was inspired by Lucas's close associations with commercial partners in Perth.[60]

While connections with businesses that fielded women's workplace football teams in Western Australia appear to underpin the reasons why the Lucas company staged a match in Ballarat, it does not adequately explain the involvement of their opposing team. The employees of the Commonwealth Clothing Factory, nearly all single women, were responsible for making uniforms for the troops, hence the nickname 'Khaki Girls', but they enthusiastically devoted their time and contributed financial resources from their limited wages to the war effort. As Bruce Scates and Frances emphasise, it was not unusual for women in many female-dominated workplaces to bear heavy workloads, and the formation of special after-hours working bees to raise money and make comforts for the troops was a common scenario. However, the efforts of the Khaki Girls attracted special attention.[61] According to Scates and Frances, they were officially formed in 1918 and organised themselves into three branches – a Bugle Band, a Physical Culture Squad and a Rifle Squad – each with a distinctive uniform, strongly paramilitary in nature. These groups spent their time drilling and performing with the express purpose of raising funds and assisting AIF recruiting campaigns. Moreover, they travelled to distant regional towns such as Geelong, Echuca, Shepparton and Ballarat, where they took part in parades and militaristic displays.[62] A later interview with the leader of the Bugle Band, Lyla Barnard, reveals that it was the Rifle Squad who played in the football match against the Lucas Girls, but it was usual for the entire group of Khaki Girls to march at other venues, even though the notion of women wearing military uniforms was somewhat controversial at this time.[63]

Burke is at pains to place all of the women's matches mentioned above in the context of the growth of workplace recreation. He highlights the notion that they occurred only with the tacit, paternalistic approval of the employers concerned, and that the games were played ostensibly for the purpose of raising money for patriotic causes and to celebrate the military achievements of Australian soldiers. While this template is a valid one, there are nuances to the argument, particularly in the case of the Victorian example, which Burke only briefly considers. For instance, while the Commonwealth Clothing Factory was, like many other female workplaces, strongly anti-unionist,[64] the activities of the Khaki Girls were much more stridently military in nature than any other female football team in Australia at this time. Certainly, none of the other women's teams are lauded for their 'patriotic fire' and physical attributes in the manner that the Khaki Girls were in both verse and newspaper commentary. Seemingly with no links to the department store entrepreneurs of Perth who fostered women's football in Perth, there is also the suggestion, alluded to in newspaper reports, that the Khaki Girls had 'experience in the game'.[65] However, it is not clear whether their supposed expertise was from extensive training or previous matches against other opponents. Whatever the case may be, despite the success of the event, there is no record that either the Lucas Girls or Khaki Girls played football matches again. Indeed, with the end of the war imminent, and a consequent waning of the support and opportunities offered by employers for women's workplace football, there was a short hiatus in the women's game across Australia, an interruption given impetus by the worldwide outbreak of the Spanish influenza epidemic.[66] It was not until the early 1920s that the press began to make observations on the fact that female teams in soccer, rugby league and Australian Rules football were (re)emerging across Australia at virtually the same time.[67] Although the sport history scholarship on this period is sparse, anecdotal information indicates that not all of the women's football teams which emerged in Australia during the 1920s were as heavily associated with workplace recreation, and were mostly devoid of the hyper-patriotic, militaristic and masculine traits exhibited by groups such as the Khaki Girls.

Women's Football in South Australia during the Great War

Much of the above discussion on women's football in Western Australia and Victoria has been based largely on previously published work on the topic. However, it is indicative of the nascent research on the women's game that there are no academic studies which make mention of women's football in South Australia during the Great War. In fact, despite a listing of almost 60 Honours, Masters and PhD theses dealing with the history and/or management of Australian Rules football in a comprehensive bibliography, none are concerned with the women's game in South Australia, and only two Honours dissertations are specific to the general history of the code in South Australia.[68] The official history of the South Australian National Football League makes no mention of women's football, and only a few pages are devoted to the impact of the Great War on the Adelaide's senior men's competition, noting that while most clubs disbanded for the duration of the conflict, a number of League and amateur teams combined to form the Patriotic League in 1916, which continued operating until the end of the 1918 season.[69] In this context, it is relatively easy for developments in women's football in South Australia to 'fly under the radar', with an assumption that females took up the game at a later stage.[70]

One solution to this problem is to rely on searches of digitised newspaper databases, where key terms such as 'women's football', 'ladies' football', 'girls' football' and 'female footballers' help to reveal some anecdotal evidence for the development of the game. Thus, it is possible to sketch something of a framework for the growth of the women's code in South Australia. A necessarily patchy narrative drawn from sometimes quite isolated newspaper articles is, however, an important one, for it helps to confirm that the diffusion of the women's game (based on the available evidence) seemed to occur in a west-to-east direction across the nation, albeit with some notable differences in the examples from Adelaide.

What follows is not a comprehensive listing or discussion of all references to women's football in South Australia. Rather, it is an indicative sampling of the types of games that were occurring across the state. As expected, some of the earliest records related to women's football in South Australia are, as they are in other states, short on detail and open to speculation as to the form of the game, the identity of the participants and the level of organisational or public support. It is also difficult to gauge whether or not the players and officials involved were necessarily aware of other related developments elsewhere in Australia (or the rest of the world), although press reports of women's soccer in Britain certainly appeared in some Australian newspapers during the 1890s and it was not uncommon for obscure or novel events such as female participation in local football games to be reproduced in newspapers far away from their point of origin. Many of the reports are also 'tongue-in-cheek', so it is not always clear that the games or women being referred to were real or fictional. For example, in 1906, the *Burra Record*, in an aside to a regular 'gossip column', mentions that ' . . . a girls' football club' was to be organised in the town. Located in the mid-north of South Australia and originally settled as a mining town in the mid-nineteenth century, Burra later became a pastoral centre. However, there is no evidence that a club was formed or any matches played, although the same column makes special mention of female interest in the code by noting the presence of 'girl barrackers' in the town.[71] A little more substantive in terms of anecdotal evidence is the reference to the picnic of the Saddleworth Total Abstinence Society in September 1911, where 'A ladies' football match resulted in Miss Daley's team beating Miss Friebe's team by about 3 goals', with 'Mr H. Blunt' officiating as the umpire.[72] As the report reveals, the picnic was held in the nearby 'scrub' and was preceded by races and games. Saddleworth is also located in the mid-north of South Australia (on the road to Burra), but such isolated references, and their matter-of-fact reporting, simply reveal not so much any supposed link between games played in close geographical proximity, but rather that low-key 'scratch' matches involving females, or plans to form a women's football club, were episodes occasionally deemed to be noteworthy. These sorts of unsubstantiated rumours about the formation of clubs, or the examples of women playing in impromptu games, are examples of the type of de-contextualised circumstantial evidence that a search of digitised press sources can reveal.

By 1916, however, the Great War was providing a context for a particular type of women's football game. Novelty football matches involving females, with funds raised to be forwarded to such charities as the 'Soldiers' Fund', were now being reported in a number of newspapers.[73] Unlike the contests in Perth, though, where most games were played by women in uniform with scores and best players sometimes recorded in a loosely based competitive framework, a 'ladies' football match' in Adelaide, played at the University Oval on Friday, July 28, 1916, was a costume match organised by Miss N. McCartney. In this case:

> The players were picked promiscuously from all parts of the city and suburbs, and were attired in various grotesque costumes. Some represented Indians, negroes, and clowns, while others appeared in neat costumes which facilitated a quick run on the wing or an effective dash through the centre line.[74]

Indeed, it was the 'absurdity of the situation' that appealed to the spectators, indicating that not only did the novelty of women playing football have appeal, but also the 'fancy dress' nature of the contest added to the spectacle of the occasion and helped to attract interested onlookers. These less than serious contests were, in fact, part of a long line of sporting activities where both males and females masquerading in fancy dress costumes in a carnival-type environment signified not so much the desire to play sport, but the desire to suspend accepted social hierarchies for a limited time, ostensibly for entertainment or fund-raising purposes.[75]

By 1917, with the war still in full swing, matches featuring women continued to take place in Adelaide, with some games now under the auspices of the Young Men's Christian Association,[76] while in the following year, reports of games in country towns such as Gawler, north of Adelaide, were reported, featuring evening practice sessions and supported by claims that '[r]ecognized football colours' would be worn.[77] In the latter case, on the day of the match, 'Each player was designated with the "pet" name of her brother who had shown prowess in the football field before the days of the war, most of them now being away serving the colours', and all 36 players, divided into the 'Excelsiors' and the 'Bing Girls', were listed in the press.[78] However, given the example of Miss McCartney's costume match (mentioned above), it was not always initially clear to the crowd what sort of contest they were going to witness at such matches. In this instance, according to the press, even while the players were 'distributed to their respective places in the field', 'the spectators treated the whole as a burlesque, and created much merriment by addressing the fair ones, adorned in Jerseys, short skirts and bloomers, by their new titles of Jerry, Dinny, Chook, Squash, etc.'.[79] While the first quarter was seen as 'highly amusing', and the crowd was often 'in roars of laughter', it did not take long for the barracking to become characterised by encouragement rather than shouts of derision. As the reporter noted, 'the girls settled down to play' and the spectators became 'surprised with the skill that was exhibited'.[80] Four quarters of 15 minutes each were played, notably on a full length ground, 'the girls disdaining a shorter course'.[81]

The above discussion implies that there was a type of linear progression in football games involving women. From impetuous, non-descript scratch games played as part of picnics or social gatherings, to fancy dress matches where women (and also sometimes men) donned theatrical costumes (emphasising the absurdity of their contest) in order to provide novelty entertainment for a crowd, to more serious competitions, where the participants were perhaps part of a workplace or other social grouping and practised beforehand, were usually coached by men, and often surprised onlookers with their skill and determination on the field of play. While on the surface this represents a tempting pattern for the development of women's football, it is too simplistic and does not take adequate account of the diversity of contests that were occurring. That is, there were several types of football competition, involving women versus women, and men versus women (not to mention men dressed as women), that coexisted, both during the Great War and afterwards.

Amongst this mixture of football games involving women was also the high profile, officially sanctioned, overtly patriotic fund-raising event, usually staged on a much grander scale. The prime example of this is the heavily promoted match between North Adelaide and South Adelaide at the Jubilee Oval on Saturday, September 21, 1918. The advertisement for this game highlights 'the distinguished patronage' for the event, which included luminaries such as the governor and his wife, the mayor and his wife, a brigadier general and an army captain (see Figure 3). The patriotic purpose behind the 'Girls' Football Carnival' was also explicit, as the event was staged 'By permission of the Department of Repatriation' and with the 'sanction of the Red Cross Society'. All proceeds were to 'provide comforts for the Anzacs' and the potential audience were assured that they would be 'helping our soldiers by coming to the carnival'.[82] Worthy of note is that the game was not played between workplace teams, as most similar matches in Western Australia at this time seem to have been. Also notable is the fact that the Red Cross Society was directly involved in endorsing the contest. While this organisation was involved in supporting other wartime football games elsewhere in Australia, including the match in Ballarat, the fact that the Adelaide contest was officially 'sanctioned' by the Society sets this match apart.

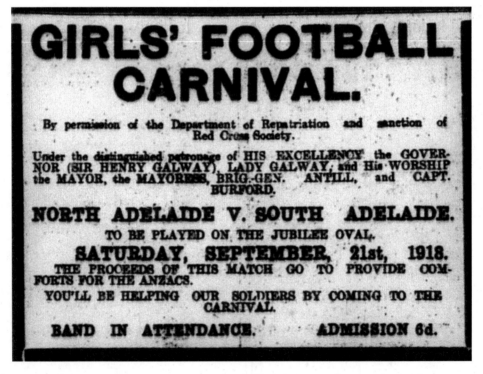

Figure 3. A match between North Adelaide and South Adelaide in 1918 was played under the patronage of the governor, the mayor and military officers. Advertisement from the *Register*, September 20, 1918.

According to a recent centenary history, the Australian Red Cross Society was officially formed nine days after the outbreak of the war, although it was initially mooted in Adelaide in 1909, and had the support of leading citizens, including the mayor of the city. A local 'German and Samaritan Red Cross Society' was formed in Adelaide in 1911, a city that had historically attracted many German immigrants throughout the nineteenth century.[83] However, it was Lady Helen Munro Ferguson, the wife of recently appointed Australian governor-general Ronald Munro Ferguson, based in Melbourne where the national parliament was located, who was the catalyst for the formation of a network of independent 'state divisions' of the Red Cross.[84] In Adelaide, explains Melanie Oppenheimer, the South Australian division was formed at a meeting convened jointly by Lady Marie Galway, the wife of the state's governor, and Mrs A.A. Simpson, the wife of the mayor. Galway was part German, and in Oppenheimer's view this 'cultured, intelligent, charming' woman went out of her way to make sure that the conveniently located Government House was open to the cause of the Society.[85] To add further context to the involvement of these two women as patrons of the 'Girls' Football Carnival', it should be noted that the Australian Red Cross raised money in a variety of ways. While Oppenheimer mentions Church collections, dances, socials, gymkhanas, race meetings, raffles, art unions, carnivals and fairs as charitable events, she also specifically adds 'football matches' to her list and notes that 'Having vice-regal patronage certainly assisted [the] Australian Red Cross in their fundraising'.[86] While no specific football matches are mentioned in her book, the role of Galway and Simpson in fostering the women's football match in Adelaide must have been an exemplar of this type of activity.

Following the match, Adelaide's *Daily Herald* provided a comprehensive report of the game, including a list of all participants, goal kickers and best players. It was a positive and eager report, including such descriptive phrases as 'Moments of intense excitement were frequent, and many of the onlookers were enthusiastic in their encouragement'. There were no derogatory asides in the report and there was no crowd misbehaviour worthy of mention, with special reference of the military band that 'rendered selections' throughout the afternoon.[87] In a male football landscape decimated by the war, a heavily promoted, well-patronised women's game, held for a patriotic cause on one of the city's main ovals, was clearly favourably received by the press, and as a contest it stands apart from some of the other games that were staged in South Australia during the Great War.

One other aspect makes this match significant, even distinct. Unlike most other matches from South Australia during the Great War, it appears that a photograph has survived of the North Adelaide versus South Adelaide game. While no images seem to be traceable in digitised press sources from South Australia in this period, there are a small number of relevant photographs of female footballers that do exist. These images, recently uncovered in the Searcy Collection at the State Library of South Australia by Matthew Stephen, feature one action shot of a women's match.[88] The catalogue entry describes the photograph as 'Girls playing football on Jubilee Oval, Adelaide' and the date provided is 'ca 1918'. Given that one of the players is wearing a jersey with a square, white patch featuring a red cross on their back, it seems highly likely that this is a photograph of the game played under the sanction of the Red Cross Society and with vice-regal patronage. A male figure, presumably the umpire (wearing what seems like a suit and hat), stands to the right of the action, as a loose ball is chased by several women. The teams, one in light colours and the other in a dark uniform, are wearing stockings, dresses and jumpers, with the light-coloured team members visible in the shot all wearing what appear to be beanies. A sizeable crowd is looking on in the distance.[89]

At least two other images of female footballers from the Great War period are also in the vast Searcy Collection, and both are dated 'ca 1917'. One, labelled as 'A team of young sportswomen in South Australia' in the catalogue entry, depicts three rows of women, all wearing a white uniform similar to that worn by one of the teams in the 1918 image described above. The ball is slightly indistinct in terms of shape (it could be round or oval), but the fact that 18 women are in the outdoor shot (with what looks like some type of barracks in the background) would indicate that these women were dressed and ready for a game of Australian Rules football rather than soccer (which only requires 11 persons on a team).[90] The second image also features 18 women in three rows, but they are in a studio setting and the photograph also includes two well-dressed women (one wearing a fox-fur) and three men in suits and ties. A large flag with some sort of embroidered insignia is cradled by one of the players in the front row. The catalogue describes the image as 'Studio view of a team of sportswomen, the captain holds a large ball; identities not known'. The date is 'ca 1917'.[91] It cannot be ascertained with certainty, but it is possible, despite the variance in the approximate dates provided in the catalogue entries, that all three photographs relate to the women who played in the North Adelaide versus South Adelaide game that took place in 1918. This assumption is partly based on the observation that the uniforms worn in the 'ca 1917' images are very similar to those depicted in the 'ca 1918' action shot.

Space does permit a discussion of all the examples of women playing football in South Australia during the Great War. However, several other matches are worth mentioning in terms of an embryonic typology that is being presented. Although participants in the Jubilee Oval game from September 20, 1918, were not demarcated as being affiliated with workplace teams, there were several contests where female players were associated with Adelaide companies, similar to the situation in Western Australia. For instance, on August 12, 1918, a report, titled 'Feminine Football. A Jolly Exhibition by Women', appeared in the *Register*. It described a 'Women's Patriotic Football Match' at Jubilee Oval, and the two teams represented, respectively, James Marshall and Company and Charles Moore and Company. Players were listed by name, and the uniforms ('jerseys, bloomers, and short pleated skirts') were described as purple and white (Marshall), and two blues with a scarlet monogram (Moore). The report noted that 'Both players and public contributed to the feast of mirth', with squeals by the players that 'delighted the crowd', and the barracking itself said to be entertaining.[92] Importantly, the presence of a 'cinema operator' and 'several photographers' was noted. A return match between the same teams was reported in the *Advertiser* on September 9, 1918, although this time the game was played at the Adelaide Oval in the presence of 'about 3,000 people'. Players were again listed by name and scores were recorded. On this occasion, the umpire was nominated as Mr Black and funds from the match were donated to the Red Cross Society.[93] Significantly, in between the two matches, the 'Wondergraph', a 'Splendid Moving Picture' of the August game between the teams representing the firms of James Marshall and Charles Moore, was screened, and widely advertised in the press.[94] The James Marshall company was a major store in Adelaide, selling footwear, linen, wallpaper and furniture, while the Charles Moore company lauded itself as 'The Premier Store', specialising in 'Tempting Manchester Bargains'.[95] Both companies would have benefited commercially from the exposure garnered from the football games themselves, not to mention the subsequent cinematic coverage. This suggests that, as in Perth, support for women's football may not have been altogether altruistic and that matches featuring workplace teams were an important part of the commercial, social and sporting environment during the war years in particular.

Conclusions

The exact influence of females playing Australian Rules football for the first time during a period when established gender roles were under some strain due to the social ructions of the Great War must always remain notional. However, by piecing together scattered fragments of information, including several photographs that do not yet appear in digitised newspaper databases, as well as some filmic evidence, it is possible to sketch a typology, if not a framework, for the development of the women's code in South Australia (and beyond). Significantly, these hitherto 'missing' developments in South Australia (of which only a few have been discussed in this paper) all occurred before the match that took place between the Lucas Girls and the Khaki Girls in Ballarat, Victoria, on September 28, 1918. Until further evidence is uncovered and greater contextualisation provided, perhaps from currently non-digitised press sources, it would seem that Victoria, traditionally the heart of football culture in Australia, lagged behind other states, notably Western Australia and South Australia, in terms of initiatives related to women playing Australian Rules football.

Acknowledgements

The author wishes to thank colleagues Peter Burke, Roy Hay, Brunette Lenkić, Ken Mansell, Michael Riley, Trevor Ruddell, Matthew Stephen, Ian Syson and Nikki Wedgwood for their practical assistance and ongoing interest in this project.

Notes

1. In terms of nomenclature, it should be acknowledged that the conflict was commonly known as the 'Great War', with international and Australian newspapers referring to 'the next Great War' or 'the coming Great War' in the decade before the war in Europe was declared. See Garton and Stanley, "The Great War and Its Aftermath," 40.
2. Winter, *The Cambridge History*.
3. The acronym 'ANZAC' is often used in lower-case format, as it is throughout this paper. For the entomology and use of the term, see Dennis et al., *The Oxford Companion*, 32.
4. Robson, *Australia and the Great War*.
5. Gammage, *The Broken Years*.
6. McKernan, *The Australian People*.
7. Adam-Smith, *The Anzacs*; Carlyon, *Gallipoli*; and Carlyon, *The Great War*.
8. For a brief discussion of how the 'Anzac legend' developed, see Dennis et al., *The Oxford Companion*, 37–42. For a more detailed treatment, see Seal, *Inventing Anzac*. Blair looks specifically at myths associated with the experience and character of Australian 'diggers' in "'An Army of Warriors, These Anzacs'."
9. Smart and Wood, *An Anzac Muster*.
10. Luckins, *The Gates of Memory*.
11. Beaumont, *Broken Nation*.
12. Beaumont, *Australia's War*.
13. Damousi and Lake, *Gender and War*.
14. Lake and Reynolds, *What's Wrong With Anzac?*
15. Carl Bridge claims that Anzac Day is 'Australia's most important public festival and has become over time the country's de facto national day'. See his entry on 'Anzac Day' in Dennis et al., *The Oxford Companion*, 32–7 (quotation from page 32). For wider considerations of commemoration associated with the Great War, see Sumartojo and Wellings, *Nation, Memory and Great War Commemoration*.

SPORT, WAR AND SOCIETY IN AUSTRALIA AND NEW ZEALAND

16. For recent discussion of these topics in the press, see, for example, King, "Time to Honour Sacrifices," 29. See also Scates, "Finding the Missing of Fromelles," for a more substantive overview. It is significant to note that the Gallipoli campaign lasted only eight months, whereas Australian divisions fought on the Western Front in France and Belgium for two-and-a-half years.

17. For details of these projects, and related conferences, publications and websites, see http://artsonline.monash.edu.au/anzac-remembered/

18. A further 23 women also reflect on World War II in the anthology. See Klein, *Beyond the Home Front.*

19. Adie, *Fighting on the Home Front.*

20. British National Archives, "Women and the First World War," http://www.nationalarchives.gov.uk/pathways/firstworldwar/document_packs/women.htm

21. See, for example, Frances, *The Politics of Work*; Oppenheimer, "'Fated to a Life of Suffering'"; and Oppenheimer, *Australian Women at War.*

22. The most comprehensive book on Australian women and sport contains only fleeting references to women's sport in the 1914–1918 period. See Stell, *Half the Race*, passim.

23. Australian losses in World War I eventually totalled almost 62,000, with an additional 155,000 wounded (although this figure excludes many soldiers who were gassed but did not seek treatment). For an overview of the impact of the conscription debate and its potential impact on men playing Australian Rules football during the war years, see Blair, "'The Greater Game'"; Blair, "Will They Never Come?"

24. Hess, "'Ladies are Specially Invited'."

25. See, for example, Booth and Tatz, *One-Eyed*, 89–107; McKernan, "Sport, War and Society"; Phillips, "Football, Class and War"; Moore, *The Mighty Bears!*, 76–82; and Noonan, "Offside."

26. See, for example, Rodwell and Ramsland, "Cecil Healy"; Phillips and Moore, "The Champion Boxer Les Darcy"; and Main and Allen, *Fallen.*

27. Phillips, "Sport, War and Gender Images," 78.

28. Ibid., 81.

29. Ibid., 84.

30. Ibid., 89.

31. The Australian Red Cross was established on August 13, 1914, with women comprising 80% of its members. The Australian Comforts Fund, also heavily reliant on women, was an umbrella body for most of the voluntary organisations set up after the outbreak of the war. See Dennis et al., *The Oxford Companion*, 59, 67.

32. Hess, "Playing with 'Patriotic Fire'."

33. Hess, "Chinese Footballers and Female Players," 46. For useful discussions of the relevant literature, see Hess, "'For the Love of Sensation'," 20–30; Hogan et al., "Women and Australian Rules Football"; and Wedgwood, "Doin' It for Themselves!"

34. Burke, "A Social History of Workplace," 119.

35. Ibid., 127. See also Burke, "Patriot Games."

36. Burke, "A Social History of Workplace," 128.

37. Ibid., 129.

38. Ibid., 130, 133.

39. Ibid., 133. For a succinct summary of the trenchant opposition to men's football in Western Australia during the Great War, see Barker, *Behind the Play*, 50–1.

40. Burke, "A Social History of Workplace," 141.

41. See the National Library of Australia's Trove website at http://trove.nla.gov.au/newspaper?q=

42. See, for example, the impressive website of Michael Riley (assisted by Ken Mansell), 'Boyles' Football Photos', which has a section devoted to women's football at http://boylesfootballphotos.net.au/tiki-index.php?page=Womens+Football+-+Overview. This is currently the most comprehensive online guide to women's football matches in Australia.

43. See, for example, reports of games in the *Western Mail*, October 26, 1917, and the *Western Mail*, July 5, 1918, where a match between men and women is recorded.

44. Burke, "A Social History of Workplace," 142, 147.

45. Ibid., 142.

46. See http://catalogue.slwa.wa.gov.au/search~S2?/Xwomen%27s+football&searchscope=2&SORT=D/Xwomen%27s+football&searchscope = 2&SORT = D&SUBKEY = women's +

SPORT, WAR AND SOCIETY IN AUSTRALIA AND NEW ZEALAND

football/1%2C48%2C48%2CB/frameset&FF=Xwomen%27s+football&searchscope=2&
SORT=D&4%2C4%2C

47. See, for example, Ross, Hutchinson, and Associates, *Sporting Life*, 86–7, where there is an incorrect, and misleading, claim that the image depicts a 'Women's Football Team, Perth, 1900'.

48. Hess, "Playing with 'Patriotic Fire'," 1394–7.

49. Hough, *Boans for Service*, 23. For details of Boan's life, see also Manford, "Boan, Henry (1860–1941)."

50. Hough, *Boans for Service*, 26–8.

51. *Western Mail*, October 5, 1917. The uniform of the team from the Boan Brothers department store is remarkably similar to that worn by the team from the Foy and Gibson department store.

52. The actual date of origin for Australian Rules football is contested, since various forms of football were being played in Victoria considerably earlier than the much lauded 'first match' in August 1858. For the contours of the debate, see Hess et al., *A National Game*, 1–19; Hay, "Football in Australia before Codification"; and Syson, "The 'Chimera' of Origins."

53. For example, a football match involving men and women on roller skates was played on the Richmond Skating Rink. See the *Richmond Australian*, May 8, 1889. The *Illustrated Australian News*, August 1, 1894, featured an image of men and women from a theatrical troupe playing football on the Melbourne Cricket Ground.

54. *Williamstown Chronicle*, July 17, 1886. One newspaper, as part of a report on women's soccer in Britain, also asserted (without supplying evidence) that 'a match between ladies was played recently in Melbourne'. See *West Australian*, May 23, 1895. Although the focus of this paper is women playing Australian Rules football, it should be noted that there is photographic evidence that females were formally involved in games of soccer in New South Wales from at least during the time of the Great War. See Baxter, "West Wallsend Ladies Soccer Teams," 27. For the best substantive overview of women's soccer in Australia, see Hay and Murray, *A History of Football in Australia*, 264–82.

55. Hess, "Playing with 'Patriotic Fire'."

56. "The Ballarat Arch of Victory and Avenue of Honour," Heritage Information Guide, no date. See also www.ballarat.com/avenue.htm

57. White, *The Golden Thread*, 15, 22.

58. Ibid., 17.

59. Frances, *The Politics of Work*, 97, 194.

60. Burke, "A Social History of Workplace," 158–9.

61. Scates and Frances, *Women and the Great War*, 56.

62. Ibid.

63. Bassett, "Lyla Barnard," 271–4.

64. Frances, *The Politics of Work*, 98.

65. *Ballarat Courier*, September 30, 1918.

66. The pandemic severely disrupted social life in Australia with around 12,000 fatalities recorded. See Garton and Stanley, "The Great War and Its Aftermath," 55–6.

67. Table *Talk*, July 21, 1921. For discussion of the rise and fall of women's soccer during the interwar period in an international context, and its links with the feminist movement of the time, see Michallat, "Terrain de Lutte."

68. For a listing and discussion of a typology of PhDs on Australian Rules football, see Hess, "Unpublished Theses."

69. Whimpress, *The South Australian Football Story*, 31–2.

70. See, for example, Wood, "Blast from the Past," 18, where it is stated that one of the earliest women's matches in South Australia (between two teams representing 'Charles Moore and Co.' and the 'Mirror Shirt and Pyjama Factory') occurred in 1929.

71. "They Say," *Burra Record*, June 6, 1906.

72. "Saddleworth Picnic," *Adelaide Advertiser*, September 4, 1911. While the reference to 'about 3 goals' could be assumed to be a soccer-type scoreline, the bush location is probably indicative of the fact that goalposts were rudimentary at best (and were more likely to be prominent trees), and behinds (for shots either side of the goalposts), as awarded in Australian Rules football, were not recorded.

73. "Ladies' Football Match," *Daily Herald*, July 28, 1916.

74. "Ladies at Football," *Daily Herald*, July 29, 1916.

75. It is beyond the scope of this paper to consider the notion of 'carnival' as explicated by twentieth-century Russian intellectual, Mikhail Bakhtin, who derived his theories on carnival, and the suspension of social hierarchies, through examining the sixteenth-century novels of Rabelais. In this schema, masquerading in fancy dress at public events, including sporting contests, can be construed as a form of social deviance. For further discussion of carnival in the context of the development of Australian aquatic sport in the late-nineteenth and early-twentieth century, see Winterton, "'Feats of Fancy'," 63–109.
76. "The Red Triangle: Splendid YMCA Effort," *Daily Herald*, September 1, 1917.
77. "Ladies' Football Match," *Bunyip*, July 19, 1918.
78. "Ladies at Football," *Bunyip*, August 23, 1918.
79. Ibid.
80. Ibid.
81. Ibid.
82. *Register*, September 20, 1918.
83. Oppenheimer, *The Power of Humanity*, 12.
84. Ibid., 13, 15.
85. Ibid., 23.
86. Ibid., 33.
87. *Daily Herald*, September 23, 1918.
88. According to Matthew Stephen, Searcy was 'a senior customs inspector in Palmerson (Darwin) from the 1880s to 1895'. He returned to Adelaide after his spell in Darwin and died in 1925. Email correspondence from Matthew Stephen, February 14, 2012.
89. The image can be viewed at http://images.slsa.sa.gov.au/searcy/09/PRG280_1_9_298.htm
90. The image can be viewed at http://images.slsa.sa.gov.au/searcy/09/PRG280_1_9_237.htm
91. The image can be viewed at http://images.slsa.sa.gov.au/searcy/09/PRG280_1_9_228.htm
92. "Feminine Football," *Register*, August 12, 1918.
93. "Patriotic Girls' Football," *Advertiser*, September 9, 1918.
94. See an example of an advertisement for the screening of the 'Ladies' Football Match' in the *Register*, September 3, 1918.
95. See examples of advertisements from both companies in the *Register*, September 3, 1918. As noted above, teams from 'Charles Moore and Co.' continued to play games into the 1920s.

References

Adam-Smith, Patsy. *The Anzacs*. Sydney: Thomas Nelson, 1978.
Adie, Katie. *Fighting on the Home Front: The Legacy of Women in World War One*. London: Hodder and Stoughton, 2013.
Barker, A. J. *Behind the Play … A History of Football in Western Australia from 1868*. Perth: West Australian Football Commission, 2004.
Bassett, Jan. "Lyla Barnard: Khaki Girl." In *Double Time: Women in Victoria – 150 Years*, edited by Marilyn Lake and Farley Kelly, 268–275. Ringwood: Penguin Books, 1985.
Baxter, Carole. "West Wallsend Ladies Soccer Teams c 1916." *Australian Family Tree Connection*, April 2012.
Beaumont, Jean, ed. *Australia's War, 1914–18*. St Leonards: Allen & Unwin, 1995.
Beaumont, Jean. *Broken Nation: Australians in the Great War*. St Leonards: Allen & Unwin, 2013.
Blair, D. J. "'An Army of Warriors, These Anzacs': Legend and Illusion in the First AIF.". PhD diss., Faculty of Arts, Victoria University 1998.
Blair, D. J. "'The Greater Game': Australian Football and the Army at Home and on the Front During World War I." *Sporting Traditions* 11, no. 2 (May 1995): 91–102.
Blair, D. J. "Will They Never Come? A Study of Professional Football in Melbourne during the Great War, 1914–1918." Honours diss., Department of History, La Trobe University 1993.
Booth, Douglas, and Colin Tatz. *One-Eyed: A View of Australian Sport*. Sydney: Allen & Unwin, 2000.
Burke, Peter. "Patriot Games: Women's Football during the First World War in Australia." *Football Studies* 8, no. 2 (2005): 5–19.
Burke, Peter. "A Social History of Workplace Australian Football, 1860–1939." PhD diss., School of Global Studies, Social Sciences and Planning, RMIT University 2008.

Carlyon, Les. *Gallipoli*. Sydney: Macmillan, 2001.

Carlyon, Les. *The Great War*. Sydney: Macmillan, 2006.

Damousi, Joy, and Marilyn Lake, eds. *Gender and War: Australians at War in the Twentieth Century*. Cambridge: Cambridge University Press, 1995.

Dennis, Peter, Jeffrey Grey, Ewan Morris, Robin Prior, with Jean Bou. *The Oxford Companion to Australian Military History*. 2nd ed. South Melbourne: Oxford University Press, 2008.

Frances, Raelene. *The Politics of Work: Gender and Labour in Victoria, 1880–1939*. Cambridge: Cambridge University Press, 1993.

Gammage, Bill. *The Broken Years: Australian Soldiers in the Great War*. Canberra: Australian National University Press, 1974.

Garton, Stephen, and Peter Stanley. "The Great War and Its Aftermath 1914–22." In *The Cambridge History of Australia. Volume 2: The Commonwealth of Australia*, edited by Alison Bashford and Stuart McIntyre, 39–63. Cambridge: Cambridge University Press, 2013.

Hay, Roy. "Football in Australia before Codification, 1820–1860." *The International Journal of the History of Sport* 31, no. 9 (May 2014): 1047–1061.

Hay, Roy, and Bill Murray. *A History of Football in Australia: A Game of Two Halves*. Richmond: Hardie Grant Books, 2014.

Hess, Rob. "Chinese Footballers and Female Players: Discontinuous and Marginalized Histories." In *Football Fever: Grassroots*, edited by Bob Stewart, Rob Hess, and Matthew Nicholson, 31–49. Hawthorn: Maribyrnong Press, 2004.

Hess, Rob. "'For the Love of Sensation': Case Studies in the Early Development of Women's Football in Victoria, 1921–1981." *Football Studies* 8, no. 2 (2005): 20–30.

Hess, Rob. "Ladies are Specially Invited': Women and the Culture of Australian Rules Football." *The International Journal of the History of Sport* 17, nos 2–3 (June/September 2000): 111–141.

Hess, Rob. "Playing with 'Patriotic Fire': Women and Football in the Antipodes During the Great War." *The International Journal of the History of Sport* 28, no. 10 (July 2011): 1388–1408.

Hess, Rob. "Unpublished Theses." In *Reading the Game: An Annotated Guide to the Literature and Films of Australian Rules Football*, edited by Tim Hogan, 223–235. Melbourne: Australian Society for Sports History, 2005.

Hess, Rob, Matthew Nicholson, Bob Stewart, and Gregory de Moore. *A National Game: The History of Australian Rules Football*. Camberwell: Penguin/Viking, 2008.

Hogan, Tim, Rob Hess, Nikki Wedgwood, Ian Warren, and Matthew Nicholson. "Women and Australian Rules Football: An Annotated Bibliography." *Football Studies* 8, no. 2 (2005): 77–88.

Hough, David. *Boans for Service: The Story of a Department Store 1895–1986*. Claremont: Estate of F.T. Boan, 2009.

Klein, Y. M. ed. *Beyond the Home Front: Women's Autobiographical Writing of the Two World Wars*. London: Macmillan Press, 1997.

King, Jonathan. "Time to Honour Sacrifices on the Western Front." *Age*, April 24, 2014.

Lake, Marilyn, and Henry Reynolds, eds. *What's Wrong with Anzac?: The Militarisation of Australian History*. Sydney: New South, 2010.

Luckins, Tanya. *The Gates of Memory: Australian People's Experiences and Memories of Loss and the Great War*. Fremantle: Curtin University Books, 2004.

Main, Jim, and David Allen. *Fallen: The Ultimate Heroes – Footballers Who Never Returned from War*. Melbourne: Crown Content, 2002.

Manford, Toby. "Boan, Henry (1860–1941)." *Australian Dictionary of Biography*, Accessed March 20, 2014. http://adb.anu.edu.au/biography/boan-henry-5274

McKernan, Michael. *The Australian People and the Great War*. West Melbourne: Thomas Nelson, 1980.

McKernan, Michael. "Sport, War and Society: Australia 1914–18." In *Sport and History*, edited by Richard Cashman and Michael McKernan, 1–20. St Lucia: University of Queensland, 1979.

Michallat, Wendy. "Terrain de Lutte: Women's Football and Feminism in 'Les Anneés Folles'." *French Cultural Studies* 18, no. 3 (October 2007): 259–276.

Moore, Andrew. *The Mighty Bears! A Social History of North Sydney Rugby League*. Sydney: Macmillan, 1996.

Noonan, Rodney. "Offside: Rugby League, the Great War and Australian Patriotism." *The International Journal of the History of Sport* 26, no. 15 (December 2009): 2201–2218.

Oppenheimer, Melanie. *Australian Women at War*. Canberra: Department of Veterans' Affairs, 2008.

Oppenheimer, Melanie. "'Fated to a Life of Suffering': Graythwaite, the Australian Red Cross and Returned Soldiers 1916–39." In *Anzac Legacies: Australians and the Aftermath of War*, edited by Martin Crotty and Marina Larsson, 18–38. North Melbourne: Australian Scholarly Publishing, 2010.

Oppenheimer, Melanie. *The Power of Humanity: 100 Years of the Red Cross 1914–2014*. Sydney: HarperCollins, 2014.

Phillips, Murray. "Football, Class and War: The Rugby Codes in New South Wales, 1907–1918." In *Making Men: Rugby and Masculine Identity*, edited by John Nauright and T. J. L. Chandler, 158–180. London: Frank Cass, 1996.

Phillips, M. G. "Sport, War and Gender Images: The Australian Sportsmen's Battalions and the First World War." *The International Journal of the History of Sport* 14, no. 1 (April 1997): 78–96.

Phillips, M. G., and Katherine Moore. "The Champion Boxer Les Darcy: A Victim of Class Conflict and Sectarian Bitterness in Australia during the First World War." *The International Journal of the History of Sport* 11, no. 1 (April 1994): 102–104.

Robson, L. L. *Australia and the Great War, 1914–1918*. Melbourne: Macmillan, 1969.

Rodwell, Grant, and John Ramsland. "Cecil Healy: A Soldier of the Surf." *Sporting Traditions* 16, no. 2 (May 2004): 39–54.

Ross, J., G. Hutchinson, and Associates. *Sporting Life: Sport in Old Australia*. Noble Park: Five Mile Press, 2000.

Scates, Bruce. "Finding the Missing of Fromelles: When Soldiers Return." In *Anzac Legacies: Australians and the Aftermath of War*, edited by Martin Crotty and Marina Larsson, 212–232. North Melbourne: Australian Scholarly Publishing, 2010.

Scates, Bruce, and Raelene Frances. *Women and the Great War*. Cambridge: Cambridge University Press, 1997.

Seal, Graham. *Inventing Anzac: The Digger and National Mythology*. St Lucia: University of Queensland Press, 2004.

Smart, Judith, and Tony Wood, eds. *An Anzac Muster: War and Society in Australia and New Zealand 1914–18 and 1939–45*. Clayton: Monash University, 1992.

Stell, M. K. *Half the Race: A History of Australian Women in Sport*. North Ryde: Angus and Robertson, 1991.

Sumartojo, Shanti, and Ben Wellings, eds. *Nation, Memory and Great War Commemoration: Mobilizing the Past in Europe, Australia and New Zealand*. Bern: Peter Lang, 2014.

Syson, Ian. "The 'Chimera' of Origins: Association Football in Australia before 1880." *The International Journal of the History of Sport* 30, no. 5 (2013): 453–468.

Wedgwood, Nikki. "Doin' It for Themselves! A Case Study of the Development of a Women's Australian Rules Football Competition." *The International Journal of the History of Sport* 22, no. 3 (May 2005): 396–414.

Whimpress, Bernard. *The South Australian Football Story*. West Lakes: South Australian National Football League, 1983.

White, Mollie. *The Golden Thread: The Story of a Fashion House, E. Lucas & Co. Pty. Ltd., 1888–1963*. Melbourne: E. Lucas, 1963.

Winter, Jay, ed. *The Cambridge History of the First World War*. Vol. 3. Cambridge: Cambridge University Press, 2014.

Winterton, Rachel. "'Feats of Fancy' and 'Marvels of Muscle': A Social History of Swimming in Late Colonial Melbourne." PhD diss., School of Sport and Exercise Science, Victoria University 2010.

Wood, John. "Blast from the Past: Women's Football in South Australia – Part One." *South Australian Football Budget* 18 (June 5, 1993): 18.

Fronting Up: Australian Soccer and the First World War

Ian Syson

College of Arts, Victoria University, Melbourne, Australia

> Soccer is rarely remembered as a vital part of Australia's military history and the Anzac legacy. Yet, soccer contributed greatly in the First World War. In terms of moral support, enlistment, participation and 'sacrifice', soccer was at the forefront of sporting-body commitment. Using recently digitised newspaper archives, this paper will outline soccer's place in the Australian armed forces during the First World War, especially in relation to the Australian Rules states of Western Australia and Victoria, as a part of an overall project intending to reveal soccer's place in Australian culture.

This paper emerges from my interest in the cultural representation of soccer, along with the rhetorical, journalistic and historiographical practices that have contributed to the game's assumed position on the edge of Australian culture and society. This interest is attuned to the cultural and political struggles between football codes and is focused largely (though not exclusively) on the states in which Australian Rules football has become a powerful and hegemonic football code.

The paper is also one of a new kind, the post-digitisation research paper which, given the widespread availability of searchable and digitised newspaper archives, is more easily able to identify and capture archival material than in previous times. This capacity is both a strength and a weakness of such research. The technology facilitates and promotes the quotation and assimilation of a great volume of primary text into the body of the paper. This is advantageous to my interests because it enhances the texturing of the paper using the language of the period in question. It enables the easy representation of both the content and the form of the material being cited. Given that the rhetoric of inclusion and exclusion is one of my central themes, this new-found efficiency of capture is a boon.

The weakness of this technology is that it can enable a departure from more conventional historical research methods. If the tendency is to quote material and let it 'speak for itself' rather than explicate such material, then a new form of unconventional historiography is generated. My task is to balance my interests in displaying the rhetorical and stylistic with those of the reader interested in a more generalised story.

Soccer and Australian Cultural Memory

In 1931, soccer authorities in Hobart sought access to the North Hobart football ground, normally reserved for Australian Rules. They requested its use for representative games on the two days of the season when it was not needed by the Southern Tasmanian [Australian

Rules] Football Association for first-grade matches. Typically, there were expressions of resistance to this desire, one of which was a letter to the *Mercury* penned by 'Derwentside'. He argued that:

> 'Soccer' players and followers in Hobart are in a minority only a self-centred, and, which is worse, a selfish, player or supporter, would deny. Whatever merits 'Soccer' has as a winter game, it has not here the following, status, or genuine sportsman-like appeal to the average Australian as the game which some fifty odd years has evolved under the name of Australian football. The proper development of a nation's national pastimes, particularly the winter ones, does more to build up a virile nation than attempts to foster – or is it foist? – an exotic pastime upon them. Among the many thousands of Australians who manned so doggedly the trenches and trudged the fields of France and Flanders – to say nothing of the Gallipoli campaign – not a small percentage got the qualities which made the A.I.F. world renowned from the fields in at least four States devoted in winter to football played under Australian Rules.[1]

This is one more letter published in relation to one more moment in the interminable squabble for playing space in Australian sport. And it articulates many of the sentiments that had come to take hold in the Australian sporting imaginary: soccer is low, unpopular, unestablished, minor, foreign ('exotic' in fact) and is being imposed/foisted on Australians by selfish and self-centred agents of foreign influence.[2]

The letter also raises an interesting and new basis for exclusion. 'Derwentside' claims that Australian Rules supplied many of the troops who fought in the First World War and his necessary implication is that soccer did not. Accordingly, Australian Rules should have prior claim on whatever sporting fields over which it has established patterns of usage. Australian Rules paid for this access with the blood, sweat and sometimes the lives of many of its adherents who enlisted in the Australian Imperial Force (AIF). While the validity of the argument is questionable, it has been a persuasive one, then and now.

Four years earlier, in 1927, a letter to the editor of the *Sunshine Advocate* in Melbourne also invoked the Anzac[3] spirit. 'Dinkum Aussie'[4] revealed:

> It was stated by two returned soldiers, and reported in your paper, that an attempt is being made by some Johnny-Come-Latelys to supplant our national game of football with an importation. On making inquiry, I find that a local school teacher is working might and main against the national game, and I am told that at least one of the local soccer team is an Australian. I should like to suggest that the local football club report the matter to the head office in town, so that it may be brought before the Minister. If Victoria is good enough to live in, its games should be good enough to play.[5]

Many of the usual tropes are deployed: the national is game being supplanted by a 'Johnny-come-lately'. The 'when-in-Rome' argument is invoked. And those pesky 'Pommy' schoolteachers are up to their usual tricks.[6] Moreover, we get a hint of treachery insofar as an 'Australian' lad has been tempted into tasting the forbidden fruit. Amplifying this is the prefatory fact that it was reported by two returned soldiers, as if their being moved to comment proves the outrage.

Both writers suggest that soccer was a marginal game in post-war Australia. Moreover, it can be inferred that they think it is a game with very little to do with the Anzac history or spirit. A vital question is the extent to which the sentiments expressed by 'Derwentside' and 'Dinkum Aussie' represented significant popular thought and the extent to which they have stuck in Australian cultural memory.

Australian soccer neither was nor is a marginal game in participatory terms, having been popular and widely played for over 100 years. The cross the game has to bear is that it is often *considered* marginal and foreign, for a vastly complex set of reasons. Ultimately, soccer is absent from most of the positive stories Australians tell themselves about themselves and has failed to embed itself as a component of the national cultural-mythological discourse, especially when it comes to military history.[7]

These arguments are important because in contemporary Australia sport and war have obtained a close emotional connection. Relying on assertions of their cultural centrality and intimations of their contribution to war service, the two dominant football codes have assumed the right to put the sport/war connection front and centre. The Australian [Rules] Football League and the National Rugby League each conducts intensely publicised and popular Anzac Day matches.[8] It is a tradition to which supporters of both codes have been drawn in large numbers and which coincides with the rejuvenation of the Anzac legend in Australian cultural life over the past 20 years.[9]

Through this connection, the dominant football codes have been able to insert themselves into mythologised narratives of the past and the present. One implied narrative is that Rugby League players from NSW and Queensland and Australian Rules players from the rest of Australia made up large sections of the fighting force, to the extent that in mythological terms the spirit of the soldiers and the footballers have crossed over and merged.[10]

Yet any present-day understanding that the two codes dominated military preparation stems ironically from the poorly subscribed Sportsmen's Battalions, a push that effectively covered up the apparent tardiness in the enlistment of Australian Rules and League players.[11] Murray G. Phillips points out that:

> Several sports, like rugby league, boxing and Australian rules football, used the military units of sportsmen to rebut criticisms about continuing their activities during war time; other sports, which ceased their programmes, were involved because they considered it was their patriotic duty.[12]

Some contemporary retellings of the role of football in war also help to cloud the issue. Dale Blair's 'Beyond the Metaphor: Football and War, 1914–1918', published in 1996, conveys the sense that Australian Rules was the most significant sport played by Australian troops.[13] Blair's article is based on the sound premise that 'Sport and war have long been synonymous with Australia's national identity and the "ANZAC" legend provides one of the great pillars upon which that identity has been built. Of equal, if not greater standing, is the nation's penchant for sport'. He also makes the important observation that given 'the extent to which Australia's First World War experience permeates the national psyche, it is somewhat surprising that the implications of and influence of sport during this period have been largely neglected'.[14]

However, while Blair acknowledges 'the various football codes' and gestures towards the complex geneses of football in Australia, he nonetheless makes a too-easy transition from the generalities of sport and football to the specificities of Australian Rules without properly negotiating the minefield of exclusion and forgetting what such a move involves. Sometimes he transitions from one generalised discussion of Australian Rules football to the next by citing specific evidence of a game or a practice that had no necessary connection with Australian Rules. For example, he discusses the practice of 'mobbing':

> The lack of proper playing fields, particularly of the large size required for Australian football, was always a problem. The 40th Battalion, a Western Australian unit, resolved the problem by devising their own game which they called 'mobbing'. It was played with a hessian bag filled with straw, and the game had no rules other than that the bag could not be kicked. The basic object of the game was to force or throw the bag through the opposition's goal. The beauty of the game was that it could be played 'on any old ground'.[15]

Assumptions run deep in this passage. Blair seems not to countenance the possibility that the soldiers were not looking for a next-best activity to Australian Rules but were creating a game, from scratch, out of the equipment and conditions that were available to them. He possibly assumes that because they were a Western Australian Battalion they were

Australian Rules footballers by default. Blair's elisions are symptomatic of a whole range of cultural practices through which hegemonic football codes assert and justify their contemporary dominance while rewriting the past in their own image.

Reports from the Front

Sporting contests were significant activities within the AIF during the First World War. Members of the armed forces gravitated to them in great number, whether as participants or spectators. Military authorities saw these contests as an important means of maintaining good morale and letting off steam, and the AIF went to great lengths to facilitate competition and even recognise sporting excellence with awards and trophies. Blair suggests that 'the Army patronised sport in many ways – including creating facilities and ovals and organising regimental teams and competitions – because sport enhanced fitness, boosted morale, provided a physical outlet and countered boredom'.[16]

There are a number of means through which this assertion can be sustained. Substantial official reports, and photographic and officer-diary records are housed at the Australian War Memorial.[17] These demonstrate a virtual Olympiad of sport across the theatres of war.

A significant indicator of sport's general role in the overseas AIF is not contained in detailed formal and informal accounts but in a simple brief list published broadly across Australia. Among many other newspapers, the *Camperdown Chronicle* contained a report in May 1916 claiming to have seen 'a cable from Cairo to headquarters'. The cable had urged: 'Send immediately six tents, 10 small pianos, 5,000,000 printed letter paper and envelopes, 50 sets of cricket material, 50 soccer footballs, 50 association footballs'.[18]

An underutilised but particularly valuable source of information about how servicemen identified with this culture of military sport is contained in the many 'From the Front' letters published in the Australian press during the war. The recent digitisation of Australian newspaper archives has made the discovery and collation of this genre a relatively easy matter.[19]

A typical letter 'From the Front' contained much discussion of sport, particularly football, played or observed by the author. Or it spoke glowingly of a footballer who had performed heroically and sometimes a strong correlation was constructed between prowess on the football field and in battle. The Adelaide *Register* noted that a number of letters:

> from soldiers at the front state that Pte. Stanley F. Carpenter has been recommended for the Victoria Cross. He is a native of Newcastle, and one of the best-known footballers in New South Wales. He has been playing football for 20 years, although only 36 years of age, and has represented New South Wales and Australia in interstate and international matches. He has always played with the East Newcastle Club and is a life member of the New South Wales Rugby League.[20]

Soldiers from the northern states were often identified as Rugby players or advocates. The following letter published in the *Warwick Examiner and Times* in February 1917 uses a group of Australian soldiers' familiarity with Rugby to explain their poor performance against an English soccer team:

> We all went down to a Tommies' camp recently and played a football match with them. They played 'soccer'. Of course Rugby is our game so the Tommies scored an easy win. We enjoyed ourselves very well looking on, as some very good players were on the field.[21]

The Barassi line[22] is often drawn in the letters, with those from the northern states naturalising the rugby codes and those from the south and west naturalising Australian Rules. Some of the letters of soldiers from the Australian Rules states refer to the good-natured rivalry they have with advocates of the rugby codes.

Servicemen from the southern and western states sometimes expressed their frustration that games of Australian Rules were hard to come by in England. Similarly, they voiced a longing to see games at home. Private 'Jack' Brown wrote such a letter from Gallipoli on August 17, adding the rider that the footballers at home might be better placed in the armed forces:

> We get great instructions in case gas comes here, but so far they are playing the game. Good old North Launceston! Guess they will nearly be premiers this season, though it's time they gave up football and came along here. The more that come the sooner we will get home.[23]

The *Emerald Hill Record*, a newspaper that ran only for the duration of the war, was a vehicle for many such letters. Published in and to the South Melbourne district, it kept tabs on the South Melbourne Australian Rules footballers at the front. In 1917, it published a Roll of Honour for the club listing those players who had served and noting who had been killed.[24]

A number of these players wrote letters home 'from the front' and were published by the *Emerald Hill Record*. Wal Laidlaw was published around 15 times in 1917 and 1918 and invariably mentioned football:

> A few more lines to let you know that I'm well. I am still receiving the [*Football Record*] regularly, which is most welcome. I was sorry to hear poor Bruce Sloss was killed. He was one of the best, but these things must be expected … Things were fairly quiet a week ago, so we had a football match between a couple of picked teams. We played in mud about six inches deep. One side played in sheepskin jackets and the other in shirts. After the first quarter it was hard to distinguish the difference between the players, as all were caked in mud. Our side won by seven points after the hardest day's toil I've ever done.[25]

> I will be looking forward to future papers for the results of the football. We are having a short rest, and we concluded our football season after playing eight matches, losing two.[26]

In the main the *Emerald Hill Record*'s focus is on Australian Rules football, though other codes and games get an occasional mention. Laidlaw wrote again: 'We have finished football, and were undefeated after playing twelve matches. Sport was booming through the winter, and our brigade had the champion Rugby and Australian team, besides the heavy weight boxing champion, so we did well'.[27]

The *Record*'s function of keeping track of the South Melbourne players at the war is exemplified in the following letter from Private Frank Arnold, who had played for South Melbourne Football Club in the 1890s:

> I witnessed a football match between two battalions. It was a match well worth going to see. It was in the danger zone, but that did not make much difference. Tich Bailes was playing. He kicked four goals, but he is not the Tich of old. The —th had not been beat for two years. It was a terrible shock to them. One of our prominent officers took £30 to £90, and the rank and file all had their few francs on. I captained the —th Battalion. We won by a point just on time. This was when we were training on Salisbury Plains. Poddy Hiskins is not very far from where I am camped. I saw poor Bruce Sloss's grave. I would, very much like to send you a photo of it. I will do my best to do so. I have two of the old South footballers with me – Joe Lowrey and Bert Mills. Both wish to be remembered to you and all the old boys.[28]

A few months later, Wal Laidlaw regretted to say: I haven't come across any of the boys yet. At the present time it is difficult to get in touch with any of them. I suppose you will be thinking of the football season by the time this reaches you. I hope you have better luck this year. Kind regards to all.[29]

Soccer obtains some direct mention in the letters. Private Marshall Caffyn was another ex-South Melbourne player, published a number of times in the *Emerald Hill Record*. Here, he reports on his own participation in a game of soccer:

> I had a game of footer the other Sunday – soccer. They put me in goals, and thought I was a marvel when kicking off – I used to put the old round ball half way up the ground every time – the game is not much good. Give me the good old Australian rules every time. I have also played rugby over here. The games aren't to be compared.[30]

Les Turner, also a South Melbourne player, wrote from Scotland, 'I went to see a British Association football match last Saturday. It was a good display of their football and I enjoyed it, but give me our game every time for top place'.[31]

This was an echo of a letter from Laidlaw, two years previously. He had been 'to see an English soccer football match'. He thought the game was 'interesting to watch', and that 'both teams were evenly matched. They had some top-notch men, and the game was played at great speed'. But, in the end he felt 'there is nothing like our Australian game'.[32]

Soccer is acknowledged and enjoyed to an extent but the letters display a felt need to remind readers that it is an inferior, replacement activity for what they would rather be doing. It is an interesting prefiguring of a significant mode of the *Football Record*'s anti-soccer rhetoric in years to come.[33]

As Stan Hiskins writes, some bluntly refused to participate: 'Every Sunday we have a game of soccer. We enjoy it too, although most of our boys won't have it on any account'.[34] It is notable that a Victorian Football League (VFL) footballer is happy to try the game and enjoy it, whereas some of his less-accomplished comrades refuse. Perhaps they would not 'lower' themselves; or perhaps their self-image as sportsmen would be compromised in the likely event that they were to play soccer badly.

Other sportsmen also took the opportunity to play soccer, while expressing a yearning for their main sport at home, in this case cycling in Queensland:

> I am O.K. Still in the same old place, and not likely to shift yet. I often get 'Sports' and read up the cycling. I suppose the racing season is starting again in Brisbane. The only sport we are able to take up is football, and we had a good game of soccer today.[35]

When soccer is discussed fully it is sometimes as a curiosity. The following piece from Turner reports positively on a game he observes but is written with a sense of the shock of the new:

> I saw a great football match here the other day between an Egyptian and a British army team. Football here is very different to Australian. It is purely foot-ball – hands are not allowed to touch the ball, which is perfectly round. I can see it is a far more scientific game than ours, and the Egyptians are particularly clever with their feet, and very active. The game is called soccer, and was introduced by the British 10 years ago. As it happened the British team won, but there was very little difference between the two teams.[36]

While Turner is complimentary towards, the game he nonetheless sees soccer as exotic. His writing exemplifies the way that soccer has a curiosity status in many of the letters and, while it was often played by Australian troops, it is seen as a game to be played for secondary reasons. It is what the locals played; it was the best available, but second-best to Australian Rules or a version of Rugby – and so could be enjoyed on that basis. Some letters also make it clear that when an opportunity to play their preferred code presented itself, soldiers took it with glee.

If the evidence presented in many of these letters constructed soccer as a necessary yet tolerated secondary indulgence, another stream of letters made a different point. They spoke to soccer's ordinariness (or unextraordinariness) in the military context.

Sometimes when Australian servicemen attended soccer matches they referenced a familiar 'home' code but came away with less certainty about the superiority of that code and felt less inclined to offer judgements. Private Edward J. Ryan wrote to his uncle in 1916:

Well, I can tell you that football does not worry me much at present, but I went to look at a game of 'soccer' while I was in Edinburgh, and I wouldn't like to pass my opinion as to which is the best game – Australian or 'soccer'.[37]

One soldier's letter to the *Euroa Advertiser* alludes to home football colours (probably to Euroa Magpies Australian Rules FC) but fails to cast a judgement on what he had observed – apart from the inferred mild disappointment that his adopted team lost – 'Had a stroll through the glorious gardens and saw the teams from the H.M.S. *Swiftsure* playing soccer, and as one side appeared in black and white I got a bit excited. The red team won'.[38]

Many of the letters 'normalise' soccer without comparative reference to any other code. A soldier in Egypt in February 1915 describes soccer as explicitly un-exotic: 'They then started their football match. They played English soccer, so it wasn't anything novel'.[39] A letter from HMAS *Australia* bandsman, Jack Richardson, in September of the same year speaks with the fatalism of a genuine supporter about his team's prospects in an upcoming game: 'We are going to play them at soccer, but I think they will win, and give us a hiding as they are the best band team in the Navy'.[40]

Farrier Bob Anderson, who played soccer for Moonyoonooka (outside Geraldton) before the war,[41] was published in the *Geraldton Guardian* in March 1916:

We have plenty of football (soccer).[42] We have formed a team out of this company, but it's the same old story only about half of us know the game. We have had three matches and haven't been beaten – two wins and a draw. Duncan got a team out of the 11th. He also got the old Queens Park centre (Swan) to play for them. He didn't play himself but he had a better football team than ours. However, it is not always the best team that wins, and they were very lucky to get a draw. They only scored in the last five minutes. Our goalkeeper thought the ball was going past, but it struck the post and went through. I was playing back and had plenty to do. I stopped Swan a few times. No doubt he is a good player and a dandy shot, but I think he is a bit rough. We will be playing next Saturday, so we may get knocked. I'm captain of this lot, and it's not too easy a job, as sometimes the best men either go to town (Cairo) or are out on duty. News is scarce, and a man can't say too much, as all letters are censored now. I met McPhie. He came over a week or ten days ago. I hope this finds all of you Geraldton boys in the pink. Give one and all my kindest regards. I'm afraid I won't be back in time for the football this season, so *au revoir*.[43]

Anderson indicates a flourishing soccer culture within the armed forces, even if not all of the participants were from soccer backgrounds. While Anderson complains that half do not know the rules, he might have rejoiced in the fact that half *did* know the rules.

Anderson's letter also raises the suggestion that the Australian teams are at least competitive. Lance-Corporal Gates reported that 'Our soccer football team lost to a team from an English regiment, by one goal to nil'.[44] Mr T. Jones, YMCA secretary with the troops 'who had both "Tommies" and "Kangaroos" in his charge' on the Sinai Peninsula, reiterated the familiarity many had with soccer. He wrote that 'Football matches are arranged about twice a week, both "Soccer and Rugby", and the excitement displayed is intense, and reminiscent of the old days at home'.[45]

In May 1916, Unomi wrote that he had:

received letters from several soccerites on active service. Courcey O'Grady, Jimmie Cutmore, and Bert Shellat are all late officials of the J.B.F.A. They were all well at date of writing and desire to be remembered to their many soccer friends. Needless to add, they have been taking an active interest in football, particularly O'Grady and Cutmore who were members of an Egyptian team that did well in competition.[46]

Suggested in this latter gathering of letters is an extensive and coordinated soccer programme within the AIF.

As a whole, the letters 'From the Front' reveal that soccer was available for Australian servicemen to play and/or observe – and they did one or the other, in their thousands. However, there are three tonalities in these letters: soccer subdominant, soccer neutral and soccer dominant. Further research will help to ascertain the regional factors in these tonalities and answer the vital question of whether Australian troops participated in soccer as a second-best to their preferred sport or as their preferred option.[47]

Soccer Enlistments

A significant and potentially contradictory point lost in the contemporary mythologisation of Anzac is that many of those in the very first Australian troopships were British-born, a good number of them recently arrived migrants. E.M. Andrews, in *The Anzac Illusion*, argues that the 'AIF had a large minority of British-born in it'. With C.E.W. Bean and other 'purveyors of the Anzac legend' very much in his sights, he suggests that a 'fact often overlooked' is that the British-born made up:

> 13.3 or 15.65 per cent of the Australian population, but either 18 or 22.25 per cent of the AIF for the whole war, depending on whose figures are taken. They were more numerous in some formations, however, being 27 per cent of the first contingent, and 50 per cent of the 28th Battalion, from Perth ... Whatever figures are accepted, the British-born clearly volunteered in higher proportions than the Australian-born, and considerably higher in the opening days of the war.[48]

Bean concedes that many of those who enlisted were British-born, but suggests that their relative numbers were severely whittled down prior to embarkation. The following reads like a bad-faith rendering of statistics, over-determined as it is by Bean's idea of the superiority of the Australian bushman:

> Since the only places for enlistment were in the capital cities, many men had been recruited who would not have been taken had the time been longer. The floating population of these towns probably secured too large a proportion of the acceptances. Immigrants from Britain who happened to be about the cities showed an extraordinary preponderance in the earlier stages – Colonel MacLaurin left it on record that at one period 60 per cent of the recruits for his brigade were British born; before it sailed, 73 per cent of the men in the first contingent were Australian born.[49]

And Bean suspects that many of the remainder would be as near as good as Australian-born, their having 'lived in Australia since childhood'.[50] It is not clear what Bean makes of the fact that of the first 58 to fall at Gallipoli (from the 11th Battalion) only just over half (31) were Australian-born or had Australian domiciled parents. Most of the remainder were recently arrived, British-born, adult migrants.[51]

The widespread enlistment of British-born soldiers invites the question of the percentage of the British-born enlistments who were also soccer players, given the extent to which these migrants represented the overwhelming majority of Australian soccer players. John Williamson in *Soccer Anzacs* – a book that tells the story of the Perth Caledonians' contribution to the war effort – claims a direct nexus between the British-born, soccer and enlistment. Citing P.S. Reynolds' report, *The New History of Soccer*, he claims that '300 players and officials enlisted from the Western Australian soccer community and this is not surprising in light of the high proportion of Anzacs who were born in the United Kingdom'. It is possible that this figure sells WA soccer enlistments short.[52]

Exemplifying Williamson's point is the following excerpt from the *Daily News* in April 1915, prior to the Gallipoli landing. The Perth YMCA:

Soccer Club has responded splendidly to the call for men to serve our King and country abroad. By about the end of January the following members of the team had volunteered: Harry Amos, J. W. Balsdon, Herbert A. Bell, Frank M. Gill, James F. Jack, Cyril Jeans, J. S. Neale, A. Sage, Sid. Stubbs, P. Wrightson. Three are in Egypt, five are still in camp here, and two are waiting to be called up by the military authorities. The club is proud of the large number of soccer boys who have enlisted, and we are looking forward to seeing them return safe and sound. An interesting letter is to hand from Frank Gill, now in Egypt. He is fit and well, but anxious to get to the front. He says he has climbed the Pyramids.[53]

A willingness to enlist was a prevalent attitude found in soccer clubs in Western Australia and beyond – a commitment that had significant long-term ramifications for both the Caledonians Club and for the game across Australia.

In October 1915, Perth soccer journalist Unomi was able to report some astounding figures from WA:

The European war has played havoc with all winter pastimes, for every branch of sport has nobly responded to the country's call, and Westralian soccerites in particular have well maintained their name of sportsmen by giving of their best to the army at Gallipoli, as a glance at the list hereunder will testify. On looking back on the past year, the uppermost feeling of the soccer community must be sadness with a measure of pride. Pride in the knowledge of the self-sacrifice made by many of our comrades in answering the appeal of the nation, and regret at the pitiless sacrifice of life. A number of those who were with us this time a year ago will no longer play the game. They fill honoured graves on the heights of Gallipoli, and much as I would like to write an appreciation of their courage and devotion of their country I do not feel equal to the task. From time to time the names of those players who enlisted have appeared in this column, it may therefore be fitting to give the number that has gone, or about to go, from each club. In doing so, however, it is not with any spirit of boastfulness, nor is it with the object of inviting comparisons, but in view of the somewhat disparaging statements made some time ago about football, I think it only my duty to show that soccer has done its bit and has nothing to reproach itself with. The list, which includes both associations, is:

Club	Enlistments	Wounded	Killed
Austral	17	4	1
Caledonians	7	0	0
Casuals	11	1	2
Claremont	46	3	4
City Rangers	13	3	3
College	25	4	3
Fremantle	6	0	1
Perth	14	1	6
Referees	7	1	2
Thistle	11	1	1
Y.M.C.A.	23	0	2
Leederville	11	0	1
Other Clubs	50	14	7
Total	241	32	33[54]

On the resumption of soccer in Geraldton in 1919:

Mr J. G. Scott, Hon. Secretary, in an interesting report to the meeting of the British Football Association, referred to the difficulties under which the last playing season, 1915 was concluded, owing to so many of the players going to the war, and which caused the game to be suspended the following seasons. From the lists he had been able to secure he found that 62 of their players went to the front, and 16 of these had made the supreme sacrifice in defence of the Empire.[55]

In 1933, informed by Scott, R.C. Webb, then president of the Geraldton Soccer Association, revised these figures upward, claiming that 80% of its players had enlisted:

> At a recent club meeting Mr. J. G. Scott, past president of the Association, in speaking of the formation of the soccer code in Geraldton, mentioned that in 1914, at the outbreak of the Great War, there was just over one hundred players on the books of the Association. Over eighty of these men answered the great call and saw active service.[56]

Like their Western Australian brethren, soccer players across the country enlisted in droves, many of them prior to the Gallipoli campaign. Harry Dockerty, president of the Victorian British Football Association, claimed in February 1915 that 'his organisation, numbered 500 members, and 200 had already gone to the front'.[57] These numbers are questionable given that in July, after the Gallipoli campaign began, it was claimed by another representative that 'they had a total of 170 out of 550 players (30%) serving with the colors or out at Broadmeadows'.[58]

Despite the *Emerald Hill Record*'s tendency observed above to focus on Australian Rules footballers, it sometimes acknowledged the commitment of soccer players to the enlistment process. It reported the day before the Gallipoli invasion:

> Considerable difficulty has been experienced by the council of the 'Soccer' clubs in providing a satisfactory competition for the forthcoming season, and it is only quite recently that they have been able to draw up a complete fixture list. As is generally known, the chief reason of this is the fact that so many clubs have been hard hit by the large number of players who have joined the Expeditionary Forces that it has been extremely doubtful whether some of them would be able to raise a team of any description.[59]

In July 1915, it reported (going so far as to break standard practice and name individual soccer players) that more 'than a dozen players of the Thistle club have joined the forces this week, and the senior team had to take the field without the services of Goodson, Hogg, G. Brown, and Raitt'.[60]

According to the *Argus*, when soccer resumed in Melbourne in 1919:

> At the first annual meeting of the British Association, on June 16, the report covering a period of four years commencing 1915 disclosed the interesting fact that 90 per cent. of the players had enlisted for service abroad or at home. No competitive football had been played during the war.[61]

The Hobart *Mercury* recollected prior to the resumption of the interstate rivalry between Tasmania and Victoria in 1921: 'The last occasion on which a Victorian team visited Tasmania was in August, 1914, and it was at Hobart when war was declared. Seven of the team volunteered for active service immediately on return to Melbourne'.[62]

In March 1915, the *Mercury* claimed that 'Soccer football stood out as a fine example to all sporting organisations in Tasmania. The Elphin Club had sent every one of its playing members to the war'.[63] Fifty players from the top 10 soccer clubs in Tasmania, north and south had enlisted by April 1, 1915.[64]

In South Australia, player enlistments were also mounting. In April 1915, the Sturt Club reported losing 'the services of eight of last year's players, who have enlisted in the Expeditionary Forces, and are now in Egypt, but several new men having been secured the prospects are bright'.[65]

While these departures were causing the game to wane, the clubs 'happily' sent their members off to the AIF with a sense of duty and pride, as well as a semblance of propriety. The Adelaide Tramways team placed its enlisted members in a prominent position in its 1914 team photo.[66]

In the Queensland town of Toowoomba (population 13,000 in 1914) the commitment was remarkable. On the resumption of soccer in Toowoomba in 1919, at 'the annual meeting of the British Football Association it was reported that 140 members of the association had gone to the Front'.[67]

In NSW the soccer enlistments were vast. Typical of the Sydney clubs, the Granville Magpies contributed heavily to the war effort. In total, 17 out of 22 Magpie players in 1914 could 'be accounted for as having done or are doing their bit for King and country in foreign parts'.[68]

Australian soccer players were as (if not more) keen as the players of other codes to do what they perceived as their duty. The next question is to ask how well the players were 'embedded' in the mechanics of war. Were they *there*?

Soccer over There

For good or ill, Gallipoli is at the centre of the Australian story of sport and war. As the first major site of Australia's participation in the invasion of Turkey, it is commemorated as a tragic and courageous beginning of Australia's war campaign. As suggested earlier, it is also a location for a powerful contemporary imagining of Australian nationality and cultural development. If 'ANZAC' can convey a general sense of Australian spirit, then 'Gallipoli' is the place of that spirit's founding.

And soccer was also at Gallipoli, and not merely in the actions of the soccer players (Allies and Australians) who fought and died there. It was played there. The image of a soccer match being played at Gallipoli[69] is the kind of picture that leaves nothing to be said. An organised game of soccer was played between Allied troops and they were being cheered on by hundreds of others.

While more evidence is needed to connect this visual image directly with Australian troops, they certainly played soccer on Lemnos in December 1915. Lemnos was loaned by Greece as a base 'for operations on the Gallipoli Peninsula'. An image collected by the Australian War Memorial shows members of the 6th Battalion playing there against a team from *HMS Hunter*.[70] The men were likely *en route* to Egypt after participating in the Gallipoli campaign.

Former Geelong VFL footballer Leo Healy reported on his recuperation in Lemnos after having a tumour removed from his leg – resulting from an injury at Gallipoli. Healy described 'Lemnos as quiet, but the natural harbour is beautiful. The men chiefly amuse themselves playing cricket and Soccer football'.[71] Not only was soccer played at Gallipoli, it was used as a means of refuge, recovery and relaxation by Australian troops in the aftermath of the events that created the legend of Anzac.

More symbolic evidence of soccer's intimate connection with Gallipoli lies in the remarkable story of the Soccer 'Ashes'. They were conceived in 1923 during New Zealand's tour to Australia:

> Mr. Mayer (manager of the New Zealand soccer team) took back to the dominion the ashes in a box with a history attached to it. Mr. W. A. Fisher (secretary of the Queensland association) possessed a silver safety razor case presented to him when he left for the war, and it was with him when he landed with the Anzacs. He presented it to Mr. Mayer, and it contains some of the soil of Queensland and New South Wales, whose representatives played in the test matches. Mr. Mayer intends to have it mounted in New Zealand woods so that it may be a prized memento in connection with international matches between Australia and New Zealand.[72]

The 'Ashes' tag appeared to be a typical symbolic nod to the cricketing Ashes until it was revealed by the *Sydney Morning Herald* 13 years later that the case literally contained ashes:

> The 'Ashes', incidentally, are a genuine trophy. They are a relic of the New Zealand team's visit to Australia 13 years ago, when the ashes of cigars smoked by the captains of the New

SPORT, WAR AND SOCIETY IN AUSTRALIA AND NEW ZEALAND

Zealand and Australian team were placed in a plated safety-razor case, which, in turn, was enclosed in a casket of New Zealand and Australian timbers, honeysuckle and maple, suitably ornamented and inscribed. This trophy bears a record of the test games between the two countries since 1922, and was won three years ago by Australia, which beat the visiting New Zealand team in every test.[73]

The Sydney *Sun-Herald* reiterates the story of the Australia–NZ soccer 'Ashes' during the 1954 New Zealand tour of Australia:

> Ashes of two cigars, smoked in 1923, have become the Soccer Test 'Ashes', won by Australia yesterday.
>
> The cigars were smoked at a Soccer dinner by the Australian captain, Alec Gibb, and the New Zealand captain, George Campbell, after New Zealand had won the 1923 Test series. They are contained in a silver safety razor case which was carried in the landing on Gallipoli by a New Zealand soldier.
>
> The razor case is set in a casket made of Australian and New Zealand woods inscribed with a kangaroo and the New Zealand fern leaf. The 'Ashes' were presented to the Australian team at a dinner in honour of the New Zealand side last night.[74]

Frequent test series for more than 30 years between the two Anzac nations, playing for a trophy that 'witnessed' action at Gallipoli and is inscribed with powerful cultural icons, seems to be clear evidence of a deep and abiding relationship between soccer and the Anzac story. Richard Cashman wonders why this tradition died out in 1954 without ever stopping to marvel that it lasted as long as it did or ponder the mechanics of its gestation.[75]

Indeed, this is a vital question because even as Australian soccer's quality, profile and professionalism were starting to rise in the 1950s, the game's connection with the *Australian* past and its status within legend and mythology were undergoing erasure.

Corners in Foreign Fields

The final grisly question is to ask: what sort of toll did the fighting take on Australian soccer players? In May 1915, Unomi wrote ecumenically about the unfolding tragedy of the war and its impact on local Perth soccer:

> At the great match now raging in the Dardanelles the enemy is no respecter of codes. It is all the same to them whether their bullets find billets in an adherent of the Australian, Rugby or Soccer games. Therefore, with so many of our players at the front British Associationists must expect to contribute towards the blood toll now being exacted. That we are doing so is evidenced in the fact that since the declaration of war no less than five have passed hence. Two, Private Courtney and Major Parker through illness, and three in action – namely Private Amos (Referees' Association), Major Carter (Perth Club), and Private Algy Hale (Claremont Glebe). At the usual meeting of the association on Wednesday last, reference was made to the loss sustained, and a motion to the effect that letters of condolence be sent to the relatives of the deceased was passed. Amongst those reported on the injury list is Lieutenant Rockliffe. Old timers will remember Mr. Rockliffe as being the first secretary of the Junior Association and also a great enthusiast in schools football. I am sure every soccerite will wish him a speedy recovery.[76]

Ultimately, the most powerful (and harrowing) evidence of soccer's 'being there' lies in the bodies of the men who 'stayed there', those who died in the carnage. When the Toowoomba British Football Association re-gathered in 1919, they noted their own toll:

> During the evening the Chairman extended a hearty welcome home to the returned men present, and Mr. S. Morgan responded on behalf of the returned men. The secretary stated that the British Football Association ('Soccer') was the only football association that had an honour roll in Toowoomba. The names of Syd. Cousens, Lit. Groom, A. Dundas[ch], Colin

Groom, W. Bury, and J. McManus were recorded in the minutes as having paid the supreme sacrifice in the late Great War.[77]

Pre-war soccer had not only grown in the metropolitan and larger regional centres. It had taken root in the country as well. Towns like Broken Hill, Rockhampton, Charters Towers and Warwick had established bustling soccer cultures that were all inevitably truncated by the war effort.

Mildura's developing two-team competition in this period resuscitated a game that had flowered there briefly in the mid-1890s. Weekly matches were played between clubs based in Mildura and the neighbouring town of Irymple. This microcosmic competition provides its own story of the war's impact on small towns and sport. Of the 11 players in the Irymple team of 1913, at least seven enlisted. Of this number, five lost their lives.

Yet, the scale of this tragedy is sadly exceeded by the example of the Caledonian team in Perth. Eight members of the club (six first team players) lost their lives in active service. John Williamson's *Soccer Anzacs* documents the Caledonian story from origins to the club's final demise.

Williamson concludes poignantly, making a claim for soccer's centrality to the legend of Anzac and radically defining Australian heritage in terms of actions and commitment rather than birthplace:

> Few sporting clubs in Australia were so decimated in the War's bloody battles as the Caledonian Soccer Club. Practically every player and official enlisted and served under the Australian flag in the First World War. They took part in battles that are remembered throughout Australia every year on 25th April – battles burnt into the Australian psyche.
>
> These Caledonians were Anzacs and what started off as a Scottish strand was woven into the fabric of Australia society by the deeds of its gallant youth. If we reflect on the sacrifice of this team we realise that it paid in blood for the right to use the name Caledonians and be accepted as part of our Australian heritage.[78]

How might 'Derwentside' have responded to such a claim?

Conclusion

Australian soccer historians rarely write about the First World War. It is usually a mere lacuna in their narrative. Yet as I hope to have shown, it needs to be far more than that. It is, first, the place of another dislocated kind of rich soccer history that reveals a game far more central to Australian stories than has been hitherto acknowledged. Australians played and observed games of soccer during the war and many were newly introduced to the game solely because of their participation in the war. Second, the war is that which prevents, perhaps more than any other force, the game's then seemingly inevitable rise to a degree of prominence across Australia. After the war, with more migrants and with renewed enthusiasm, soccer set off once more on its merry course of rebuilding. But this time the enemies within the other football codes were forewarned and forearmed.

The migrants of the 1920s were greater in number but perhaps lesser in commitment to spreading the 'British game of football'. History was once more unkind[79] and despite the seemingly better organised streams of migration, it was not until after the Second World War that the kind of ferocious passion for soccer generated by a migrant boom was seen again.[80] Future research may well reveal that this 30-year break was a great developmental blockage for the game of soccer in Australia. It may also reveal that the elision of soccer and its British-born adherents in the construction of the Australian legend of the First World War was a significant factor in this limit to soccer's growth.

SPORT, WAR AND SOCIETY IN AUSTRALIA AND NEW ZEALAND

Acknowledgements

I would like to thank Paul Mavroudis for his vital assistance in pulling this paper into shape, Roy Hay for his general inspiration and Damian Smith for his exemplary commitment to the project of researching Australian soccer soldiers.

Notes

1. *Mercury*, April 3, 1931, 8. The name 'Derwentside' is derived from the Derwent, Hobart's main river.
2. These issues are canvassed by Hay in "'Our Wicked Foreign Game'."
3. Anzac stands for the Australian and New Zealand Army Corps and in Australian mythological terms often stands metonymically for the entirety of Australian military history. Moreover, the term is sometimes deployed as a symbol of 'Australian spirit' in general.
4. 'Dinkum' means 'authentic' in Australian slang. A 'Dinkum Aussie' is an authentic Australian.
5. *Sunshine Advocate*, November 5, 1927, 1. This letter is so extreme that it is possible that it was a hoax – what might be called trolling today.
6. 'Pommy' is the derogatory Australian slang for 'English'. English schoolteachers were seen as especially proactive in illicitly introducing soccer to Australian schoolboys. Prior to the war, this tension came to a head in Perth, Western Australia. A retrospective on the death of J.J. Simons, the founder of the Young Australian [Football] League mentions this attitude in relation to 1905: 'Soccer was firmly established in the schools, but Mr Simons fought for the national game until he had overcome the prejudices of English schoolteachers'. *Daily News*, October 25, 1948, 6.
7. Philip Mosely and Bill Murray put it another way: 'it has not entered the Australian soul'. Roy Hay claims that 'there has been a failure to make the game Australian' on the part of its custodians. Mosely and Murray, "Soccer," 214; Hay, "'Our Wicked Foreign Game'," 172.
8. Since 1995, Collingwood and Essendon have battled for AFL Anzac supremacy at the MCG. St George and Eastern Suburbs commemorate the day in the NRL. In recent years, a cross-Tasman NRL game between Melbourne Storm and New Zealand Warriors has also been added to the Anzac Day mix. In 2013, AFL club St Kilda FC played their inaugural Anzac Day game in Wellington.
9. See Lake, Reynolds, and McKenna, *What's Wrong with Anzac?* for a thoroughgoing history and critique of the rise of Anzac Day in this period.
10. Green, "Anzac Day." Green sees a great deal of transference involved in the sporting co-option of Anzac:

    > The deeds of our veterans are at once honoured and dragged down to the humdrum of ordinary life through constant acts of easy equivalence. The further we travel from those great wars that saw the mass involvement of ordinary men and women, the more we see their sacrifice, their often terrible sacrifice, as analogous to the recognisable struggles of our modern lives: the valor of footballers, something as universal and banal as 'mateship'.

11. Less than 1% of Australia's fighting force was recruited via the Sportsmen's Battalions. Booth and Tatz, *One-Eyed*, 100.
12. Phillips, "Sport, War and Gender Images," 81.
13. Blair, "Beyond the Metaphor."
14. Ibid.
15. Ibid.
16. Ibid.
17. A term search for 'sport' limited to the First World War in the Australian War Memorial's web site http://www.awm.gov.au/ obtained 691 hits, the vast majority being photographs.
18. *Euroa Advertiser*, July 21, 1916, 5; see also: *Horsham Times*, June 21, 1916, 3; *Warrnambool Standard*, July 29, 1916, 8; *West Gippsland Gazette*, July 25, 1916, 4; *Traralgon Record*, July

SPORT, WAR AND SOCIETY IN AUSTRALIA AND NEW ZEALAND

21, 1916, 6; *Bairnsdale Advertiser and Tambo and Omeo Chronicle*, July 22, 1916, 6; *Prahran Telegraph*, May 27, 1916, 5; *Camperdown Chronicle*, April 20, 1916, 2; *Cumberland Argus and Fruitgrowers Advocate*, May 16, 1916, 3; *West Australian*, October 3, 1916, 8.

19. Perhaps the long-standing historiographical prejudice against history from below and a healthy distrust of editorial practices during wartime have also militated against the widespread and systematic use of these letters.

20. *Register*, June 16, 1915, 7.

21. *Warwick Examiner and Times*, February 12, 1917, 1.

22. The 'Barassi Line' is an imaginary line drawn across Australia that divides the country culturally into Australian Rules and Rugby zones. A good outline is available in Fujak and Frawley, "The Barassi Line," 94.

23. *Launceston Examiner*, September 3, 1915, 8.

24. *Emerald Hill Record*, February 10, 1917, 2.

25. Ibid., May 26, 1917, 2.

26. Ibid., September 15, 1917, 2.

27. Ibid., June 8, 1918, 30.

28. Ibid., February 23, 1918, 2.

29. Ibid., June 29, 1918, 2.

30. Ibid., November 17, 1917, 2.

31. Ibid., March 16, 1918, 2.

32. Ibid., January 15, 1916, 2.

33. See, for example, the *Football Record* 8, June 4, 1928, 3. This edition contained the following statement from 'Chatterer':

> Australia's game is recognised by people from other lands who have followed the codes of those countries as the most spectacular of any winter game of the kind, and the Soccer and Rugger lads who have settled among us and have taken to Aussie's football will tell you that it is the best of all.

34. *Emerald Hill Record*, February 5, 1916, 3.

35. *Queenslander*, April 22, 1916, 18.

36. *Euroa Advertiser*, May 19, 1916, 3.

37. *Barrier Miner*, December 31, 1916, 2.

38. *Euroa Advertiser*, March 19, 1915, 3.

39. *Barrier Miner*, February 7, 1915, 1.

40. *Gippsland Times*, September 27, 1915, 2.

41. A player listed as B. Anderson played for the Moonyoonooka soccer team in 1914. *Geraldton Guardian*, May 21, 1914, 3.

42. Probably the newspaper's parenthesis.

43. *Geraldton Guardian*, March 7, 1916. 4.

44. *Nepean Times*, May 27, 1916, 6.

45. *Daily News*, January 15, 1917, 2.

46. *West Australian*, May 20, 1916, 9.

47. In my research so far, soccer dominant letters seem at this stage to come mainly from Western Australia, with some from Queensland and NSW. Soccer subdominant is very much the tonality from Victoria. Further work needs to be done to establish patterns and emphases.

48. Andrews, *The Anzac Illusion*, 44.

49. Bean, *Official History of Australia*.

50. Ibid.

51. These figures are drawn from the 'First to Fall' web site: http://www.anzacsite.gov.au/11 anding/first-to-fall/11battalion/index.html.The remainder were made up of English (14) and Scots-born (6), with 2 Irishmen, 1 Englishman born in Brazil, 1 Maltese, 1 man whose parents were domiciled in India. All those without a given place of birth and with next of kin domiciled in Australia have been attributed Australia-born status.

52. Williamson, *Soccer Anzacs*, vii. It is not clear whether the Geraldton numbers are included in this figure.

53. *Daily News*, April 3, 1915, 8.

54. *West Australian*, October 16, 1915, 9. These figures are by no means accurate or up to date at the time. The Caledonian figure is clearly incorrect given their tragic story.

55. *Geraldton Guardian*, June 14, 1919, 4.
56. *Geraldton Guardian and Express*, June 3, 1933, 4.
57. *Barrier Miner*, February 13, 1915, 6.
58. *Malvern Standard*, July 3, 1915, 6.
59. *Emerald Hill Record*, April 24, 1915, 3.
60. Ibid., July 17, 1915, 4.
61. *Argus*, June 23, 1919, 9.
62. *Mercury*, August 19, 1921, 4.
63. Ibid., March 31, 1915, 5.
64. *Examiner*, April 1, 1915, 6.
65. *Register*, April 1, 1915, 10.
66. State Library of South Australia, "The Adelaide Tramways British Football Club, 1914 team photo," http://images.slsa.sa.gov.au/mpcimg/35750/B35670.htm
67. *Brisbane Courier*, April 4, 11.
68. *Cumberland Argus and Fruitgrowers Advocate*, September 15, 1917, 10.
69. *Youtube*, "World War I: Gallipoli Campaign 4/4," see the image at 5.49–5.52 in this video, http ://www.youtube.com/watch?v=SQsCQ4k8WTA. The game was conducted as part of the illusion that the Allies were carrying on as normal when in fact plans were being made to evacuate the Gallipoli Peninsula.
70. The team from the destroyer *HMS Hunter* playing a game of soccer against a 6th Battalion team at a camp on the Aegean island of Lemnos. Australian War Memorial, http://www.awm. gov.au/view/collection/item/C01191/.
71. *Geelong Advertiser*, November 12, 1915, 2.
72. Adelaide *Register*, August 10, 1923, 7.
73. *Sydney Morning Herald*, July 3, 1936, 16.
74. Sydney *Sun-Herald*, September, 1954, 41.
75. Cashman, *Sport in the National Imagination*, 109.
76. *West Australian*, May 22, 1915, 9.
77. *Brisbane Courier*, April 4, 1919, 11.
78. Williamson, *Soccer Anzacs*, 113.
79. Hay and Syson, *The Story of Football*, 10–11.
80. This 'boom' is discussed in-depth by Kallinikios, *Soccer Boom*.

References

Andrews, E. M. *The Anzac Illusion*. Cambridge: Cambridge University Press, 1993.
Bean, C. E. W. *Official History of Australia in the War of 1914–1918 – Volume I – The Story of ANZAC from the Outbreak of War to the End of the First Phase of the Gallipoli Campaign, May 4, 1915*, 11th ed. 1941, http://www.awm.gov.au/collection/records/awmohww1/aif/vol1/ awmohww1-aif-vol1-ch5.pdf.
Blair, Dale. "Beyond the Metaphor: Football and War, 1914–1918." *Journal of the Australian War Memorial*, Apr. 28, 1996, http://www.awm.gov.au/journal/j28/j28-blai.asp.
Booth, Douglas, and Colin Tatz. *One-Eyed: A View of Australian Sport*. Sydney: Allen & Unwin, 2000.
Cashman, Richard. *Sport in the National Imagination: Australian Sport in the Federation Decades*. Sydney: Walla Walla Press, 2002.
Fujak, Hunter, and Stephen Frawley. "The Barassi Line: Quantifying Australia's Great Sporting Divide." *Sporting Traditions* 30, no. 2 (Nov. 2013): 93–109.
Green, Jonathan. "Anzac Day is About Their Deaths, Not Our Lives." *The Drum*, Apr. 25, 2012, http ://www.abc.net.au/news/2012-04-25/green-anzac-day-lest-we-forget/3971574.
Hay, Roy. "'Our Wicked Foreign Game': Why Has Association Football (Soccer) Not Become the Main Code of Football in Australia?" *Soccer and Society* 7, nos 2–3 (2006): 165–186.
Hay, Roy, and Ian Syson. *The Story of Football in Victoria*. Melbourne: Football Federation Victoria, 2009.
Kallinikios, John. *Soccer Boom: The Transformation of Victorian Soccer Culture 1945–1963*. Sydney: Walla Walla Press, 2007.
Lake, Marilyn, Henry Reynolds, and Mark McKenna. *What's Wrong with Anzac? The Militarisation of Australian History*. Sydney: University of NSW Press, 2010.

Mosely, Philip, and Bill Murray. "Soccer." In *Sport in Australia: A Social History*, edited by Wray Vamplew and Brian Stoddart, 213–230. Cambridge: Cambridge University Press, 1994.

Phillips, Murray G. "Sport, War and Gender Images: The Australian Sportsmen's Battalions and the First World War." *The International Journal of the History of Sport* 14, no. 1 (1997): 78–96.

Williamson, John. *Soccer Anzacs: The Story of Caledonian Soccer Club*. Applecross: John Williamson, 1998.

The Role of Sport for Australian POWs of the Turks during the First World War

Kate Ariotti and Martin Crotty

School of History, Philosophy, Religion and Classics, The University of Queensland, Brisbane, Australia

Nearly 200 Australians were taken prisoner by the Turks during World War I, some 76 of them during the Gallipoli campaign and the remainder over the succeeding three years during the ongoing campaigns against the Ottoman Empire. Approximately a quarter of them died in captivity. In contrast to the experiences of Australians taken prisoner by the Japanese during the Pacific War, Australian history and collective memory, and Australian commemorative activities, have almost totally overlooked the Australian prisoners of the Turks. This article redresses the balance somewhat by looking at an important aspect of the prisoners' lives; the games they played while in captivity. The article suggests that sports and games were an important part of their methods for coping with the captivity experience, although there were some significant differences in the role sport played for captives of the Turks as compared to the role it played for those taken prisoner by the Japanese in the next World War.

In March 1918, Maurice Delpratt wrote a letter to his sister in Queensland about his recent participation in a multinational sporting competition in Turkey. Delpratt outlined the events in which he had participated – 100 yards dash, shot put and long jump – and proudly explained that he had beaten 'a big field of French and British competitors' to win the sprint race.[1] He also boasted that he had placed second in the jumping and won the egg-and-spoon race.[2] As the presence of an egg-and-spoon race suggests, Delpratt was not writing home about an event of Olympic proportions. Instead, he was describing a sports carnival organised as part of extended Easter festivities by Allied prisoners of war (POWs) held captive by the Turks during the First World War.

One hundred and ninety-six Australians, including 21 officers, became prisoners of the Turks during the First World War. Sixty-eight soldiers and the entire crew of the *AE2* submarine were captured during the Gallipoli campaign, while the remainder were taken prisoner in various battles across the Sinai-Palestine front and in Mesopotamia. These men from the infantry, the Navy, the Light Horse/Camel Corps and the Flying Corps were the first Australians to experience prolonged wartime imprisonment, and the first to be imprisoned by captors from a different ethnic and distinctly unfamiliar cultural and religious background. As POWs of the Turks, they ventured not just into captivity but also into a distinct physical, cultural, social and ethnic environment. They were at the vanguard of Australian mass wartime captivity experiences, they suffered high mortality rates and they engaged with and experienced foreign cultures to a degree unmatched by the vast majority of Australian soldier-travellers in the twentieth century. They were much more immersed in foreign-ness than, for example, other Australian servicemen in Egypt, Britain and France.[3]

Yet we know remarkably little about these captives as they have largely escaped both public interest and historical scrutiny. They are rarely mentioned in any general analysis of the war and usually warrant only minimal mention in generic POW histories.[4] Non-academic authors have afforded the prisoners the most attention, but these works tend to rely on either memoirs or diaries to focus on one particular POW.[5] The post-war significance of the Anzac legend – against which surrender and captivity sat rather awkwardly – and the developing idea of the Turks as an 'honourable enemy', coupled with the relatively small size of the prisoner cohort, has meant the prisoners of the Turks have long been overlooked in the history and memory of Australian experiences of the First World War.[6]

Moreover, overwhelming public and academic interest in World War II POWs of the Germans and Japanese has ensured the continued historiographical neglect of Australians who experienced captivity in different wars. The prisoners of the Japanese, in particular, have gained almost legendary status in Australian history because of the privations and misery of their experiences, and because of the extent of the publications detailing and documenting their time in captivity. From the many memoirs, diaries and television dramas about their experiences, coupled with the considerable academic scrutiny they have received from scholars such as Hank Nelson, Joan Beaumont and Christina Twomey, the prisoners of the Japanese and their time in captivity are now reasonably well understood.[7] We know how they were taken POWs, where they were held, how they were treated and how those fortunate enough to survive and return to Australia were affected in the long term. Thanks to the work of historians such as Kevin Blackburn, we also know a lot about how they played, and the purposes that sport and other physical recreations performed for them.[8] Our understanding of them and their lives while in captivity is far more advanced than for their counterparts held captive by the Turks in the First World War.

This article goes some way to redress this imbalance in Australian POW literature by focussing on one aspect of the captivity experience of the Australian prisoners of the Turks – the playing of sports and sporting events like that described by Delpratt. It outlines how, like their counterparts in other conflicts, the POWs of the Turks used sport to help them endure both the physical and psychological challenges of prolonged imprisonment and argues that, for them, sport also helped fulfil another specific imperative: the normalisation of the inversion of the racial hierarchy. Capture and imprisonment at the hands of the Turks represented a major challenge to the sense of cultural superiority felt by the Australians. Emphasising their Britishness, through the playing of sport and other cultural performances, offered a way to mitigate this shaken sense of power and status.

Kevin Blackburn, in his history of Australian sport at Changi, notes that the image of POWs organising and playing sport while in captivity is somewhat striking.[9] Popular perceptions of POWs, fuelled largely by images and stories of the prisoners of the Japanese, are that they are passive and powerless, and usually undernourished, exhausted and brutalised. But sport has a long association with military endeavours, including wartime imprisonment. Scholarship regarding sport and Australians in captivity has thus far focussed on the form and function of games, physical exercise and sporting competition in World War II POW camps and has highlighted the key roles that sport fulfilled for these POWs in terms of recreation, exercise and the expression of cultural identity.

Peter Monteath writes that sport rapidly became the most popular pastime among Australians in German captivity during World War II.[10] Team sports, including cricket, rugby, soccer and Australian Rules football, were played to a high standard by Australian captives in Germany. Athletics carnivals, boxing matches and 'remarkably' golf were other common sporting pursuits. Equipment and facilities were generally provided by organisations such as the YMCA and Red Cross, or were improvised by the prisoners. Cricket balls were fashioned by wrapping string around pebbles, soccer goals were constructed from Red Cross parcel string, and team outfits were made from scraps of fabric and old uniforms. In some instances, the Germans provided the POWs with sporting gear. At a camp for merchant seaman in northern Germany, for example, the Germans worked with the POWs to build a proper cricket pitch. According to Monteath, the facilitation of sports among POWs by the Germans was only partly based on altruism. German camp Commandants were mindful of the potential use of POWs as a labour force, and encouraged sporting activities and events as a way to ensure prisoners maintained health and fitness, thus making them better, stronger workers.[11]

But sport fulfilled needs and met imperatives for the prisoners too. Australian prisoners in Germany poured their energies into organising and playing sport because it offered an opportunity to let off steam and momentarily forget their troubles. As Monteath writes, sport 'brought with it the prospect of transcendence, an escape from the cruel monotony and troubles of kriegie life to the comforting certainties of their most elemental, physical selves'.[12] Sport also allowed the Australians to express their national identity in an environment of mixed cultures and ethnicities. Australian prisoners competed against their British counterparts in mock Ashes Test series in several camps, sometimes playing in front of crowds of up to 2500.[13] At Hohenfels in 1943, Australian POWs established an Australian Rules football league which comprised teams named after native Australian animals including the Kangaroos, Emus, Kookaburras, Wallabies, Snakes and Goannas.[14] At one camp, Australians used a water reservoir built for fire-fighting purposes for playing water polo, holding swimming carnivals and giving a demonstration of a quintessentially Australian sport – surf life-saving.[15] Several pre-war sporting stars were among those captured, and they contributed their skills to the competitions. For example, Keith Carmody, a batsman who captained an Australian XI against England in 1943 before his capture, led the Australian cricket team at *Stalag Luft III Sagan.*[16]

Intense scholarly interest in the POWs of the Japanese means we also know how and why sport became a key component of their captivity between 1942 and 1945. Sport was central to the lives of these POWs even before they were captured. Gordon Bennett, commander of the Australian forces (AIF) in Singapore and Malaya, believed that sport was good for fitness and morale and, along with other officers of the 8th Division, he encouraged sporting competitions between various units. In Singapore, such competitions continued into captivity as conditions, initially at least, were comparatively favourable. Large numbers of prisoners – some 50,000 Australian and British POWs entered Changi POW camp on 17 February 1942 – meant that enthusiasm and ability abounded, while the prisoners' occupation of pre-war British military barracks meant that equipment and facilities, including three playing fields, were also available.[17] Moreover, the Japanese effectively left the prisoners to organise and run the camp as they saw fit, meaning that officers could combat lassitude and stupor among the men, as well as a potential loss of discipline and morale, by encouraging and facilitating a range of entertainments, educational activities and games. Sports such as football began within days, probably on a 'scratch' basis between sides got together on the spur of the moment, with more organised contests followed soon after. As in Germany, cricket, basketball, tennis, hockey and rugby league were played to a high standard, while swimming and running competitions were also popular.[18] However, the number of sporting competitions in Changi declined in mid-1942. The population of the camp shrank rapidly as prisoners were moved to labour camps on the Burma-Thai Railway, in Japan itself and to other locations. Officers instigated bans against playing rugby and Australian Rules football because of the risk of injuries and the consequent drain on limited medical supplies, while poor nutrition and illness meant many prisoners lost the will to play.[19] In 1944, the Japanese restricted Changi inmates to the civilian gaol, cutting off access to the playing fields, and in early 1945, in a final blow to sporting life in the camps, they officially prohibited prisoners from participating in any sport and other forms of entertainment.[20]

Despite its decline in prevalence, sport performed important functions within Changi. As in the camps in Germany, it played an obvious role in relieving monotony and offered opportunities for entertainment. Blackburn suggests that for Australians in Japanese captivity sport also allowed for the expression of national sentiment. Matches between Australian and British teams drew on and continued the interwar rivalry of the two nations, which allowed for the release of some of the tension associated with the fall of Singapore. Sport allowed for the expression of Australian anger at the capitulation on the rugby field or cricket pitch, rather than in more violent or disruptive forms. Matches against their Japanese captors were also reasonably common and performed a similar function. Participating in, watching or supporting Australian teams in their diverse sporting encounters provided a wide scope for nationalist sentiment at Changi.[21] 'Australianness' was performed through sport and the maintenance of Australian sporting traditions, such as the Melbourne Cup or, as Roland Perry details, the Changi Brownlow, where the best and fairest player in the camp competitions was awarded a version of the Brownlow Medal, replicating a practice of the Victoria Football League.[22]

Playing sport at Changi also gave the prisoners a way to reaffirm their masculinity in the wake of devastating military defeat at the hands of a stereotypically feminised Asian enemy. The Australian troops viewed their Japanese counterparts as racially inferior. World War II propaganda posters often portrayed Japanese soldiers as primitive beings analogous to monkeys or apes, and popular impressions of the Japanese among Australian troops included ideas about their lack of ability to see in the dark and their outdated and ineffective weaponry. As Nelson writes, 'the reputation of the Japanese as the copiers of the tinsel and the tinny from the West precluded their being taken seriously as an enemy of the full might of the British Empire and the United States'.[23] The decisive victory of the Japanese throughout Southeast Asia and the capture of thousands of Allied troops in the early months of 1942 drastically altered these ideas and impressions. Agnieszka Sobocinska argues that the imprisonment of Australians at the hands of the Japanese represented a major challenge to the established colonial racial hierarchy of the region.[24] The Australians' white bodies – symbols of their pre-war superiority in the Pacific – were at the mercy of an Asian power. Playing sport between each other and against their captors allowed the POWs to reclaim power over their bodies, and both redeem their manliness and mitigate the stigma of being passive captives.

While the men at Changi were well aware of their military heritage, for they were after all the *2nd* AIF, it is highly unlikely that they had any awareness that they were not the first significant group of Australians to be taken prisoner by an ethnically and culturally foreign enemy, for the experiences of those Australians taken prisoner by the Turks made little impact on post-war public memory. Nearly 200 Australians were interned in Turkey during the First World War, and despite some significant differences, many aspects of their experiences would have resonated with their successor generation of captives, including their sporting and recreational activities. They were housed in a variety of prison camps that varied in purpose, from temporary work and convalescent to more permanent camps designed to hold prisoners until the end of hostilities. These camps were established from Constantinople (Istanbul) in the west to the Taurus Mountains in the east, and in many major towns and smaller villages in between, including Angora (Ankara) and Afyonkarahissar. Such geographic diversity and difference in the purpose of the camps led to varied conditions. Officers generally fared better than the enlisted men. In accordance with the 1907 Hague Conventions, the international laws that regulated the behaviour of belligerents during the war, officers could not be made to work while in captivity, and so the majority of Australian officers lived out their imprisonment in the relative comfort of the prison camp at Afyon.[25] Here they were accommodated in the houses of displaced Armenians and enjoyed a degree of freedom and autonomy. The majority of the men, on the other hand, were used for some form of labour – mostly on the Berlin–Baghdad Railway project – and often endured harsher conditions. The more remote nature of these work camps made access to food and other provisions, including health care, difficult, and diseases such as malaria and dysentery, as well as accidents and problems associated with wounds sustained during capture, took their toll. A total of 54 Australians perished as prisoners.

Sport was a significant feature of Australians' captivity experiences under the Turks. Many of the prisoners' diaries, letters home and repatriation statements make it clear that there were facilities and opportunities to engage in physical activity and sporting competition, often on a reasonably regular basis, though in a far less structured and more improvised manner that in Changi. Obtaining equipment was a chief issue. In their letters to their families and the Australian Red Cross POW Department, the aid agency responsible for the welfare and comfort of all Australian POWs during the First World War, the prisoners requested sporting gear such as footballs, boxing gloves and cricket apparatus be sent to the camps. In November 1918, William Cliffe's brother, Charles, wrote to the POW Department explaining that he had received two letters from William: 'In both of these he begs me to try and get someone to send out to them a football bladder'.[26] Cliffe's brother and the POW Department recognised the importance of such equipment and organised for its distribution. It is not clear, however, if William Cliffe ever received his football. Indeed, restrictions on mail, the inefficiencies of the Turkish postal system and British War Office limitations on the types of goods that could be sent to Allied troops in enemy hands meant that the prisoners could not rely on receiving sporting equipment from the Red Cross or other external sources. Often, improvisation or modification was necessary. James Brown, an Australian medical student serving as part of the Royal Australian Medical Corps, captured at Katia in 1916, remembered officers at Afyon creating a form of badminton, called *Burfu*, using tennis rackets and balls made from old stockings.[27] British officer Elias Henry Jones also wrote in a post-war memoir that 'busy penknives' created items to pass the time, including chess pieces, draughts and hockey sticks and pucks.[28]

Regardless of how it was obtained, the prisoners put what sporting equipment they had to good use. At Belemedik, a work camp in the Taurus Mountains, prisoners played in inter-service football teams and later established a boxing tournament.[29] Officers and men obtained permission to play cricket matches against each other at Afyon, though only on the condition that the two teams did not speak to each other. Brown and others surmised this restriction was due to the Turkish fear that the POWs could hatch an escape plan.[30] As Brown and Jones' comments suggest, officers were keen participants in sporting activities; indeed, their greater amount of free time meant that sports were more common in officers' camps than in work camps. Changing seasons and weather patterns also influenced the types of sports that were played. Cricket was a popular warm weather sport and even the presence of large numbers of sandflies around the field used as a cricket ground at Afyon did not deter players.[31] With the coming of winter, cricket was replaced by hockey and football. Extreme cold brought snowfalls and froze water, which also led to skiing and tobogganing on improvised equipment – novelty sports for most Australians. Both officers and enlisted men remembered winter snowball fights with particular fondness. George Kerr reported in his diary that heavy snowfalls at Afyon early in 1916 had led to 'much fighting and a good deal of snow-balling between the Russians and us and the French'.[32] The frequency of complaints from returned prisoners about lack of access to, or provisions for, sport and exercise while in captivity suggest that more prisoners would have played more sport had the facilities and provisions been more favourable.

There were several key factors behind the organisation of and participation in sport in the Turkish camps. Just as their POW successors would discover in World War II, sporting activities provided relief from the boredom of daily life as a captive. Like POWs in all conflicts, the Australians in Turkey suffered from the sense of lassitude and ennui caused by the monotony of enforced imprisonment.[33] Several prisoners reported that boredom was one of the chief causes of depression among the POW population. For Thomas White, a pilot with the Australian Flying Corps captured in Mesopotamia in November 1915, 'time ceased to be' as the days of his captivity melded into one long, continuous drag.[34] One Australian witnessed the breakdown of a fellow officer POW at Afyon: 'One day I found Lieutenant LF ... walking up and down the promenade, cursing imprisonment ... and striking such an attitude as to suggest he was about to tear his hair and rend his clothes'.[35] Famous British ex-POW of the Germans during World War II, Pat Reid, who managed the rare feat of escaping from Colditz, later wrote that 'inactivity could lead to idiocy' in a prison camp, and it would seem that several prisoners in Turkey felt the strain.[36] Sport offered a means with which to combat this sense of stultification and tedium, and provided an opportunity for physical – and to some degree psychological and emotional – exercise under conditions in which these were in short supply. As Kerr confided in his diary in May 1916, captivity caused him to suffer periodic 'fits of the blues', which he managed to combat by engaging in physical activity and sports. He established a routine whereby he performed 'physical culture' classes at night before bed and then donned boxing gloves for some sparring with fellow POWs in the morning.[37] For Kerr, sport offered a way of overcoming potential depression.

Sport also offered entertainment. The Australians in Turkey often mentioned sporting events and activities in the same breath as other amusements such as concerts or other cultural and social events, and in many instances sport was used to mark special occasions. Daniel Creedon's first Christmas in captivity was made memorable by the combination of sports and a concert, and on New Year's Day 1916 he likewise noted in his diary that the day 'was spent quietly. There was a football match and sport, also a concert at night'.[38] Similarly, Albert Knaggs, one of the crew of the *AE2* submarine captured in the Dardanelles in April 1915, noted of Christmas Day 1915 that

> it was made as bright as possible by our Turkish Officers who gave us permission to play football outside in a field. We played a match Navy versus Army in which Army won 4 goals to 1. A concert was held in the evening.[39]

George Handsley recalled of Christmas 1916 at Afyon that a football game in the snow proved entertaining for both players and spectators: 'this was the only occasion we saw many of our fellow prisoners smile'.[40] Part of the entertainment factor inherent in playing or watching sporting activities was the opportunity it provided for prisoners to engage with fellow POWs – and sometimes their captors. Charles Woolley, a British officer who later became famous for his archaeological work in Egypt, stated that at Kedos, an officer's camp in which several Australian POWs worked as orderlies, prisoners played football against Turkish boys from a local school until camp officials cancelled the competition 'as it wasn't seen to be right'.[41] In May 1918 William Randall wrote from a Railway work camp to his sister and brother-in-law in Melbourne that he participated in various forms of physical activity, including a daily swim in the local river.[42] He also stated that he was part of a football team that played against the German employees of the company responsible for overseeing the construction of the Railway: 'We played the German transport fellows at football yesterday and beat them, scoring five goals to nil. Next week we have another match'.[43] After the games, the prisoners were provided with 'a feed and free drinks'.[44] Playing football allowed Randall the chance to mingle with others in his camp – POWs and those in positions of authority – both on and off the sporting field.

Sport also offered a means through which the Australians could express their cultural identity, though it is in this respect that the experience of the POWs of the Turks differs markedly from other Australian POW experiences. Unlike Australian POWs in German or Japanese hands from 1939 to 1945, no particular Australian sporting identity emerged in Turkey. The far smaller number of Australians held prisoner in Turkey precluded the formation of football leagues, Test cricket series or any equivalent. Moreover, a number of prisoners would have been indisposed through injury or illness, or simply not inclined, to take part in any sort of Australian sporting competition or form any sustainable Australian sporting teams. Nor did the prisoners of the Turks have the same access to facilities and equipment comparable to those in the Changi barracks. Importantly, they also lacked the same sense of unit cohesion. This is an important distinction between the captivity experiences: at Singapore, Malaya and elsewhere in the Pacific, and in many instances in Greece, Crete and North Africa, Australian POWs were taken in large groups, meaning that they could, to some extent at least, continue on their pre-captivity sporting associations, competitions and connections. Australians taken prisoner by the Turks, however, were generally captured individually or in small groups and came from a wide range of battalions, divisions and even services. The urge to express masculinity as an antidote to the experience of mass surrender must also have been less. Australians taken prisoner by the Turks had been in combat and were already widely regarded as heroes, and the Turks, unlike the Japanese, were not depicted as particularly feminine or seen as lacking masculine attributes.

The Turks were, however, popularly perceived by the POWs to be racially and culturally inferior. Though the Turks were not depicted as feminised in the same way the Japanese would later be, they were perceived to be racially and culturally inferior. The history of Western Christian and Eastern Islamic relations in the century preceding the First World War forms what Jeremy Salt calls 'a tangled skein'.[45] European impressions of the Turks during the nineteenth century varied due to circumstance, oscillating between admiration for Turkish soldiers' resolve and stoicism during the Crimean War to outrage at their perceived innate bloodthirstiness during the Bulgarian massacres of the 1870s.[46] By the time of the outbreak of war in 1914, the Turks were widely held in contempt for their supposed despotism – a characteristic believed to be the key contributing factor behind the decline of the Ottoman Empire.[47] Years of internal conflict, political instability and economic stultification had brought the Empire to the brink of bankruptcy, and earned it the nickname of 'the Sick Man of Europe'. The entry of the Ottoman Empire into the war on the side of the Central Powers was dismissed as inconsequential. Newspapers labelled Turkey 'Germany's Catspaw' and one assured readers that the Turks posed no serious threat. The *Sydney Morning Herald* published an article in November 1914 stating that the Turkish declaration of war would 'hardly affect the general situation … the creation of a new sphere of hostilities will not involve the detaching of a single army corps from either of the old fronts'.[48] For Australians, it was the Germans who were the real enemy.

Alongside this belief in the inferiority of their captors, the Australians were also largely ignorant of their Turkish enemy. Australians had only limited experience with Turkish people prior to the First World War. In the 1911 census, the last taken before the outbreak of war in 1914, only 311 people identified as Turkish out of a population of more than 4.5 million.[49] White Australians, however, did have some experience with others of Islamic background. Peta Stephenson argues that Australia has a long history of contact with the Muslim world, from Indonesian fisherman to Malayan pearlers and Afghan cameleers. Stephenson estimates that between 2000 and 4000 Afghan cameleers settled in Australia from the mid-1800s to the 1930s.[50] Despite their important role in trade and exploration, white Australians believed the cameleers were 'barbaric, immoral, "pagan" and unclean'.[51] Their cultural practices, religious beliefs and different appearance made them the objects of ridicule and derision and, as Christine Stevens writes, 'the term Afghan began to embody a notion of contempt, of racial inferiority, of uncleanliness, brutality, strangeness and fear'.[52] Thus, at the outbreak of war, Australian popular perceptions of the Turks were largely based on public discourse relating to the cameleers and British impressions, which, in turn, reflected contradictory and contested Orientalist ideas and the Social Darwinist belief in the superiority of the white 'race'. As Peter Stanley has written, 'the Australia that raised and constituted the first Australian Imperial Force was a deeply racist society'.[53]

The Australians held POW by the Turks were therefore confronted by a major challenge to their sense of cultural superiority and their ideas of the racial hierarchy. The principal Hague laws that related to POWs directed that all POWs were to be treated on the same footing as soldiers of equivalent rank from the captor nation.[54] This law meant that, for many Allied prisoners, their lives as captives in wartime Turkey would be very different from what they were used to. Cultural clashes were the cause of many of the challenges associated with the Australians' time in Turkish captivity. Vast cultural differences regarding food, accommodation, modes of transport, health care, work and punishment emphasised for the Australians the inferiority of their captors and engendered concern over their ability to cope with the perceived uncivilised conditions. Forced to live in the same manner as a people whose culture they felt was inferior to their own, the prisoners were deprived not just of much of their freedom, agency, customs and culture, but also of the status their 'race' was supposed to confer. However, the prisoners actively challenged their situation. To reassert their shaken sense of racial pride and bring a semblance of normality to their abnormal lives in Turkey, the Australians developed and implemented measures to modify and manage – in effect, to normalise – their camp conditions and culture and shape their experiences of internment.

One of the key ways in which the Australians in Turkey normalised captivity was by enacting their Britishness. Emphasising their membership of British culture helped mitigate the trauma of the inversion of the racial hierarchy. Though some cultural differences were noted, and at Afyon several Australian officers banded together and nicknamed their residence 'Australia House', the Australians in Turkey were effectively seen as British by their captors, by their fellow prisoners and, significantly, by themselves. The Australians were housed in British sections of camps – distinct from the French and Russians – they joined in with British messes and they contributed to theatrical and musical performances that centred on British culture.

The Australians also asserted their Britishness in their relations with captives of other national groups. The Turks had also captured troops from France, Russia and India during the First World War, many of who lived alongside the Australians in the bigger work and convalescent camps, as well as at officers' camps and in hospitals. Opinions of their fellow prisoners were often couched in racial terms that emphasised the cultural superiority and civility of the Britishers. The French were noted for their ability to throw a decent party, but were also often scorned for their attitudes towards imprisonment. One Australian POW wrote about the French that '[l]ike us they can be firm but they are quicker at knowing the time for meekness, and the assumption of it doesn't seem to go so much against the grain as it does with us', while the Russians were also viewed with pity and condescension.[55] The reproduction of colonial power relations also offered the Australians opportunities to exert, and assert, superiority in the camps. The Turks captured thousands of Indian troops in Mesopotamia and other theatres. In keeping with the hierarchy of the Indian Army, Indian troops were separated from their British superiors in the camps but often remained under their administrative control regarding the division of money and comforts. In several instances Australian POWs assumed quartermaster-like positions over groups of Indian POWs or other Railway labourers. In one case, Trooper Edgar Hobson was made responsible for a contingent of 500 Kurdish workers.[56] The authority that the Australians, as white Britishers, maintained over their comrades lower on the colonial and racial orders went some way towards reaffirming their own racial pride and status.

Sport was another of the measures through which the prisoners expressed their British identity. The Australians often competed as British within camp sporting competitions. When Delpratt competed in the Easter sports carnival at Belemedik in March 1918, he did so as a Britisher. His triumph in the 100-yard dash was seen as a victory for the British in the camp; indeed, as he proudly told his sister at home, he was pleased his efforts earned him the nickname of 'the Wallaby who upheld the British prestige'.[57] That his Australianness was subsumed into Britishness in sporting performance in the camps did not seem to bother Delpratt, as it indicated both his membership of a superior 'civilised' culture and his distinction from his Turkish captors.

Similar alignment with their British fellows does not appear to have occurred to the same extent with their counterparts in German captivity. Australian POWs in Germany during the First World War appear to have maintained more of an Australian identity rather than becoming subsumed into Britishness, even in the playing of sport. One factor influencing this could be that opportunities to do so were more limited. David Coombes, the author of the most recent analysis of Australian POWs in Germany during the First World War, argues that the Germans deliberately mixed their prisoners to challenge any existing sense of cultural affinity among the population.[58] Australian prisoners often found themselves, according to Coombes, sharing quarters with POWs of diverse nationalities, including Russian, Belgian, Italian and French. Alongside this deliberate mixing of cultural groupings, there were far greater numbers of Australians captured by the Germans than by the Turks during the war, with some 3867 Australians taken prisoner on the Western Front between 1916 and the cessation of hostilities.[59] The effects of this larger cohort on the organisation and playing of sport is reflected in the accounts of POWs who describe Australian prisoners playing games of Australian Rules football. Such matches were, in the words of one Australian, 'a novelty to the Pommies and French'.[60]

Moreover, the desire to enact Britishness as a way of mitigating the inversion of the racial hierarchy was perhaps lessened by the fact that the Germans, though portrayed as barbaric Huns in wartime propaganda and undoubtedly perceived to be the 'real' enemy in the conflict, were white, Christian Europeans. Marilyn Lake suggests that prior to the First World War Australians and Germans shared a strong sense of cultural unity based on their common Anglo-Saxon heritage. The Germans were seen as 'Teuton cousins' and the outbreak of war was lamented as a fracturing of a long tradition of racial and cultural affinity.[61] The differences between captive and captor in Germany – religiously, culturally and historically – were thus nowhere near as great as in Turkey, thus minimising the need for the prisoners of the Germans to reassert any sense of cultural superiority.

Sport played a key role in making captivity in Turkey bearable. Like the generation of POWs held captive by the Germans and Japanese during World War II, the Australian prisoners in Turkey used sport to relieve boredom, offer opportunities for physical and psychological exercise, provide entertainment and allow engagement with others in the camps. For these reasons alone, sport contributed to making extended wartime imprisonment a more tolerable, and perhaps even more meaningful, experience. But, in Turkey, sport also assumed deeper significance as it was used as a means to normalise the prisoners' abnormal situation. Capture and imprisonment at the hands of the Turks inverted the racial hierarchy in which white Australians of the time placed much stock. Playing sport alongside other white individuals, or against their captors, allowed the Australians to reassert their power, status and racial superiority and mitigate the trauma this inversion caused. In this sense the purpose of sport differed between the experiences of POWs in Turkish and, specifically, Japanese captivity. Rather than using sport as a means of expressing national sentiment, the Australians in Turkey actively emphasised their Britishness while playing sport, often at the expense of any sense of Australianness, in order to perform their membership of a perceived superior culture. While they waited to return home, the prisoners recreated as much of home as they could in their camps, much as their counterparts in World War II did. Despite the great differences in numbers, facilities and organisation, and the more British identity that was expressed in Turkey, the processes of attempting normalisation and alleviating boredom were shared: herein lies the significance of the sport played by Australian POWs of the Turks in the First World War.

Notes

1. M. Delpratt to E. White, March 29, 1918. Maurice George Delpratt Correspondence, John Oxley Library, State Library of Queensland.
2. Ibid.
3. On the soldier as traveller and tourist see Richard White's two articles: "Cooees Across the Strand" and "The Soldier as Tourist."
4. Examples include Adam-Smith, *Prisoners of War*; and Neave and Smith, *Aussie Soldier*.
5. Examples include Kerr, *Lost Anzacs*; and Brenchley and Brenchley's two books: *Stoker's Submarine* and *White's Flight*.
6. This trend is changing. Jennifer Lawless completed a PhD about the experiences of Australians taken POW on Gallipoli at the University of New England in 2011, while Kate Ariotti is in the final stages of her PhD thesis about how the prisoners of the Turks, their families and various

other groups felt about and coped with the unprecedented challenges brought about by captivity at the hands of a radically different enemy. See Lawless, "Kizmet"; and Ariotti, "Coping with Captivity."

7. Scholarly studies into the prisoners of the Japanese began in the 1980s with the groundbreaking work of historians Hank Nelson and Joan Beaumont. See Nelson, *Prisoners of War*; and Beaumont, *Gull Force*. Since then there has been a steady stream of work devoted to their experiences, ranging from studies of specific groups of captives, such as Hearder, *Keep the Men Alive*, and Kenny, *Captives*, to analyses of specific camps such as Gamble, *Darkest Hour*, studies of the Burma–Thai Railroad including Nelson and McCormack, *The Burma-Thailand Railway*, and investigations into the trials of those accused of war crimes against prisoners such as Rowland, *A River Kwai Story*.

8. Blackburn, *The Sportsmen of Changi*.

9. Ibid., 2.

10. Monteath, *P.O.W.*, 215.

11. Ibid., 215–6. While this may have worked during the early years of captivity, by late 1944 the effects of poor diet and disease had weakened the prisoners to the point that many sports, including rugby and Australian Rules football, were abandoned.

12. Monteath, *P.O.W.*, 220.

13. Ibid., 217–8.

14. Ibid., 218–9.

15. Ibid., 219.

16. Ibid., 218.

17. Ibid., 124.

18. Blackburn, *The Sportsmen of Changi*, 128. Blackburn argues that rugby league took precedence over the official game of the AIF, rugby union, for several reasons ranging from connotations of class to the fact that league is typically a faster game, and thus more enjoyable for spectators.

19. Ibid., 131–3.

20. Ibid., 142–3. Two of the three fields had already been lost to the POWs: one had been turned into a runway and the other had an aircraft hangar built on it.

21. Ibid., 129–30.

22. Perry, *The Changi Brownlow*.

23. Nelson, *Prisoners of War*, 12.

24. Sobocinska, "'The Language of Scars'," 58.1–58.19.

25. Article 6 of "Annex to the Convention: Regulations Respecting the Laws and Customs of War on Land (Hague IV); October 18, 1907," http://avalon.law.yale.edu/20th_century/hague04.asp.

26. C. Cliffe to M. Chomley, November 20, 1917. ARC POW Dept. Case File of William Cliffe, AWM3DRL/428 Box 39.

27. Brown, *Turkish Days and Ways*, 178.

28. Jones, *The Road to En-dor*, 118.

29. Kerr, *Lost Anzacs*, 139 (diary entry for December 28, 1915). Army versus Navy was a popular competition.

30. Brown, *Turkish Days and Ways*, 237.

31. Ibid., 241. John Beattie stated that the field used by the prisoners at Afyon was approximately half a mile's walk from the town. Repatriation Statement of John Beattie, AWM30 B1.3.

32. Kerr, *Lost Anzacs*, 147 (diary entry for January 14, 1916).

33. Swiss doctor and International Red Cross Representative Adolf Vischer visited many POW camps in Europe and Turkey during the First World War. In the aftermath of the conflict, he published a book in which he argued that the specific restrictions of wartime captivity caused prisoners to suffer from a recognisable psychological illness he termed 'barbed wire disease'. See Vischer, *Barbed Wire Disease*.

34. White, *Guests of the Unspeakable*, 157.

35. Brown, *Turkish Days and Ways*, 214.

36. Reid, *Prisoner of War*, 157.

37. Kerr, *Lost Anzacs*, 189 (diary entry for May 12, 1916).

38. "Diary Written by D.B. Creedon," 15. Creedon Diary 1915, OM90-138, John Oxley Library, State Library of Queensland.

39. "Diary of A.E. Knaggs," 12. Papers of A.E. Knaggs *AE2*, AWM PR85/96.

40. Foster, *Two and a Half Years*, 39–40.
41. Woolley, *From Kastamuni to Kedos*, 110–1.
42. W. Randall to Mr & Mrs W. Wangemann, May 27, 1918. Papers of Trooper E. Randall 6th ALH and Pte. W. Randall 14Bn., AWM 3DRL/7847.
43. Ibid.
44. Ibid.
45. Salt, "Johnny Turk Before Gallipoli," 17.
46. Ibid., 19–20. See Gladstone, *Bulgarian Horrors and the Question of the East*, for a contemporary – and influential – view of the Bulgarian massacres.
47. On Western European perceptions regarding the decline of the Ottoman Empire see Asli Cirakman, *From the "Terror of the World" to the "Sick Man of Europe,"* 164–72.
48. "War with Turkey," *Sydney Morning Herald*, November 7, 1914.
49. Jupp, *The Australian People*, 709; Knibbs, *Census of the Commonwealth of Australia*, 85.
50. Stephenson, *Islam Dreaming*, 35. "Afghan" was used as a collective term for the cameleers, regardless of whether they came from Afghanistan, Baluchistan or what is now Pakistan. Their common religion bound them together as one group in the eyes of white Australians.
51. Stevens, *Tin Mosques and Ghantowns*, 239.
52. Ibid., 150.
53. Stanley, "'He Was Black, He Was a White Man, and a Dinkum Aussie'," 221.
54. Article 7 of "Annex to the Convention: Regulations Respecting the Laws and Customs of War on Land (Hague IV); October 18, 1907," http://avalon.law.yale.edu/20th_century/hague04.asp.
55. M. Delpratt to E. White, December 16, 1917. Maurice George Delpratt Correspondence. For Australian POW perceptions of their Russian counterparts, see Halpin, *Blood in the Mists*, 180–1. Halpin states that the Russians were abandoned by their country – the Bolshevik Revolution of 1917 meant there was no aid agency to assist Russian prisoners of war.
56. Repatriation Statement of Edgar Hobson, AWM30 B2.2. Maurice Delpratt also assumed responsibility for a camp of Indian POWs in the Taurus Mountains.
57. M. Delpratt to E. White, April 1, 1918. Maurice George Delpratt Correspondence.
58. Coombes, *Crossing the Wire*, 280.
59. Pegram, "Introduction," xii.
60. Pte Frank Sturrock cited in Coombes, *Crossing the Wire*, 294.
61. Lake, "British World or New World?" 36–7.

References

Adam-Smith, P. *Prisoners of War: From Gallipoli to Korea*. Melbourne: Viking, 1992.

Ariotti, K. "Coping with Captivity: Australian POWs of the Turks during the First World War and the Impact of Imprisonment." PhD diss., University of Queensland, 2014.

Beaumont, J. *Gull Force: Survival and Leadership in Captivity, 1941–1945*. Sydney: Allen & Unwin, 1988.

Blackburn, K. *The Sportsmen of Changi*. Sydney: NewSouth, 2012.

Brenchley, F., and E. Brenchley. *Stoker's Submarine*. Sydney: HarperCollins, 2001.

Brenchley, F., and E. Brenchley. *White's Flight: An Australian Pilot's Epic Escape from Turkish Prison Camp to Russia's Revolution*. Brisbane: Wiley, 2004.

Brown, J. *Turkish Days and Ways*. Sydney: Halstead Press, 1940.

Cirakman, A. *From the "Terror of the World" to the "Sick Man of Europe": European Images of Ottoman Empire and Society from the Sixteenth Century to the Nineteenth*. New York: Peter Lang, 2002.

Coombes, D. *Crossing the Wire: The Untold Stories of Australian POWs in Battle and Captivity during WWI*. Newport: Big Sky, 2011.

Gamble, B. *Darkest Hour: The True Story of Lark Force at Rabaul*. St Paul: Zenith Press, 2006.

Gladstone, W. E. *Bulgarian Horrors and the Question of the East*. New York: Lovell, Adam, Wesson, 1876.

Hearder, R. *Keep the Men Alive: Australian POW Doctors in Japanese Captivity*. Sydney: Allen & Unwin, 2009.

Foster, J. R. *Two and a Half Years a Prisoner of War in Turkey – Related by G.W. Handsley*. Brisbane: Jones and Hambly, 1920.

Halpin, J. *Blood in the Mists*. Sydney: The Macquarie Head Press, 1934.

Jones, E. H. *The Road to En-dor: Being an Account of How Two Prisoners of War at Yozgad in Turkey Won Their Way to Freedom*. London: The Bodley Head, 1930.

Jupp, J., ed. *The Australian People: An Encyclopedia of the Nation, Its People and Their Origins*. Cambridge: University Press Cambridge, 2001.

Kenny, C. *Captives: Australian Army Nurses in Japanese Prison Camps*. Brisbane: University of Queensland Press, 1986.

Kerr, G. *Lost Anzacs: The Story of Two Brothers*. Melbourne: Oxford University Press, 1997.

Knibbs, G. H. *Census of the Commonwealth of Australia: Volume 1: Statistician's Report*. Melbourne: McCarron, Bird, 1917.

Lake, M. "British World or New World? Anglo-Saxonism and Australian Engagement with America." *History Australia* 10, no. 3 (2013): 36–50.

Lawless, J. "Kizmet: The Fate of the Gallipoli POWs." PhD diss., University of New England 2011.

Monteath, P. *P.O.W.: Australian Prisoners of War in Hitler's Reich*. Sydney: Macmillan, 2011.

Neave, D., and C. Smith. *Aussie Soldier: Prisoners of War*. Brisbane: Big Sky, 2009.

Nelson, H. *Prisoners of War: Australians Under Nippon*. Sydney: Australian Broadcasting Corporation, 1985.

Nelson, H., and G. McCormack. *The Burma-Thailand Railway: Memory and History*. Sydney: Allen & Unwin, 1993.

Pegram, A. "Introduction." In *Both Sides of the Wire: The Memoir of an Australian Officer Captured during the Great War* [originally published as *At All Costs*], edited by A. Pegram. Sydney: Allen & Unwin, [1919] 2011.

Perry, R. *The Changi Brownlow*. Sydney: Hachette, 2010.

Reid, P. *Prisoner of War: The Inside Story of the POW from the Ancient World to Colditz and After*. London: Hamlyn, 1984.

Rowland, R. *A River Kwai Story: The Sonkrai Tribunal*. Sydney: Allen & Unwin, 2008.

Salt, J. "Johnny Turk Before Gallipoli: 19th Century Images of the Turks." In *Before and After Gallipoli: A Collection of Australian and Turkish Writings*, edited by R. Akcelik, 15–27. Melbourne: Australian-Turkish Friendship Society, 1986.

Sobocinska, A. "'The Language of Scars': Australian Prisoners of War and the Colonial Order." *History Australia* 7, no. 3 (2010): 58.1–58.19.

Stanley, P. "'He Was Black, He Was a White Man, and a Dinkum Aussie': Race and Empire in Revisiting the Anzac Legend." In *Race, Empire, and First World War Writing*, edited by S. Das, 213–230. Cambridge: Cambridge University Press, 2011.

Stephenson, P. *Islam Dreaming: Indigenous Muslims in Australia*. Sydney: University of New South Wales Press, 2010.

Stevens, C. *Tin Mosques and Ghantowns: A History of Afghan Cameldrivers in Australia*. Melbourne: Oxford University Press, 1989.

Vischer, A. L., Trans. from German *Barbed Wire Disease: A Psychological Study of the Prisoner of War*. London: John Bale, Sons and Danielsson, 1919.

White, R. "Cooees Across the Strand: Australian Travellers in London and the Performance of National Identity." *Australian Historical Studies* 32, no. 116 (2001): 109–127.

White, T. *Guests of the Unspeakable: The Odyssey of an Australian Airman – Being a Record of Captivity and Escape in Turkey*. Sydney: Angus & Robertson, 1932.

White, R. "The Soldier as Tourist: The Australian Experience of the Great War." *War and Society* 5, no. 1 (1987): 63–78.

Woolley, C. L. *From Kastamuni to Kedos: Being a Record of Experiences of Prisoners of War in Turkey 1916–1918*. Oxford: Basil Blackwell, 1921.

Men Who Defaulted in the Greatest Game of All: Sport, Conscientious Objectors and Military Defaulters in New Zealand 1916–1923

Greg Ryan

Faculty of Environment, Society and Design, Lincoln University, Christchurch, New Zealand

During the Great War most New Zealand sports bodies restricted their competitions in some way. A rhetoric against 'sporting shirkers' proliferated and was reinforced when the New Zealand government introduced military conscription in 1916 and adopted a trenchant attitude against any who were unwilling to serve. After the Great War the New Zealand Returned Soldier's Association (RSA) requested that regional and national sports bodies ban known conscientious objectors and military defaulters from all sporting competitions. Subsequent actions by sports bodies were largely if not wholly symbolic in that the number of conscientious objectors was small and there is scant evidence of any individual actually being removed from sporting competition. But they are nevertheless a potent expression of the nexus between sporting prowess and blood sacrifice that developed throughout the British Empire during and after the Great War. But not all followed the wishes of the RSA. Some were concerned that an onus was being put on sporting administrators to fulfil a role that was the responsibility of the government, while militant trade unionists took exception to such punitive treatment of those who had had the courage to stand by their convictions.

Sport has been variously examined as a physical and moral preparation for active service during the First World War[1] and as a focus for recruiting and maintenance of morale on the home front.[2] Horse racing and rugby league, with their respective elements of gambling and payment for play, have also been subjected to particular scrutiny against contemporary perceptions that they were somehow less patriotic or less committed to the war effort in view of their relative reluctance to suspend normal competition.[3] But nothing has been said of the links between sport and avowed anti-militarism during the war. Certainly this was not a dominant theme. Indeed, the evidence is decidedly fragmented and has only come within the grasp of historians with the significant digitisation of newspapers in recent years.[4] Yet the debates in 1920s New Zealand in which returned soldiers and their supporters challenged the participation of conscientious objectors and military defaulters in organised sport provide another valuable perspective on the conventionally understood nexus between sport and war.[5] If sport was training for war, then it apparently followed that those who had eschewed war service had forfeited their rights, sporting and otherwise, within post-war society. But just as some had resisted the war effort generally and the demands of conscription in particular, there was a vocal minority after the war who insisted that such 'political' interventions had no place in sport.

SPORT, WAR AND SOCIETY IN AUSTRALIA AND NEW ZEALAND

Although strong elements of emergent national identity were evident in New Zealand from the late nineteenth century, this was offset by a perhaps greater emphasis on enduring loyalty to the British Empire. New Zealand troops distinguished themselves in the South African war and in 1907 the Prime Minister Sir Joseph Ward left no doubt that further contingents would be forthcoming in any time of crisis and especially so as the Anglo-German naval race intensified. 'Our country is very anxious and willing to assist the Old Land in the event of trouble arising, to do so voluntarily by men or money and ... always would be ready to do its share in fighting for the defence of the Motherland in any portion of the world'.[6] True to his word, on March 22, 1909, Ward informed Britain that New Zealand would defray the cost, some £1.7 million, of the immediate building of one dreadnought class battle cruiser to be gifted to the British Navy.[7] In a further show of military preparedness an assessment of New Zealand's defence capability during a tour by Lord Kitchener led to the passing of a Defence Act in 1909. This introduced compulsory military training (CMT) for males aged 12–20 (later 14–25) and established an active territorial force.[8]

But the passing of the Defence Act also gave focus to various strands of anti-militarism. Unlike Australia, exemptions on the grounds of conscience were not permitted. Almost immediately strong opposition emerged. Christian-based movements including the New Zealand Peace Council, the Anti-Militarist League and the Freedom League were formed to oppose CMT. Meanwhile, successive iterations of what became the New Zealand Labour Party coordinated strong opposition on socialist and ideological grounds amid a wider climate of industrial unrest during the immediate pre-war period. In Christchurch, working-class apprentices at the Addington railway workshops also formed a Passive Resisters' Union, although they were unsuccessful in an attempt to have its hockey team accepted into the local competition.[9] On the rugged West Coast of the South Island, coal miners, including an influential if not numerically strong socialist element at the core of the most militant 'Red' Federation of Labour, were especially vigorous in their opposition, regarding the Defence Act as a weapon of capitalist imperialism.[10] By 1914 almost 5000 men had been convicted for failing to register or otherwise resisting CMT. While most were fined, some were imprisoned in military defaulters' camps such as Rīpapa Island in Lyttelton Harbour near Christchurch.[11]

At the outbreak of war in August 1914 New Zealand's previous military preparations were apparently vindicated and much opposition to CMT quickly receded. A combination of patriotism, adventure and peer pressure triggered a rush to enlist. A total of 14,000 men joined within the first week and a force was rapidly dispatched to take German Samoa. More than 100,000 men served overseas by the end of 1918. Even as the confident predictions that the war would be 'over by Christmas' evaporated into the brutal realities of stalemate at Gallipoli and on the Western Front, the vast majority of the population remained firm in their support for the war effort and the inevitability of sacrifice.[12] Nevertheless recruiting campaigns soon failed to meet enlistment targets. In October 1915 the government created a National Register of all males between the ages of 17 and 60 years with details of their willingness or otherwise to serve. But only 30% of men eligible for military service had volunteered by early 1916. In July, with opposition from only four MPs, the National coalition government passed the Military Service Act establishing the Expeditionary Force Reserve consisting of every male European between the ages of 20 and 46 years from which all future reinforcements were to be selected by ballot. The first ballot took place in mid-November 1916. The Act was extended to Maori in June 1917. By the end of the war 30,000 men had been conscripted into the Expeditionary Force for service overseas.[13]

The Military Service Act quickly became a tool to force conformity to the war effort as those who were deemed to be 'shirking' their obligations were now subjected to formal sanction and ultimately conscription of any who actively refused to serve. The Act made only limited allowance for exemption from service on religious grounds for groups that had, prior to the outbreak of war, declared military service 'contrary to divine revelation'. Even then, those exempted had to be prepared to undertake non-combatant service in New Zealand or overseas. Only 73 exemptions were granted to Quakers, Christadelphians and Seventh-day Adventists. But there was no sympathy for any who objected on political, moral or non-recognised religious grounds. By the end of the war 273 men were in prison in New Zealand for refusing to serve. Included was the West Coast Labour MP Paddy Webb who was one of several sentenced to hard labour. He epitomised a strong feeling among the militant mining communities that conscription of men was a direct attack on the working class as there was no corresponding conscription of wealth for the war effort and, indeed, evidence of profiteering as prices of basic commodities rose. The last of the imprisoned objectors were deliberately not released until after the last New Zealand troops had returned home in 1919. In total 2600 conscientious objectors, including many who had gone into hiding during the war to avoid conscription, were subsequently stripped of their civil rights including denial of voting rights for 10 years and being barred from employment by government or local bodies.[14]

The most extreme manifestation of official determination to enforce conformity to the war effort came in July 1917 when Colonel H.R. Potter, the Trentham Military Camp commandant, sent 14 of the most recalcitrant conscientious objectors to Britain aboard the troopship *Waitemata*. One, Mark Briggs, refused to walk onto the ship and was dragged. Under a regime of mistreatment and threats most of the group eventually relented and agreed to become stretcher-bearers or take other non-combatant roles in France. Four, including Briggs and Archibald Baxter, remained defiant. They endured repeated sentences of Field Punishment No. 1 which involved being tied to a post in the open with their hands bound tightly behind their backs and their knees and feet bound for up to four hours a day in all weather. In February 1918 Baxter and Briggs were forcibly taken to front-line trenches under heavy shellfire. It was scarcely surprising that by mid-year they were deemed unfit for military service due to the privations they had suffered.[15]

The establishment and growing political influence of the New Zealand Returned Soldiers' Association (RSA) ensured that condemnation of conscientious objectors and shirkers more generally did not abate when war ended. Wounded soldiers returning to New Zealand from Gallipoli from July 1915 formed various local groups that came together in the formation of an Association in Wellington on April 28, 1916. At the outset it stressed that it was non-sectarian and non-political and was initially concerned with the repatriation of soldiers and the rights of disabled soldiers. But agitation, especially from the Auckland and Christchurch branches during 1919, led to a shift from non-political to non-party-political enabling the RSA to pose questions of election candidates regarding their support for its aims. Membership peaked at 57,000 in 1920, more than two-thirds of all returned soldiers, then declined sharply to 24,000 in 1922 and a low of 6000 by 1927 as men successfully reintegrated into society.[16] Yet what the RSA lacked in numerical strength as the 1920s progressed was more than offset by a consolidation of its vocal political influence. Under the presidency from 1921 of Major-General Sir Andrew Russell, former commander of the New Zealand Division, the RSA became a well established and influential force, constantly lobbying central government for more comprehensive rehabilitation schemes within a wider post-war reconstruction of the

New Zealand economy. At the same time, the Association exerted some degree of social control over its membership by encouraging respectable pastimes such as sport and discouraging an association with more disreputable aspects of wartime male culture. During the 1920s RSA teams entered many local competitions in cricket, hockey, rugby and soccer as some men sought to retain the strength of wartime bonds rather than integrating back into local clubs. The Palmerston North RSA team won the local senior rugby competition in 1920.[17]

Most importantly for present purposes, the RSA augmented its welfare focus with strenuous efforts to safeguard the memory of the war and of those who had not returned. This was especially evident in the campaign to have Anzac Day observed as a full national holiday, achieved in 1922, and in the poppy appeal and range of solemn rituals associated with the day. It also revealed itself in an unrelenting determination to marginalise conscientious objectors and military defaulters. When, in July 1919, the Conscientious Objectors Fellowship approached the Christchurch branch of the RSA requesting an opportunity to explain their position, they were curtly informed that objectors had been dealt with by a government commission of enquiry and as the war had been won without their help, the Association had no reason to communicate with them now that the war was over.[18] The RSA again responded with hostility in late 1920 when the Military Service Amendment Act effectively declared an amnesty for conscientious objectors and military defaulters, some of whom had remained in hiding after the war. Although the denial of civil rights remained in force for objectors, the wartime process of court martial for those who had resisted active service was replaced with a civil process to deal with those, generally referred to as 'military defaulters' who continued to resist CMT. The Auckland RSA responded bitterly that those who had avoided service by hiding were now getting off scot-free while some soldiers remained in military detention for crimes, such as assault, that would scarcely have warranted a prison term in civilian life. The Wellington branch reiterated that the policy of the RSA was that all military defaulters should be made to serve their full sentence as they were 'a menace to the community'.[19] During 1921 various RSA branches sought to continue pressure against defaulters at a local level. In Taranaki it was resolved 'That, in view of increasing unemployment, this association strongly condemns the action, of certain prominent business' firms in Hawera in employing military defaulters and urges all employers of labour to give preference to returned soldiers and loyalists in fulfilment of promises given during the war'.[20] The conference of the New Zealand Farmers' Union was also asked to consider a remit from the Southland RSA protesting against military defaulters being released from prison, and urging that the union strongly support the RSA in any action that may be necessary to prevent objectors obtaining civil rights.[21] These and other calls for sanctions were generally applied to both conscientious objectors who had refused to fight during the war and those, including men who had been too young for war service, who now resisted CMT. Terms such as 'military defaulter', 'shirker' and 'conscientious objector' were frequently used interchangeably although the context surrounding each group and the penalties attending their actions were markedly different.

As in all combatant countries, New Zealand sport was significantly challenged by the war. On the one hand, sport had long been regarded as a moral and physical training ground for young men and was therefore favoured as a vital component of 'soldier-making'. Consequently sports clubs and associations became important conduits to military recruitment during the early months of the war.[22] The sentiments expressed by James Allen, Minister of Defence, in a speech at Milton on April 6, 1916, were certainly nothing original.

> It is a great game, it is a greater game than your cricket, football and hockey. It is a great test of nationality, it is a great test of citizenship for every man who is a true sort. We are proud of our national games, and we deplore and hate this terrible war, but I venture to say that the man who is a true sport, the man who understands that the stakes are high, that the stakes are nationality, New Zealand or no New Zealand, will not hesitate to answer the call of his mates in the trenches and join in the great game.[23]

But the utility of sport as a preparation for war did not guarantee universal acceptance of its continuation during the hour of conflict. As recruitment slowed, during 1915–1916 there were heated discussions especially around the notion that those who were fit to play were fit to serve, but also on the theme that horse racing in particular, with both a commercial and gambling dimension, was channelling potential revenue away from the war effort.[24] While all sports decided to continue, especially in the interests of fostering community spirit and fundraising for patriotic causes, most restricted their activities. Typical was the New Zealand Rugby Football Union which suspended inter-provincial matches aside from a small number for charity. By the 1916 season, as declining numbers of available players forced many teams to withdraw from local competitions, it was increasingly seen as practical to encourage junior sport rather than persist with meagre and mediocre senior grades. The Canterbury Rugby Football Union replaced its senior competition with two grades, under 19 and under 20, for the 1916 and 1917 seasons, and its Otago counterpart took similar action. But from late 1917 there was a gradual relaxation in these measures to allow sport for those serving at home or legitimately unable to serve and to sustain morale and fitness for those approaching military age.[25]

Perceptions of those who sought to avoid or oppose war easily intersected with the debates of the sporting community. Where sport was seen to embody the traits of masculine physicality and character necessary for the battlefield, conversely the shirker was widely regarded as effeminate and lacking both physical and moral strength.[26] In July 1916 'Normal' wrote to *The Press* to make explicit both the problem of and solution for the non-combatant.

> The non-participation of anti-militarists in games has been commented on in Christchurch. I have several friends who are strong anti-militarists, and long ago it struck me as curious that with one exception none of them played games. The young man who takes no interest in any kind of game is abnormal, a freak, and the anti-militarists' lack of interest in games is only one manifestation of his abnormality. It is a pity, for games would do these curious people a great deal of good. Their besetting sin is narrowness and rigidity of mind. For the most part they read narrowly and mix – if the phrase is permissible – in narrow circles. Now games, especially team games, are admirable instruments for rubbing off corners and bringing one into contact with all sorts and conditions of men. The little world of the anti-militarists, with its over close atmosphere, needs a whiff or two of the keen rather rough, wind of the cricket and football fields'.[27]

At almost the same time a report circulated throughout New Zealand detailing the failure of British officers in France to inspire any interest in organised sport among the non-combatant corps of conscientious objectors working behind the lines.[28]

While many clubs and governing bodies exhorted their members to enlist, and some debated steps to shame supposed shirkers into doing so,[29] there is no evidence during the war years of any formal sporting sanction against avowed anti-militarists or conscientious objectors. But as sport resumed in earnest immediately after the war, questions began to be asked. In June 1919 the *Fielding Star* urged the Manawatu Rugby Union to take action on a report that two men 'who had what are charitably termed conscientious objections to fighting for the Empire while the war was on' were playing in the club competition on the previous Saturday. It was noted that these players were in the best form and fitness compared with those recently returned from the war. One had reportedly served a period of imprisonment for military desertion. 'The colossal impudence displayed by such men in walking onto the football field cannot adequately be described. For the memory of their fallen football comrades, the soldier players would be justified in refusing to tolerate this'.[30] A year later Stipendiary Magistrate V.G. Day, in the Christchurch Magistrates Court stated that it would be a good idea if local football clubs, by which the magistrate evidently meant rugby clubs, refused to allow participation by players who had not fulfilled their obligations under the Defence Amendment Act which had reinstated CMT after the war. This was in response to one 'drill defaulter' who claimed that his non-attendance at a half day territorial parade was because he was playing rugby.[31]

The first formal intervention against objectors and defaulters from an administrative sporting body appears to have come from the Management Committee of the Wellington Cricket Association in December 1920. The secretary, Roy S. Johnson, said he had been approached by some returned soldiers who pointed out that as 'defaulters' had been deprived of civil rights, it was only appropriate to deprive them of sport and a halt must be called to the policy of 'forgive and forget'. Committee member H. Buck added that many players in his club had scars and physical disabilities from battle and it was not fair to ask them to play against those who had not served. The Secretary was directed to advise all affiliated clubs that it was 'undesirable' for those deprived of civil rights to play in local competitions.[32] At the same time a columnist for the *Free Lance* questioned the identity of H. Nunn from the Hutt club and wanted to know if he was the same H. Nunn who had served a prison term as a territorial defaulter.[33] But in a sign of attitudes to come, the *Grey River Argus* on the West Coast republished the report of these deliberations under the headline 'Sports or Jingoes: Cricket Association's Strange Stand'.[34]

Further, apparently unconnected, efforts were made to raise the issue of objectors and defaulters with provincial rugby unions in particular during 1921–1922. In May 1921 the Manawatu Rugby Union decided to ban all 'military defaulters' from competitions and to suspend any club knowingly playing one. J. Smith, representing the RSA, insisted that the motivation for debarring these men was not personal spite but their duty to represent limbless men and those fallen on the battlefield.[35] In late July the neighbouring Taranaki union received a letter from the commanding officer of the Taranaki Regimental District urging a ban on all who had defaulted during the war or were continuing to default on their CMT obligations. The Union was supplied with a list of known defaulters and agreed to ban them from competition.[36] Arguably the most comprehensive and extreme response came from the Otago Rugby Football Union at its annual meeting in July 1922. In response to a letter from the Otago District Council of the RSA it was moved 'That no military defaulter be allowed to play football under the jurisdiction of the ORFU for ten years from date'. J. Dunne of the Dunedin club questioned whether men such as most of those on the committee who had not gone to war for legitimate reasons ought to be making decisions about who could play sport. The country needed to move on, especially as the government was no longer pursuing conscientious objectors. But the majority of the meeting insisted that a firm stand had to be taken and that rugby authorities had the right to determine who could or could not play in competitions under their jurisdiction. The motion was passed 27–4, effectively meaning that any conscientious objector would be banned until July 1932, nearly four years after any official denial of civil rights had expired.[37]

The stance of some other sports was more equivocal. In August 1921 R.J.F. Aldrich, Secretary of the Wellington RSA, wrote to the New Zealand Boxing Council requesting clarification of an apparent decision to allow conscientious objectors to participate in boxing championships.

> I would point out to you that it is not necessary for a man to have been convicted to be classed as a military defaulter, as legislation was passed some time ago giving these shirkers absolution. I need hardly say that my association will protest most strongly against these people being permitted to take part in any kind of sport whatever.

What Aldrich clearly had in mind were those men who had evaded conscription and never been convicted. W.G. Talbot, Secretary of the Council, replied that a remit to ban 'defaulters' (although the target was clearly 'objectors') had been brought forward at the annual conference in Greymouth but had lapsed due to lack of support. This did not mean that boxing officials supported participation by such men, but merely that there was insufficient support for a formal sanction against them given that the government was no longer pursuing them.[38] In July 1922 a remit was put to the annual general meeting of the professional New Zealand Athletic and Cycling Union: 'That no "shirker", military defaulter or undesirable person be allowed to compete at any meeting held under the rules of the New Zealand Athletic and Cycling union'. A motion to remove the words 'undesirable person' was carried after a debate in which it was pointed out that such a designation was vague at best. Greater concern was expressed that a ban on defaulters put the onus on clubs who may not be aware that they had one among their membership. The original motion was therefore amended to read 'knowingly allowed to compete'. Finally, one delegate pointed out that those who refused CMT were being called 'military defaulters' and there was a real risk that banning all such men could leave them with no competitors. Accordingly the Union stipulated that its ban applied only to those who had 'shirked' their responsibility during the war.[39]

After two years of sporadic debate initiated at local level, the national executive of the RSA took the matter firmly in hand with a letter to a range of provincial and national sports bodies early in 1923. In essence the Association found it particularly difficult to forgive those who had not played any part in the war but continued to play a part in sport:

> Military defaulters have been deprived of civil rights for their failure to render service, and in almost every branch of sport they are to be found at the present time capable and well enough to reach representative form, many of them, while we find men who did their duty maimed for life and deprived of the enjoyment of outdoor sports for the remainder of their lives. Men there are who rendered good service in the war, and are in the top flight of our sportsmen to-day, and there are men who are enjoying just a game now and then – their disabilities probably precluding them from taking up the game thoroughly – yet the men who defaulted in the greatest game of all are on the same footing in sport as they were in 1914. Is this fair? Should this be? This association, the only organisation of the New Zealand men who served in the Great War, is strongly against the existing conditions which allow military defaulters – in other words men who in practice do not believe in justice or law and order – to take equal places with the rest of the community in the pursuits which are boasted of as being one of, if not the greatest, factors in the moulding of our race.[40]

But in making their claim the RSA, so determined to stigmatise conscientious objectors in other contexts, provided no details of those who were apparently to be found in 'every branch of sport'. Of equal significance, no such evidence was asked for by most sporting bodies or the press.

Several sports immediately declared their full support for the RSA. The New Zealand Football Association wrote to all clubs recommending that they do not allow 'defaulters of the Great War' into any competitions.[41] The New Zealand Cricket Council recommended to all affiliated associations to debar 'military defaulters' from playing in matches under their control.[42] The New Zealand Amateur Athletic Association stated that it was in favour of debarring military defaulters from participation and decided to forward a copy of the RSA letter to each club with a strong recommendation that it be supported. The Council of the New Zealand Rowing Association resolved to distribute the RSA letter to all local associations with a view to discussion at the next meeting of delegates, as the existing rules of the Council could not enforce the proposal.[43] The management committee of the Wellington Rugby Union proposed a further step in asking clubs to supply a return of any players who came within the category of 'defaulters'. In response to a query as to how such information could be obtained, it was pointed out that the government had prepared a list of defaulters after the war. The one dissenting voice at the meeting was Father Paul Kane who thought the matter scarcely came within the scope of the Union. The war was well over and he did not think that men who had once been punished under the law should now be punished a second time. Kane, an ordained Catholic priest, played one game for the All Blacks in 1921 under the surname Markham.[44] The only national sporting body to flatly reject the RSA overture was the New Zealand Swimming Council which felt that it would be too difficult to detect and deal with 'military defaulters' and therefore decided to take no action.[45]

A more concerted effort from the RSA at a national level in turn provoked the most concerted opposition from the more militant West Coast. In late 1920 as the Government proposed its amnesty, several public meetings on the Coast, dominated by coal miners and unionists, had declared their support for the Labour Party in its efforts to stop any continuing persecution of conscientious objectors by military or civil means.[46] Now the Greymouth branch of the RSA dispatched a firm rebuff to headquarters in Wellington:

> This association regrets the action of the association's headquarters in asking all Rugby unions to expel conscientious objectors from their ranks, as we are of opinion no good can come from it, and further, we submit it is outside the constitution of the Returned Soldier's Association to interfere in such matters.

A.H. McKane stated that returned men had to work alongside objectors and could not down tools because of their presence. 'If he appealed to an industrial organisation, he would probably be told the objector was a good unionist, and if he went to a private employer the latter would not dismiss a man because he was an objector. Therefore, if they had to work alongside conscientious objectors, they should be fair in other respects'.[47] In similar vein the West Coast Rugby Union debated whether they were obliged to follow the lead of their national body. It was suggested that the issue raised by the national executive of the RSA was a 'dying question' and most people were moving on with their post-war lives. The Union received the letter from the NZRFU but took no action.[48] The West Coast Football Association also declared that it had no intention of following the directive of its national body. Although there was some sympathy for the stance of the RSA, it was also the case that the Empire was again trading with Germany and they were obliged to look to the future rather than dwell on the past.[49] The most trenchant response on the West Coast came in a motion unanimously passed at a meeting of the Ngakawau Miners Union in early May 1923.

> That we the Ngakawau miners enter a very emphatic protest against the decision of the New Zealand Rugby Union and its attitude towards men who had the courage of their convictions and refused to be led by a 'mass psychology'; furthermore we realise that the action of the New Zealand Rugby Union is detrimental to the best interests of sport, and that their action has a political significance that should not be lost sight of by the working class.[50]

It is surely testimony to the status of rugby as the 'national game' in 1920s New Zealand that this resolution was aimed squarely at the NZRFU and not at the RSA or the various other sports that had supported its stance. The Miners Union secretary H.L. Evans further commented in the *Grey River Argus* that he was 'beginning to think that the workers will have to use the boycott occasionally to compel these people with the militaristic minds to realise that the workers are not going to be dictated to as to who shall be eligible to play football or any other game in this the 20th century'. He noted that conscientious objectors were allowed to sit in the British House of Commons and actively voice their opinions against any further repetition of 1914. But in New Zealand objectors were disenfranchised because the apathy of the workers allowed them to be so.[51] But rather than provoking further engagement, this riposte from the West Coast marked the end of the debate. The RSA did not respond and there is no sign of any comment on objectors and sport for nearly a year from mid-1923.

There was one last flourish from the RSA and its supporters. In June 1924 the national executive formed a sub-committee to investigate a report that a military defaulter had been selected in the All Blacks team which was about to tour Australia and Britain. In short order the committee concluded that there was not sufficient evidence.[52] But the rumour persisted, not least because the NZRFU was slow to refute it.[53] Finally on June 16 the Union issued a statement.

> If it were known that any man actually shirked war service he would not be considered a fit representative of the Dominion as a footballer. A decision to that effect was made some years ago, and the Union as presently constituted has no intention of departing from it. As far as we are aware there is no man selected in the present team who comes under this category. Rumours are current, and in fairness to members of the team, who are all more or less brought into disrepute by such rumours, we feel that a statement should be made. If anybody has any information with regard to any of the players chosen having failed to answer the call of their country for war service we shall be glad to have the fact brought before us.[54]

Ten days later it was reported that the player accused as a defaulter had merely been fined once or twice for missing territorial parades, but had never refused or evaded territorial service generally and had obtained a clean discharge from the Territorials which he had shown to the national selectors.[55] Yet it seems that not all players were so blameless. In early July D.G. Fairbrother of Timaru was charged with defaulting from drill and being 'non-efficient' for the previous four years. In his defence he explained that he was playing rugby as he wanted a trip to Britain with the All Blacks and was therefore determined to get as much practice as possible. The Magistrate, E.D. Mosley, fined Fairbrother £2 and costs and threatened him with denial of civil rights if he appeared again. He also directed that the case be referred to the Rugby Union to deal with, as a man who did not do his duty for his country should not play rugby.[56] Given that one of the most significant moments of the All Blacks tour was a visit to the grave of the 1905 'Original' All Blacks captain Dave Gallaher in Belgium, it was almost unimaginable that anyone with a dubious record of service would have been tolerated.[57]

The last recorded action against a military defaulter in a sporting context came in late 1925 when Wallace Robinson, a Taranaki representative player, was withdrawn from a match against Auckland after it was revealed that he had been deprived of civil rights for three years and fined £5 for failing to attend territorial drill over an eight-year period.[58] But by the following year it was evident that the NZRFU was softening its previously uncompromising stance. When asked to reaffirm its attitude to military defaulters, the Management Committee of the Union was quite willing to declare that 'a man who shirks parades is no good for football' but insisted that a distinction must be made between that man and 'the boy who shirks for sheer bravado'. One committee member stated that civil law dealt with defaulters and it would therefore be a mistake for the Union to deal with them as well. On the other hand, military authorities had increasingly met the needs of the Union by arranging as far as possible that drill did not clash with fixtures. Eventually the Union determined to adhere to its existing policy regarding those who had avoided service during the war, but would deal with 'drill shirkers' on a case by case basis.[59]

Fairbrother and Robinson, both defaulters rather than objectors, were the only players conclusively and publicly identified during the RSA campaign. There is no specific evidence of any individual conscientious objector being excluded from sport during the 1920s. But this is not the point. The *intent* to exclude these men is sufficient indication of a dominant state of mind whereby the service and sacrifice of the war were to be enshrined and ritualised as key components of New Zealand's national identity while elements of dissent were to be vigorously stamped out.

Why conscientious objection and sport intersected in this way in New Zealand and nowhere else is a moot point. In Britain, where conscription was introduced, and where conscientious objectors were imprisoned and sometimes subjected to Field Punishment No. 1, there is no evidence of any post-war sporting sanction against them.[60] Meanwhile, although Australia did not adopt military conscription, one should not imagine for a moment that anti-militarists and other objectors to military service were left unscathed.[61] Moreover, there was a single instance to match the campaign in New Zealand when the Returned Sailors and Soldiers' League strenuously objected to prominent rower Wally Pfeiffer who had declared himself a conscientious objector to conscription. But the campaign failed to gain substantial public sympathy and Pfeiffer held his place in the Murray Bridge crew that represented Australia at the 1924 Paris Olympiad.[62] It was perhaps that the strong devotion to Empire that drew New Zealand to adopt and vigorously enforce CMT and then conscription in the first place left in its wake a far stronger legislative framework within which the RSA felt it could exert an influence. New Zealand was 16 times more likely than Britain to arrest its citizens for conscientious objection during the war, invoked far stricter conscience clauses in its military service legislation and finally enacted a denial of civil rights twice as long as that in Britain.[63]

But the enduring legacy of the RSA stance was limited. Although the New Zealand government continued to pursue conscientious objectors with vigour during the Second World War, and the RSA enthusiastically supported this endeavour, attempts to extend penalties to sport gained no traction. A motion to the Wellington Football Association in March 1942 was almost unanimously defeated. A few days later both the Hawkes Bay and Auckland rugby unions also refused to take action ostensibly on the basis that objectors were the concern of civil and not sporting authorities.[64] There is no evidence of any other sporting body grappling with this issue or any reference to the debates of the 1920s. Perhaps perceptions of New Zealand sport were gradually moving towards the more conventional political alignment evident in the late twentieth century. Whereas in the 1920s it was the militant left, epitomised by the Ngakawau Miners Union, who insisted that 'politics' had no place in sport while more conservative elements insisted that it did. Within a generation, and especially with regard to sporting contacts with South Africa, the roles were reversed.

Notes

1. For example Campbell, "'Training for Sport Is Training for War'"; Birley, "Sportsmen and the Deadly Game"; and Veitch, "'Play Up! Play Up! and Win the War!'"
2. For example Collins, "English Rugby Union and the First World War"; Phillips, "Football, Class and War"; and Phillips, "Sport, War and Gender Images."

3. For example McKernan, "Sport, War and Society"; and Noonan, "Offside: Rugby League."
4. For New Zealand see http://paperspast.natlib.govt.nz/cgi-bin/paperspast
5. Generally contemporary accounts used 'conscientious objector' to describe those who had refused service during the war and 'military' defaulter for those who refused compulsory military training before or after it. However, the RSA tended always to use the more pejorative 'military defaulter' in both contexts.
6. Quoted in McGibbon, *The Path to Gallipoli,* 167–8.
7. Ibid., 171–2.
8. Ibid., 181–93.
9. CH342 Box 14/60, National Archives, Christchurch.
10. Richardson, "Politics and War," 128–30.
11. Grant, *Out in the Cold,* 14–15.
12. McGibbon, "The Shaping of New Zealand's War Effort."
13. Martin "Blueprint for the Future?" 517–19; and Baker, *King and Country Call,* 42–63, 79–95.
14. *Auckland Star* (hereafter *AS*), June 23, 1916, 6; Baker, *King and Country Call*, 153–210; Grant, *Out in the Cold*, 18.
15. Grant. "Briggs, Mark"; and "Baxter, Archibald McColl Learmond."
16. Clarke, "Return, Repatriation, Remembrance," 157–61.
17. Ibid., 164–79.
18. *Evening Post* (hereafter *EP*), July 4, 1919, 4.
19. *AS*, September 30, 1920, 7; *EP* October 23, 1920, 6; and *New Zealand Herald* (hereafter *NZH*), November 3, 1920, 8.
20. *EP*, June 7 1921, 6.
21. Ibid., July 11, 1921, 6.
22. Hall, "The Greater Game," 15–32; and Loveridge, "Soldiers and Shirkers," 65.
23. *The Press*, April 7, 1916, 9.
24. Hall, "The Greater Game," 33–43. See also among many examples, *Ohinemuri Gazette*, September 29, 1916, 3; *EP*, December 11, 1915, 14; *EP*, December 27, 1915, 2.
25. Hall, "The Greater Game," 103–6, 226–31. See also *Otago Daily Times* (hereafter *ODT*), December 1, 1916, 7.
26. Loveridge, "Soldiers and Shirkers," 69–71
27. *The Press,* July 8, 1916, 6.
28. For example, *NZH*, July 1, 1916, 2.
29. For example, a special meeting of the Canterbury Centre of the New Zealand Swimming Association debated a motion 'That all swimmers who are eligible for active service shall not be allowed to compete in inter-club events during the season unless they can show a satisfactory reason to the executive why they have not offered their services to the Empire'. The motion was eventually withdrawn as it was determined that there was not yet a shortage of recruits. *EP*, December 27, 1915, 2.
30. *Fielding Star*, June 16, 1919, 2.
31. *EP*, June 1, 1920, 6.
32. Ibid., December 8, 1920, 6.
33. *Free Lance*, December 15, 1920, 31.
34. *Grey River Argus* (hereafter *GRA*), December 11, 1920, 3.
35. *EP,* May 25, 1921, 4; May 26, 1921, 8.
36. *AS*, August 1, 1921, 4.
37. ORFU Committee Minutes, July 10, 1922; *ODT*, July 22, 1922, 6.
38. *EP*, August 25, 1921, 8.
39. *Hawera & Normanby Star*, July 25, 1922, 4; *EP*, September 18, 1922, 2; and *AS*, September 18, 1922, 9.
40. Quoted in NZ *Truth* (hereafter *NZT*), April 7, 1923, 1.
41. *EP*, March 23, 1923, 2; and *NZH*, March 27, 1923, 9.
42. *EP*, May 1, 1923, 4.
43. Ibid., March 28, 1923, 16.
44. Ibid., April 11, 1923, 9.
45. Ibid., May 28, 1923, 4.
46. *GRA*, August 31, 1920, 3; and *ODT*, September 28, 1920, 5.
47. *NZH*, May 19, 1923, 12.

48. Ibid., April 16, 1923, 8.
49. *The Press*, May 1, 1923, 6. See also *NZT*, March 8, 1924, 9.
50. *Maoriland Worker*, May 2, 1923, 10.
51. Ibid.
52. *AS*, June 11, 1924, 9.
53. *NZT*, June 14, 1924, 6.
54. *AS*, June 17, 1924, 8.
55. Ibid., June 28, 1924, 21.
56. *NZH*, July 10, 1924, 6.
57. Masters, *With the All Blacks*.
58. *NZT*, October 10, 1925, 11.
59. *EP*, June 17, 1926, 8.
60. This conclusion is derived from a search of the British Newspaper Archive 1918–1925. See http://www.britishnewspaperarchive.co.uk/ For discussion of conscientious objectors in Britain see Boulton, *Objection Overruled*; Kennedy, *The Hound of Conscience*; and Rae, *Conscience and Politics*.
61. See Oliver, *Peacemongers*. See also Blair, "The Greater Game," 91–2, who briefly discusses the impact of compulsory military training on sport prior to the war, but does not discuss sporting attitudes to anti-conscriptionists or conscientious objectors during the war.
62. *Sydney Morning Herald*, May 23, 1922, 8; *Sydney Morning Herald*, May 7, 1924, 16; *News* (Adelaide), November 5, 1923, 9; and *Murray Pioneer and Australian River Record*, November 17, 1923, 12.
63. In Britain 16,000 conscientious objectors were reviewed by military tribunals and 6300 arrested from a population of 46 million. In New Zealand 2600 were arrested from a population of 1.16 million. See note 14 above.
64. *EP*, March 26, 1942, 9; *AS*, March 28, 1942, 6; and *AS*, March 31, 1942, 7.

References

Baker, Paul. *King and Country Call: New Zealanders, Conscription and the Great War*. Auckland: Auckland University Press, 1988.

Birley, Derek. "Sportsmen and the Deadly Game." *The British Journal of Sports History* 3, no. 3 (1986): 288–310.

Blair, D. J. ""The Greater Game": Australian Football and the Army at Home and on the Front during World War I." *Sporting Traditions* 11, no. 2 (1995): 91–102.

Boulton, David. *Objection Overruled*. London: MacGibbon and Kee, 1967.

Campbell, James D. "'raining for Sport Is Training for War': Sport and the Transformation of the British Army, 1860–1914." *The International Journal of the History of Sport* 17, no. 4 (2000): 21–58.

Clarke, Stephen. "Return, Repatriation, Remembrance and the Returned Soldier's Association 1916–22." In *New Zealand's Great War: New Zealand, the Allies and the First World War*, edited by John Crawford, and Ian McGibbon, 157–181. Auckland: Exisle, 2007.

Collins, Tony. "English Rugby Union and the First World War." *The Historical Journal* 45, no. 4 (2002): 797–817.

Grant, David. "Baxter, Archibald McColl Learmond." In Dictionary of New Zealand Biography. Te Ara – The Encyclopedia of New Zealand, updated June 5, 2013. http://www.TeAra.govt.nz/en/biographies/3b19/baxter-archibald-mccoll-learmond

Grant, David. "Briggs, Mark." In *Dictionary of New Zealand Biography*. Te Ara – The Encyclopedia of New Zealand, updated June 5, 2013. http://www.TeAra.govt.nz/en/biographies/3b48/briggs-mark

Grant, David. *Out in the Cold: Pacifists and Conscientious Objectors in New Zealand during World War II*. Auckland: Reed Methuen, 1986.

Hall, Fiona. *"The Greater Game": Sport and Society in Christchurch during the First World War, 1914–1918*. Master's thesis: University of Canterbury, 1989.

Kennedy, Thomas. *The Hound of Conscience: A History of the No-Conscription Fellowship, 1914–1919*. Fayetteville: University of Arkansas Press, 1981.

Loveridge, Steven. "Soldiers and Shirkers: Modernity and New Zealand Masculinity during the Great War." *New Zealand Journal of History* 47, no. 1 (2013): 59–79.

Martin, John E. "Blueprint for the Future? 'National Efficiency' and the First World War." In *New Zealand's Great War: New Zealand, the Allies and the First World War*, edited by John Crawford, and Ian McGibbon, 516–533. Auckland: Exisle, 2007.

Masters, Read. *With the All Blacks in Great Britain*. Christchurch: Christchurch Press, 1928.

McGibbon, Ian. *The Path to Gallipoli: Defending New Zealand 1840–1915*. Wellington: GP Books, 1991.

McGibbon, Ian. "The Shaping of New Zealand's War Effort, August-October 1914." In *New Zealand's Great War: New Zealand, the Allies and the First World War*, edited by John Crawford, and Ian McGibbon, 49–68. Auckland: Exisle, 2007.

McKernan, Michael. "Sport, War and Society: Australia, 1914–1918." In *Sport in History: The Making of Modern Sporting History*, edited by Richard Cashman, and Michael McKernan, 1–20. St Lucia: University of Queensland Press, 1979.

Noonan, Rodney. "Offside: Rugby League, the Great War and Australian Patriotism." *The International Journal of the History of Sport* 26, no. 15 (2009): 2201–2218.

Oliver, Bobbie. *Peacemongers: Conscientious Objectors to Military Service in Australia, 1911–1945*. Fremantle: Fremantle Arts Centre Press, 1997.

Phillips, Murray G. "Football, Class and War: The Rugby Codes in New South Wales, 1907–1918." In *Making Men: Rugby and Masculine Identity*, edited by John Nauright, and Timothy J. L. Chandler, 158–180. London: Frank Cass, 1996.

Phillips, Murray G. "Sport, War and Gender Images: The Australian Sportsmen's Battalions and the First World War." *The International Journal of the History of Sport* 14, no. 1 (1997): 78–96.

Rae, John. *Conscience and Politics: The British Government and the Conscientious Objector to Military Service 1916–1919*. Oxford: Oxford University Press, 1970.

Richardson, Len. "Politics and War: Coal Miners and Conscription, 1914–18." In *Miners and Militants: Politics in Westland*, edited by Philip Ross May, 128–156. Christchurch: Whitcoulls, 1975.

Veitch, Colin. "'Play Up! Play Up! and Win the War!': Football, the Nation and the First World War 1914–15." *Journal of Contemporary History* 20, no. 3 (1985): 363–378.

'Carry On': The Response of the Victorian Football League to the Challenges of World War II

Bruce Kennedy

Private Scholar, Canberra, Australia

The Victorian Football League (VFL) was formed following an acrimonious split with the Victorian Football Association at the end of the 1896 season. Despite being based around clubs located only in Melbourne and Geelong, the VFL soon became Australia's premier football competition. Although much has been written about League players who served in the armed forces during the two world wars, less attention has been given to identifying the issues and challenges that football competitions, and the VFL in particular, had to address if they were to continue to function during times of military conflict. Trials faced by organisers of the code were logistical, political and moral. Player and administrator shortages and a restricted number of venues to play at, were the most obvious challenges. The Australian government assumed control of manpower and resources in January 1942 and placed many restrictions on discretional activities of the population. In this context, a general feeling was that there was little room for organised major sporting competitions because they could detract from the war focus. The way society reacted to the constraints shaped football's direction, and the VFL had to interpret government policy and read the mood of the public before deciding whether to continue playing. In the end, the League, despite criticism from some quarters for continuing its competition, sided with the prevailing view that the public needed a diversion to allow them some relaxation from the pressure of war. This article discusses how the VFL responded to a number of key issues during the critical period between 1942 and 1944.

Introduction

The Victorian Football League (VFL) was Victoria's, and Australia's, strongest Australian football organisation.[1] As most histories of the code explain, the League was a not-for-profit umbrella administrator of a Melbourne-based metropolitan club competition, which also included one regional centre, Geelong. The VFL was formed in Melbourne in 1896 as a breakaway from the Victorian Football Association (VFA), which had commenced operations in 1877. An ambitious League immediately assumed the mantle of having most influence over the management and development of the code and the Association maintained a hostile approach towards it throughout most of the twentieth century. The VFL's control of the code tightened when the VFA was forced into recess during both world wars.[2]

Although much has been written about League players who served in the armed forces during the two world wars,[3] less attention has been given to identifying the issues and challenges that football competitions, and the VFL in particular, had to address if they were to continue to function during times of military conflict. Trials faced by the organisers of the code were logistical, political and moral, and player and administrator shortages and a restricted number of venues to play at were the most obvious challenges. As explained below, the Australian government assumed control of manpower and resources in January 1942 and placed many restrictions on discretional activities of the population. In this context, a general feeling was that there was little room for organised major sporting competitions because they could detract from the war focus. The way society reacted to the constraints shaped football's direction, and the VFL had to interpret government policy and read the mood of the public before deciding whether to continue playing. In the end, the League, despite criticism from some quarters for continuing its competition, sided with the prevailing view that the public needed a diversion to allow them some relaxation from the pressure of war. The bulk of this article identifies and analyses how the VFL responded to a number of key issues during the critical period between 1942 and 1944, although the matters discussed are relevant to other major sporting competitions in Australia during the period of World War II (1939–1945).

Financial and Player Shortages

VFL clubs were semi-professional community-based organisations owned by several thousand individual membership holders. From 1925 until 1986, the VFL comprised 12 clubs, 11 of them located in the Melbourne metropolitan area, and another, Geelong, located 75 km away in Victoria's second largest city. The competition was self-contained and there was no promotion or relegation.

There was little money in football in the aftermath of the depression and during the war years. Funds began to flow after the war. The VFL's annual turnover from 1939 to 1945 ranged between around $10,800 (£5400) in 1940 and $7400 (£3700) in 1944. After 1945, the turnover rose steadily to around $21,400 (£10,700) in 1948.[4]

The VFL derived its income primarily from levies on its clubs and licence fees for the *Football Record*, a compact octavo-size publication sold at each ground and containing key information such as player jumper numbers and current general and individual club stories. Its main expenditures were salaries, rent, Australian National Football Council levies, grants to schools, exhibition matches, materials (including footballs) and affiliated minor leagues charges. Much of the administration was carried out by volunteers.

Individual clubs were funded almost entirely by match-day entry charges and sale of memberships. These sources dried up during the war as many family incomes declined and discretional time was limited, for instance by the absence of those on military service and extended work shifts in war industries. Although entry to football matches was relatively cheap, the public was constantly exhorted by government to divert any non-essential spending money to war loans, war savings bonds and war-related charities.

Attendances, which averaged around 15,000 per match in 1939, fell to around 8000 per match in 1942, before making a gradual recovery. All VFL clubs lost money in 1942, and any surpluses were directed to patriotic funds.[5]

Clubs were affected unevenly with regard to availability of players, both week-to-week and year-to-year. Those with many players in protected industries, such as munitions or essential services, occupations deemed essential to the war effort, and military service that allowed leave to play, were able to select teams from a wider range of regular players.

There is a strong correlation between the success of a team and the number of players used. Teams that fielded fewer players had more success because they were able to achieve more continuity through fewer changes to the team. Likewise, teams that fielded a smaller number of players who played just a few matches had more success.

Carlton, Essendon and Richmond were more fortunate in this respect. Between 1939 and 1946, those clubs fielded around 100 players. At the other end of the spectrum, North Melbourne, St Kilda and South Melbourne fielded around 150 players. During the main war years in Australia (1942–1944), Essendon, Carlton and Footscray used around 60 players or fewer. On the other hand, North Melbourne, St Kilda and Melbourne used in excess of 80 players.[6] A further indication of imbalance can be seen by comparing the average age of players between the stronger and weaker teams of the war period. The average age of players for Richmond, who finished second in 1942, was more than 26 years. The average age of players for Collingwood, who finished second-last, was under 23 years.

Community Attitudes and Government Policies

In 1939, Prime Minister Robert Menzies announced to the nation that 'as a result [of Great Britain declaring war on Germany], Australia is at war'. He stated that:

> Sportsmen can best help by completing their football programmes. A healthy, well-occupied mind is the best instrument I know with which to avoid panic. Sport plays a big part in providing this healthy outlook, so to you sportsmen I say 'Carry on'.[7]

Menzies was well attuned to the importance of playing and watching sport to the Australian community. He took an interest in a number of sports. His family home was in Melbourne, and he was an ardent supporter of the Carlton Football Club in the VFL competition.

The government's position regarding sport in Australia was reaffirmed by Menzies in early June 1940:

> We all need exercise and recreation at a time of testing like this ... I am a busy man, few are busier, but if at any time during the season I have the opportunity to see a football match I will go, and thoroughly enjoy it for the excellent recreation it provides. I would feel that I had thoroughly deserved the recreation that football gave me ....
>
> If we went the full limit and closed up all sport, as a few would have us do, what good purpose would it serve? Indeed, I fear it might serve a very bad purpose. This I would very much like to see – sport tied up with national effort in the way of increasing patriotic and war funds ... If some part of the salaries could be earmarked for war bonds, I would be happy.[8]

These words were embraced by the VFL, which sensed that it was being singled out for criticism, rather than other sports and recreations such as theatre and cinema, pubs and motoring.

Some sports, particularly cricket where the Board of Control had been willing to mothball its senior competition, the Sheffield Shield, as early as a few days after war was declared in September 1939, were keener than Australian Commonwealth and State governments to impose limitations on sport. Cricket authorities were mainly conservative in nature, felt a strong tie to the British Commonwealth and had a strong amateur ethos. However, the Australian government urged the Board of Control to proceed with its full schedule of interstate cricket matches in 1939–1940 to maintain public morale.[9]

Although Australia's involvement in the war was relatively limited in 1940, some sections of the community also believed that professional and top-level sport should be stopped until the war ended because it would divert resources and focus attention away from what was most important – winning the war. This view was not expressed uniformly by any one class, community, business, socio-economic or religious group. Some elements of the Christian community, the Establishment and British Empire proponents were vocal. They argued with indignation, righteous or otherwise, that people should be condemned if they still wanted to spend time on sport when the only real activity should be total attention on the war effort. Their message was heard, but in the cities their view did not resonate as widely through the community as it had during World War I. In country towns and rural areas, there was more support for the cessation view.

The counter argument, that sport should be encouraged as a way of involving youth, and even to prepare young men for what might be ahead of them in battle, as a distraction for those who were working long and hard, and for those who were unable to enlist – the elderly and unfit for service – emanated from other advocates of the same broad community and social groups as those calling for sport to be banned.

The two opposing views tended to neutralise each other. Until December 1941, the majority of those who had a definite opinion on the issue thought that the country was not at the point where any limitations on recreational activities could be applied for philosophical reasons. After the Japanese entered the war, the 'no sport' view gained traction when there was a new crisis, but fairly rapidly the situation would return to the prevailing uneasy balance between the two schools of thought. Most people were ambivalent about the issue.

Measured by letters to newspapers, philosophical arguments tended to predominate in the early war period. After Japan entered the war, logistical, manpower, moral and behavioural arguments tended to predominate. It is also worth noting the fact that the United Australia Party government led by Robert Menzies fell in October 1941 and the new Labor Government, led by John Curtin, came to power. Its view on sport was the same as its predecessor.

Impact of Japan Entering the War

Australians realised that the fight had come close to home at the end of November 1941 when news of the loss of the *HMAS Sydney*, with the loss of its full complement of 645 crew, at the hands of of German auxiliary cruiser *Kormoran*, a merchant raider, was made public. On December 8, Japan made a surprise simultaneous attack on Pearl Harbor, Hawaii, and a number of British possessions in the Pacific and landed at Kota Baru, Malaya. On December 9, Australia joined the USA in declaring war on Japan.

On December 10, the *HMS Prince of Wales* and *HMS Repulse* were sunk, realistically ending any hope that Britain would be able to help protect Australia. During December, the Japanese continued to make rapid progress, overrunning much of Southern and Southeast Asia. Portents for Australia became most alarming when Japan bombed Rabaul on January 4, 1941. New Guinea was an Australian protectorate at the time, so this was virtually a violation of Australia's sovereignty. The Australian government hurriedly deployed troops, both AIF and militia to New Guinea. By January 23, Rabaul was in Japanese hands.

Meanwhile, the Japanese had progressed to the Straits of Johore and threatened to take Singapore. At the time Rabaul was lost, advice from Singapore was suggesting that the situation there was desperate. The Japanese crossed the Singapore causeway on February 8, and on February 15, Singapore surrendered. Australia's first line of defence was now New Guinea where Port Moresby was bombed for the first time on February 3.

The war reached the Australian mainland when Darwin was bombed on February 19. On February 28, Brrome was bombed. Air raids on settlements across the northern Australian coastline continued over the next several months. On March 8, the Japanese landed at Lae and nearby Salamaua. Fear of invasion of Australia reached its peak. So far, there had been no sign of Japanese advances being slowed, let alone stopped.

The arrival on March 17 of US General Douglas MacArthur in Darwin after Japan had taken the Philippines lifted the spirits of the Australian people and most noticeably the Australian government. MacArthur established his headquarters in Melbourne on March 22. Americans had been arriving in Australia since December 1941 and, although the threat of invasion remained, the feeling of being alone was subsiding.

On March 26, a United (Australian and American) Command in the Pacific was established, and just over three weeks later, on April 20, MacArthur was officially placed in command of Southeast Pacific operations, which meant, in effect, that he was in charge of Australia's military effort in the Pacific region. Against this background, it is surprising that staging a senior football competition could be contemplated.

Australia's Domestic War Employment Planning

In response to the Japanese threat, the Commonwealth government established a Manpower Directorate on January 29, 1942, headed by Director-General, John Dedman, who was given extraordinary powers. His Directorate took over the responsibility for the *List of Reserved Occupations*. On February 16, Curtin announced that 'It is now work or fight as we have never worked or fought before'.[10] During the crisis of the Japanese advance in the Pacific in the early months of the year, more than 100,000 men were called up for full-time military service.

In March 1942, the *List of Reserved Occupations* was replaced by a *Schedule of Reserved Occupations and Industrial Priorities*. From April 1, 1942, all engagement of male labour was controlled and a national registration of both male and female labour was completed. The government had the power to say what every man should do whether in the armed services, war industry or civilian industry.[11]

Prime Minister Curtin, in a broadcast to the USA in mid-March, said that four of every 10 Australian men were either in the fighting services or making munitions and that would be increased to five or even six before the Australian government would be satisfied with its war effort. The priority had changed – it was not a matter of what manpower could be spared from the economic structure to build the armed forces, but what manpower and womanpower could be spared from the armed forces and from war industries to maintain the absolute minimum of non-war effort.[12] Curtin's message was received positively in Australia.

Football: To Play or Not to Play

After Japan dramatically entered the war on December 7–8, 1941, the VFL still kept its options open about continuing its competition, intimating in the press that it would continue unless the government (Australian or State) decreed otherwise. It was therefore the intention of the League to continue to be guided by the Australian government's policy to 'carry on'.[13]

The matter of whether the VFL could proceed with its fixtures was actually a matter for the Victorian Premier, Albert Dunstan, who had full power under existing regulations to make and enforce a decision. Initially, he urged the abandonment of professional wartime sport. 'We still find huge crowds attending sporting functions and theatres and the professional sportsmen taking part are still being paid huge sums', he said. However, he went on to say that he realised recreation and amusement were necessary for well-being, but that they should not be carried out to excess during wartime.[14]

By late January 1942, he had softened his stance further. When providing advice for a VFL meeting, he said that on the Saturday half-holiday, as it was called, individuals were entitled to decide how they would seek diversion from mental and physical strain. He threw the ball to the Australian government saying that unless it withdrew the half-holiday he would make no change to existing arrangements.[15] The VFL saw that it had a responsibility to provide its share of sport entertainment on the accepted half-holiday.

At that time, the Australian government was non-committal about the playing of senior level sport, provided that it did not conflict with the need for able-bodied men to put all their effort into either serving with the forces or participating in the workforce to provide essential services.

The policy affecting football was part of a broader policy spanning cultural and recreational pursuits, such as cinema, sports and carnivals. Senior football was not earmarked for any particular attention or future action. However, one important aspect of the policy was that these events should not draw significant crowds. Large gatherings of people were considered a public safety and security risk in the event of hostile enemy action.

There was still little evidence of cohesive, sustained public opposition to sport being played. Opinion about whether major sport should continue during wartime was divided, but to nowhere near the extent that it was during World War I. Some sections of the community believed that professional and top-level sport should be mothballed until the war ceased because it would divert resources and focus attention away from what was most important – winning the war. This view was not expressed uniformly by any one class, community, business, socio-economic or religious group. Some elements of the Christian community, the Establishment and British Empire proponents were vocal. They argued that people should be condemned if they still wanted to spend time on sport when the only real activity should be total attention on the war effort. Their message was heard, but in the cities their view did not resonate as widely through the community as it had during World War I. In country towns and rural areas, there was more support for the mothballing view. The counter argument, that sport should be encouraged as a way of involving youth, and even to prepare young men for what might be ahead of them in battle, as a distraction for those who were working long and hard, and for those who were unable to enlist- the elderly and unfit for service emanated from other advocates of the same broad community and social groups as those calling for sport to be banned.

As was so evident in World War I, the Australian population consisted of a sizeable minority of Irish origins, almost uniformly of Roman Catholic faith. Few with Irish heritage felt much compassion for Britain, as the events culminating in Irish independence in 1922 were still fresh in the minds of many, including those who were born in Australia. This divide, which had been a major driver for the near cessation of the VFL competition in World War I, was fuelled by the prominent presence of Catholic Archbishop of Melbourne, Irish zealot, Dr Daniel Mannix.[16] The division still existed, but was nowhere near as marked as it was 20 years earlier. There were the beginnings of a breakdown in the traditional protestant faiths. Australia was still a church-going nation, but around the edges the practices were nowhere near as rigid.

Most critics of major sport continuing in World War II spoke from a personal viewpoint. Newspaper letter writers did not claim attachment to church, political or special interest groups. Most seemed to be from the generation who fought in World War I and wanted the same attitudes as then to prevail 20 years later. Younger people did not feel the need to express their views in this way.

Much of the critical comment on sport more broadly related to sports with a heavy gaming emphasis. Racing, both horse and dog, where gambling was allowed, received about as much column space in newspapers as all other sports combined. Radio programme guides also show that racing received far more coverage than any other sport. Gambling was not permitted on any of the football codes or on cricket.

What anti-racing letter-writers did not like was the waste of time spent studying form guides and punting, the waste of money on bets that should go into war-related areas, the heavy beer-drinking culture, the feeling that punters did not care much about the war so long as they could punt, the belief that punters lacked the intellectual rigour to contribute to war activities without a big shove from government and the lack of physical activity associated with the 'sport'.

The VFL's real concern was whether it could provide a viable competition. It decided in February 1942 to defer a decision about proceeding with a full-scale competition, to give time for clubs to find out how many senior players were in essential services and would be available to form the core of each team. There was concern about how many juniors (under-18s) would be needed, whether their elevation to senior level would compromise the standard of play and affect the crowd-drawing capacity. The broad view was that some sort of competition should go ahead.

At the same time, the VFL sought the opinion of Commonwealth and State authorities. Prime Minister Curtin threw the ball back to the State premiers, claiming that permission for sporting fixtures was entirely a matter for the States.

South Australian Premier, Thomas Playford, made his government's views clear. He banned all racing in his State and allowed football to continue. His reasoning was that football was a healthy recreation, provided it did not interfere with essential work.

The Victorian Premier's position was by now far more positive. He had no objection to the VFL continuing, as long as matches were scheduled on Saturday afternoons. He also promoted the view about healthy recreation being essential and that 'outdoor amusement had much to commend it'.[17]

The VFL, having obtained sufficient reassurances from government, pressed ahead with planning for the season. Constraints would now be purely logistical. VFL Secretary, Likely ('Like') McBrien, confirmed that if a normal senior competition could not proceed, then a competition for those ineligible for war service would. He added that a number of players worked in essential services such as munitions, police and fire brigade, and in most cases worked long hours and looked forward to football for relaxation. It was also a cheap relaxation for supporters, most of whom were similarly occupied in long hours of work.

'The Ordinary Way of Life Has Gone': Prime Minister Curtin and Sport

Prime Minister Curtin announced the £35 million ($70 million) Liberty Loan in mid-February 1942. He stated that 'the ordinary way of life has gone', and added that all money, buildings and plants were now eligible to be directed to the purposes of war. His key point was that it was more important for the government to have the money than for it to remain in private hands. He said it was a threat to everyone to spend money in competition with the government, and emphasised that whatever manpower it was possible to harness from civil needs would be redirected towards strengthening war production.[18]

The Australian government continued to field questions about its stance on professional sport. In one press report, the government expressed the view that while there was no objection to amateurs playing football, it was thought that there would be a great waste of man hours in intense training of men on working days to ensure their fitness for a two-hour professional game on Saturdays.[19]

In mid-March, the government finally made clear its position on sport in wartime. The prime minister urged that organised football matches cease 'on the customary scale'. He emphasised that war had the first priority and that recreation should be for the purpose of promoting fitness for work. He said he hoped that football bodies would manage the game by giving their attention to lads too young to fight to share the production burden.

Crucially, the prime minister said that he was not asking that football should cease. He had no objection to men in the forces or those engaged in essential work who could obtain leave playing football, but they were not to spend time during the week training. Curtin added that an important safety measure for the population in time of air attack was dispersal. He did not want any great attendances, and that applied to theatres (cinema), race meetings and all entertainments.[20]

It is possible that US President Roosevelt's opinion on continuation of major sport in his country may have informed Curtin's thinking on the subject of football's continuation in Australia. Curtin would have been aware that on January 15, 1942, the US President wrote his 'Green Light Letter' to the Commissioner of Baseball, K.M. Landis, supporting the continuation of the playing of major baseball in America during the war. Landis had sought the President's direction on the matter, and Roosevelt's personal view was that it would be best for the country to keep baseball going to provide the hard-working population with a chance for recreation and take their minds off their work for a short time. He stated that 'Baseball provides a recreation which does not last over two hours and a half, and which can be got for very little cost'. At the time, baseball was America's only genuine national, professional sporting code.[21]

The Australian government's policy was seen as too ambivalent in a number of quarters. It certainly did not satisfy some, such as this letter-writer:

> We have listened to and read many claims made by our Government to swift and resolute action, and that Australia is on a complete war footing; but while race meetings, etc., are permitted, these assertions are all talk. Darwin has no sporting pleasures, and it is high time city and country fell into line. No Australian will mind being deprived of sport if the sacrifice is going to help his pals to carry on.[22]

But this was a fairly isolated and uninformed voice on the subject. Darwin did have sport at weekends played by troops and sporting events were well attended by military personnel and the few remaining locals.

Commenting on the prime minister's statement, McBrien claimed that the VFL would adapt to meet the government's wishes. It would schedule Saturday games 'unless the Government considered such weekly relaxation undesirable'.[23] Clubs would not be allowed to seek special leave for players in the forces for either matches or for training. Teams would cover vacancies with boys under military age.

The VFL suggested that consideration be given to a proposal that football be continued for a War Pennant with proceeds going to patriotic funds and a War Services Cup for competition between the members of the Defence Forces. The VFL's proposal, appropriate as it was, also contained a sweetener to help ensure that its competition could proceed.

Newspaper reports in late March suggested that play in 1942 was still not a certainty. The matter was again referred back to individual clubs for feedback. At the start of April, eight clubs said that they favoured playing and their management committees were unanimous in their support in nearly all cases. Melbourne, Collingwood and Hawthorn clubs voted against, but were prepared to participate if the majority of clubs decided to do so. Although philosophical reasons influenced these three clubs to varying degrees, the main issue was loss of players due to enlistments and call-ups. Geelong, which had been forced to withdraw due to transport restrictions, was also against continuation. Other clubs would have been reluctant to withdraw while their opponents continued to play. They would have been conscious of the difficulties faced trying to restart when normal competition resumed, presuming the war was won. The press was still uncertain about what lay ahead for the season, as this report indicates:

> If senior football is not played, VFL will concentrate on a competition for boys under 18 years, and will probably take over the management of the war services competition. It is expected that 8 camps in Victoria will provide teams, and, as most of the League [VFL] players are in one or another of them, a fairly high standard of play should be seen. Military authorities are anxious for such games to be played.[24]

Nevertheless, the VFL confirmed that its season would still start as scheduled on the second Saturday of May.

In the meantime, the VFA decided not to play in 1942, because around half of its 12 teams were unable to secure venues, could not field competitive teams and were unable to form management committees and recruit support staff to maintain their teams.

At the same time, some VFL clubs were also not well placed to proceed, although most of them were ready to give the season their best endeavours. The philosophical and logistical situations for some of the individual clubs further illustrate the difficult issues they faced.

Melbourne and Hawthorn were philosophically opposed to the season proceeding. Their committees and supporter bases were more professional and business-centred than most other clubs, and for Melbourne its parent body, the Melbourne Cricket Club, was one of the bastions of the Victorian establishment. Melbourne's view was also influenced by the fact that so many of their players from the premiership years of 1939–1941 had enlisted or were in essential production and would not be available consistently. The club had concerns about the impending decline of the team's performance on the field.

Collingwood and Hawthorn were also reluctant to continue from a logistical perspective. The clubs' player losses were substantial, although no more so than several other clubs, and they did not favour a competition taking place on such an uneven footing. They withdrew their second 18 teams from competition for 1942.

Collingwood and Melbourne contemplated a temporary merger in February–March 1942 for the duration of the war. The likelihood of a merger was fairly remote, but it shows how deeply both viewed concerns about where they, and the VFL, were headed.

All other clubs, except Geelong, which had already withdrawn from competition, favoured continuing, with negligible reservation, at least not stated in the public domain, despite some clubs suffering a heavy drain of player strength and talent.

Football Venues as Troop Accommodation

The nature and quality of infrastructure at major football grounds, such as spacious dressing rooms suitable for officers' dormitory accommodation, club rooms for office space and grandstand seating suitable as dormitories for ordinary troops, were major considerations. Access to adequate cooking, ablutions and toilet facilities were important;

in many cases, renovations were carried out to provide these facilities. Common to all the sports grounds, the arenas provided parade ground space.

Geelong's Corio Oval was the first VFL venue to be taken over by the military authorities in January 1941. Australia's 22nd Artillery Regiment was the initial occupier, and soon afterward the 2nd Cavalry Division.[25] This acquisition most likely had the blessing of local government. The Regiment had been domiciled in the South Barwon Shire from the late 1930s before going to Corio Oval. The Shire President, A.R. 'Jack' Jennings, later to become Geelong Football Club President, made a significant gesture by formally thanking the troops for their high standard of their behaviour while they were stationed in his shire. He most likely helped facilitate their transfer.[26]

Corio Oval was never again used for VFL football. Geelong had to source an alternative venue, Kardinia Park, which provided better access for fans and was more attractive for drawing business support. But the main acquisitions of VFL venues were more than a year away.

In Melbourne, the military sought venues with good access to the port and easy road access. A major factor in the soon to be acquired St Kilda Junction and South Melbourne grounds was proximity to nearby military offices and facilities on or close to St Kilda Road, the main arterial road south of the CBD.

With Japan advancing in the Pacific at an alarming rate in early 1942, the Australian Government and military had to make swift decisions about how to resource the war. There were few ready-made facilities from which to operate. Military authorities, mainly through the Department of Hirings (Hirings Directorate), expanded their operations by acquiring a range of public facilities and private business premises that were quarantined for use by the forces.

The Government, on the advice of military leaders, had to make many decisions on the run and these included what facilities should be acquired and where. Some decisions were arbitrary and involved selecting football playing venues. Understandably, military managers focused on immediate logistical needs, with little regard in most cases for community expectations or needs. They did not necessarily consider the ramifications of taking over Melbourne's major football grounds.

One of the earliest acquisitions of a Melbourne suburban football ground by the military was when the North Port Oval, home ground of the Port Melbourne Football Club (VFA), was taken over by the Army in February 1942. Significant alterations were carried out to make it suitable for occupation by troops.[27]

From mid-February, newspapers reported on a daily basis about a chaotic expansion of military takeovers of venues. From a VFL football season planning perspective, the way the occupation process evolved made it impossible to develop a weekly roster, let alone a season schedule.

In a statement which showed that military authorities did recognise that football was a major part of Melbourne's fabric, the army expressed a keenness to hold a war services competition. To facilitate this, they expected grounds to be provided. McBrien stated that:

> ... the League [VFL] would have to do so even if it meant putting on the matches as curtain-raisers. War service teams would have prior calls over players. They had suggested that Melbourne, Carlton, St Kilda, and Footscray grounds might be made available for three Army teams, one RAAF [airforce], one Navy, one essential services, and one reserved occupations and munition workers' team ... US forces would also have to be considered. They were already enjoying their national games with specially made footballs and baseball material provided by the League.[28]

The language used by the military made fans apprehensive about the VFL's capacity to proceed with its season's fixtures.

A most significant development came on April 6 when it was learned that the Melbourne Cricket Ground (MCG), Victoria's main football venue, would not be available for sport. Five days earlier, the Melbourne Football Club had advised the VFL that the MCG had been acquired by the military.[29]

The Melbourne Cricket Ground as Camp Murphy

The entire MCG facility was occupied by the US Army Forces, and was named Camp Murphy, in memory of Col William Murphy, a senior USAAF officer who died when the B18 aircraft he was on was downed over Java on February 3, 1942.

The venue was used initially by its Fifth Air Force and 11th Replacement Control Depot. The latter unit departed in late 1942. Troops were accommodated in the grandstands and tents that were pitched on the arena. Bay 18 in the Southern Stand became a picture theatre, the members' tearoom became a 'PX' (convenience store) and a floor was built for accommodation over the road in the Southern Stand which became known as 'Pneumonia Alley'. It was expected that the MCG would accommodate up to 14,000 troops at any one time.[30]

In early 1943, the USA began using the ground as a major recuperation centre for the First Regiment of the First Division of the US Marine Corps, the elite regiment which retook Guadalcanal and later Okinawa. The numbers of US troops steadily reduced during 1943 and by November they had moved out.

With the loss of the MCG to sport in 1942, apprehension about whether VFL football would be played turned into an expectation that it would not. Adding to the gloom, the military had also taken over the VFL's headquarters whose offices were occupied by the Army Inventions Directorate until 1946, while the VFL administration relocated to space elsewhere.

Only after representations from the VFL and some parliamentarians did the military decision-makers give the VFL reasonable certainty about venues. That allowed the VFL to proceed with its playing roster without having to continually look for what fresh obstacles were put in its way. The first inkling of a breakthrough came on April 16 when

> a desire was expressed in political circles that the game should be continued, from a public morale point of view and to provide relaxation for those people busy on war work. It was even said that a direction had been issued that sufficient grounds should be made available.[31]

Although prospects for the competition continuing looked secure, the venue situation was far from settled. But the outlook was more encouraging after the public learned that 'leading members of the Cabinet and leading officers in the Army have expressed a keen desire that football should continue and that sufficient grounds would be made available'.[32] There was talk that the VFL would be able to use both the St Kilda and South Melbourne grounds.

McBrien warned that 'much could happen before the opening day on May 9'. He added that 'strenuous efforts were being made by responsible authorities to provide relaxation and amusement for troops on Sunday nights, but unless grounds were available the same position might have to be faced on Saturday afternoons'.[33]

Confident that it could proceed, the VFL released its fixture for the first round of matches, noting that five grounds were available. The first round was to be played at the South Melbourne, Hawthorn, Fltzroy, Essendon and Richmond grounds. It noted that 'because of war conditions and the fact that it is not known what demands may be made on grounds available at present, the committee [responsible for fixtures] decided to announce each round weekly'.[34] A few days later, it became clear that the South Melbourne ground would be off limits for football. The VFL adjusted its schedule for the opening round to use Carlton's home ground for South's home match because Carlton had a bye in the opening round.

At the same time, the Department of Information directed newspapers and radio to say nothing further about infrastructure that had been acquired by the military. The directive stated that 'in future, references will not be made in the press or radio to buildings, racecourses, football grounds and other places appropriated for the use of the Armed Forces; their location, function or military establishment'. The direction was repeated the following week: 'In future if the military authorities take over additional football grounds or racecourses, mention will not be made in the Press or over the Radio'.[35]

Venue issues were next aired on the Monday before the season was due to start. Collingwood looked likely to regain use of its ground, but Footscray looked certain to lose the use of its ground.[36] No decision had been made by the military about its intentions for the Western Oval, and Footscray Council was pressing for a decision. Every effort was made to enable the football club to continue playing there. The training quarters were still available although the Footscray Harriers had volunteered their rooms to the military.[37]

Despite assurances that it would have access to sufficient venues, the VFL season began with uncertainty about which grounds would be available the following week, or whether the season would be able to proceed if war demands meant more grounds needed to be taken over. The public remained unsure about whether one of the few remaining diversions that made life bearable during wartime would continue.

Where cricket clubs controlled venues, particularly when backed by local councils, the prospect of military occupation was more likely. In general, cricket managers were more supportive of closing down activity that might distract people from giving a 100% focus to the war effort, and so were more likely to oppose playing professional sport during wartime.

The contrast between cricket club/local government management and football club management with regard to occupation of grounds on which football was played is seen in the way that Collingwood Football Social Club (in effect, the Football Club), as ground manager of Victoria Park, was able to regain use of its playing arena. The Social Club had been granted a liquor licence in April 1941. There appears to have been a win-win arrangement such that the military personnel could access the social club bar, and in return Collingwood was allowed to play at its home venue in 1942. The club was not paying rent for the ground, and its receipts were topped up by the drinkers. The arrangement helped Collingwood's finances markedly at a time when the club had sold fewer than 1000 memberships. Before the war, the club's membership was around 5000.

When the VFL's 1942 season started, the venues were unavailable for four clubs, namely Footscray, Melbourne, South Melbourne and St Kilda. Venues for each week's matches through the first 11 weeks of the season had to be advised to the military authorities early in the preceding week. By the end of May, the VFL was required to list its venue requirements 10 days in advance.

During the first 11 rounds, each team played each other once and had one bye. The remaining five rounds featured the same matches as in the first five rounds. This resulted in six teams playing 15 matches and five playing 14 matches. Teams were awarded four premiership points, equivalent to a win, for each bye. Teams that played 14 matches were favoured by the draw, gaining an extra four premiership points.

Halting the Japanese

Although it was not publicly known at the time, by April 1942 the USA had broken the Japanese codes enabling them to track Japanese naval and troop movements. This gave the USA an advantage helping turn the tide of the war in the Pacific with crucial victories in two major sea battles.

The Japanese sought to take Port Moresby in early May, sending a naval force including three aircraft carriers. The aim was to isolate Australia from the USA by controlling all the shipping lanes. As an air base, Port Moresby would mean continued widespread bombing of all the Australian northern and north-eastern areas. The force was intercepted by the USA on May 7, and the ensuing battle resulted in both sides suffering a similar rate of casualties. But the outcome meant that the Japanese invasion force was depleted and it had to return to Rabaul.

On June 2, the main Japanese naval fleet was heading for Midway Island to confront the USA in a virtual 'now or never' effort to break the US naval resistance, but the USA was prepared for it. The Japanese lost four aircraft carriers, while the USA lost one. The battle stopped the Japanese momentum. Japan no longer had enough air cover to protect all of its surface forces in the war theatre. The Japanese no longer had the resources to sustain any further invasion plans. However, the Japanese were not yet beaten. They continued to make inroads in New Guinea. And they maintained their aerial bombardment of Darwin and other northern Australian coastal towns.

Australia was further alarmed when three Japanese mini-submarines attempted to enter Sydney Harbour on May 31. Two were snared by protective nets and the pilots destroyed their crafts, but one did get through and attempted to torpedo a US ship but instead the weapon hit *HMAS Kuttabul*, an ex-Sydney Harbour ferry being deployed as a dormitory for Australian troops, with the loss of 21 lives. The mini-submarine pilot scuttled his craft after the attack. Furthermore, the Japanese shelled coastal suburbs of Sydney and Newcastle on June 7 in an isolated attack.

However, by July 1942, MacArthur had moved his headquarters from Melbourne northward to Brisbane, a sure sign that the war was starting to go in favour of America and Australia. The Australian public began to pick up the sense that the crisis had passed. Nevertheless, it was another 12 months before the Australian government announced that the threat of invasion was over.[38]

Melbourne Compared to Other Major Cities

The MCG and Brisbane's Woolloongabba Cricket Ground (Gabba) were not available for football from 1942, although the former facility was used again for football late in the 1946 season, and the Gabba was used for rugby in 1947. Both the Sydney Cricket Ground (SCG) (rugby and cricket) and Adelaide Oval (Australian football and cricket) were available for sport throughout the war. Some SCG and Adelaide Oval off-arena facilities were used by the military.

A major reason for the loss of Melbourne venues in 1942 was that the city was considered the least likely of all the major cities in Australia to be attacked and thus had the highest concentration of Australian and US troops in most of 1942. The US and Australian military located their key management centres in Melbourne, and MacArthur based himself there from February to July 1942, after which he relocated his headquarters to Brisbane. The move contributed to the Gabba being unavailable.

The Gabba was converted into an Army trade training centre for recruits who would serve in clerical or administrative positions in the Army. They were accommodated in tents around the perimeter of the playing field. Rugby league was moved to New Farm Park. Despite the Army occupation, the wicket block and outfield were maintained in good condition. Soldiers were only allowed on the oval in bare feet. School sport continued to be played there. Eventually, after urging from local parliamentarians, senior civilian sport was allowed back on the Gabba in 1945.[39]

Many military officers, influenced by the British tradition of playing the public school sport of rugby union, did not rate Australian football as being particularly important. There is evidence to suggest that Melbourne and Australian football were treated differently to other codes. In the 1950s when national service was still in operation, there were military establishments, even in Victoria, led by officers who banned the playing of Australian football, instead encouraging rugby union and rugby league.[40]

Attendances at big sporting events at the MCG were often very large. The 1938 Australian football grand final attracted 96,486 people. Finals attendances often drew crowds in excess of 60,000. Cricket also attracted large crowds. In 1936–1937, The Ashes Test series, the premier cricket contest between Australia and England, drew a substantial number of spectators. The Australian and State governments were mindful of the potential for large gatherings at the MCG, and the policy of minimising large numbers in one place at one time. That view may have helped make it easier to justify placing the MCG in the hands of the military in 1942, but it would not have been a major reason.

Without the MCG, Melbourne lacked a central venue able to hold a large crowd. In 1942–1944, only three matches drew more than 40,000 spectators; all were grand finals. However, massed crowds did congregate elsewhere in Australia during wartime, despite government policies. Attendances at horse racing meetings remained high. Rugby League attendances in Sydney were high, particularly in 1943 when the grand final drew 60,922, and two other finals attracted more than 40,000. Melbourne's largest football attendance in 1943 was 42,100 to the grand final.

Issues Related to the Continued Occupation of Senior Football Venues

In summary, venues for four VFL clubs became unavailable for senior football. Each had been taken over without the public being aware beforehand. Each was a community facility and now access was prohibited. There was no indication of how long they would be occupied by the military. Concerns soon arose as to their condition after the occupation ceased.

The specific reasons for military occupation varied. Footscray Football Ground was occupied by the US Forces' Chemical Warfare Service to accommodate troops.[41] It was released by the military in May 1943. After the US Marines left the MCG, it was fully occupied by the Royal Australian Air Force (RAAF) and was used mainly as a training and embarkation centre. It was released in October 1945. South Melbourne Football Ground was occupied by the US Army for accommodation of stevedores. It was released in December 1945. St Kilda Football Ground was occupied by Australia's Southern Command engineers responsible for stevedoring. It was released in early 1944.

The common factor was accommodation of troops. In that regard the relative ease with which troops could relocate without extensive renovations, repairs and improvements to existing infrastructure was important. Availability of good meal preparation areas, ablutions and toilet facilities were a necessity.[42] The public was generally unaware of these criteria, and it led to tensions between communities when one may have suffered loss of community halls and meeting places as well as sports venues, while another may have suffered minimal losses.

Politicians at local and regional levels were urged to lobby for the return of venues. It is hard to gauge the levels of success of lobbying, but it is clear enough that the representations of the Footscray Football Club, Footscray City Council and the local Australian government member of parliament, Drakeford, led to the early release of the Footscray ground. Arguments put by the VFL helped to secure the release of the St Kilda ground, but the changing nature of the war meant that there was a reduced need for the venue by the end of 1943.[43]

The Melbourne Cricket Club seemed fairly acquiescent to the RAAF continuing to occupy the MCG despite the urging of Melbourne's Lord Mayor from mid-1944.[44] Some prompting by the media may have been influential from 1945 but it may have been that the RAAF was able to vacate more or less on its terms after the end of hostilities. The MCG and the South Melbourne ground needed major structural remedial work to ready them for spectator access.

Relaxation of Policy

The Australian government's policy was designed to shift the focus of senior football competition from self-absorption to one of helping keep the population healthy. Curtin showed his hand in May 1942. He actively followed Australian football and comments he made about the code while attending the opening of the Canberra football season were reported in Melbourne. For example, Curtin claimed that 'Football is a fine means of relaxation. Those who are too old to play benefit from watching others playing as sportsmen'. He also remarked that 'football relieved the strain of wartime pressure', and expressed the hope that 'next season we will assemble as people of a victorious nation seeking to live in peace and in accordance with the traditions of sportsmanship'.[45]

Over the summer of 1942–1943, some still doubted whether VFL football would be played in 1943, but the VFL pressed on by developing its match programme 'in the hope that football can be played this year'.[46] At the start of 1943, Footscray and St Kilda were confident that their grounds would be returned. Footscray succeeded but St Kilda's hopes were dashed when the military confirmed that the venue was still needed. Richmond was happy to have Melbourne again as a tenant. South Melbourne, which had to apply to the Carlton Recreation Committee to play at Princes Park, was still waiting for an answer. Eventually, they were given permission to play at Princes Park. The tardy response was due to Carlton Football Club seeking rental fees well in excess of the previous year's rates.

The VFA again decided not to play. Its President, J.J. Liston, recommended to the Association's board of management that it would be wise to follow the example of the previous season and not resume activities on account of the drain of manpower.

By mid-1943, issues about whether or not to play had moved right away from moral and philosophical arguments. It was now all about logistics and the availability of players, officials, grounds and equipment. Governments had to ensure that scarce petrol and coal were available for industry, households and public transport to move people to and from work. The needs of fuel, food and other resources for troops to fight the war were paramount.

Conclusion

The evidence suggests that several key factors steered the directions taken by football authorities, particularly the VFL, during World War II. Logistical matters and careful liaison with the Australian government and military authorities were initially the main determinants as to whether play went ahead or not. The VFL's main consideration was to determine that its clubs had the resources to play.

The Victorian State government removed itself from the policy mix at an early stage. Australian government policy statements were important drivers of football's direction but they were not prescriptive. There was much scope for interpretation of government policies. As a result, there was considerable indecision on the part of all parties regarding making a call on whether football should continue, as they gauged public support.

International factors had some impact. The influence of military traditions, informed mainly by the British Army, at times was an impediment to the continuation of Australian football. US President Roosevelt's stance on baseball in America, embodied in his 'Green Light Letter', could have helped make up the mind of Australian Prime Minister John Curtin about the need to encourage the continuation of the VFL competition. In the end, it was social factors leading to public support, rather than government policy and other factors, which played a significant role in determining the response of the VFL to the challenges of World War II.

Notes

1. The VFL was renamed the Australian Football League (AFL) in 1990. The code was initially known as Victorian Rules football, and then Australian Rules football, but is commonly referred to today as Australian football.
2. General details of the history of the game, and the conflict between the VFA and the VFL, are covered in Sandercock and Turner, *Up Where, Cazaly?*; Pascoe, *The Winter Game*; and Hess et al., *A National Game*.
3. See, for example, Main and Allen, *Fallen*.
4. VFL Annual Reports.
5. AFL Tables website, http://stats.rleague.com/afl/afl_index.html, accessed December 13, 2013.
6. Ibid.
7. *Football Record*, Melbourne, September 9, 1939, 9.
8. Ibid., June 8, 1940, 8, quoting from the *Sporting Globe*, June 5, 1940.
9. Harte, *The Penguin History*, 382.
10. *Argus*, February 17, 1942, 3.
11. Penglase and Horner, *When the War Came*, 136.
12. *Argus*, March 16, 1942.
13. See *Age, Argus, Herald*, passim.
14. *Sun News Pictorial*, December 15, 1941.
15. VFL Minutes, January 30, 1942.
16. For discussion on the divisive conscription debate during World War I, see Blair, "'The Greater Game'."
17. *Argus*, February 12, 1942, 8.
18. Ibid., February 18, 1942, 3.
19. *Age*, March 9, 1942, 2.
20. *Argus*, March 18, 1942, 3.
21. http://www.baseball-almanac.com/prz_lfr.shtml, accessed December 13, 2013.
22. Letter written by F.V. Batten of Ballarat, *Argus*, March 28, 1942, 6.
23. *Argus*, March 19, 1942, 8.
24. Ibid., April 6, 1942, 6.

25. *Geelong Advertiser*, January 13, 1941, 5.
26. Contained in the Standing Orders file of the 2nd Cavalry Division is a note made by the Commanding Officer on April 11, 1940.
27. *Argus*, February 15, 1942, 8.
28. Ibid., April 2, 1942, 8.
29. VFL Minutes, April 1, 1942.
30. http://en.wikipedia.org/wiki/Melbourne_Cricket_Ground, accessed December 13, 2013; http://www.ozatwar.com/locations/campmurphy.htm, accessed December 13, 2013.
31. *Argus*, April 15, 1942, 8.
32. Ibid., April 17, 1942, 8.
33. Ibid.
34. Ibid., April 16, 1942, 6.
35. *Richmond, Hawthorn, Camberwell Chronicle*, April 24 and May 1, 1942.
36. *Argus*, May 4, 1942, 6.
37. For a detailed study of the impact of the war on the Footscray Football Club, see Camilleri, "*Cede Nullis.*"
38. For a more detailed overview of Japanese involvement in the Pacific War, see Dennis et al., *The Oxford Companion*, 288–92.
39. Smith, *A Superb Century*, passim.
40. For background information, see the entry on 'Rugby in the Armed Forces' in Dennis et al., *The Oxford Companion*, 473–4.
41. National Archives of Australia: Department of Air, MP742/1 Correspondence, 1943, 259/71/12, Footscray football ground – impressment reps by A.S. Drakeford.
42. Ibid.
43. *Herald*, January 21, 1944.
44. *Age*, July 5, 1944, 4.
45. Cited in the *Football Record*, Melbourne, May 23, 1942, 13.
46. *Argus*, February 1, 1943, 9.

References

Blair, D. J. "'The Greater Game': Australian Football and the Army at Home and on the Front During World War I." *Sporting Traditions* 11, no. 2 (1995): 91–102.

Camilleri, L. J. "*Cede Nullis*: The Impact of the Second World War on the Footscray Football Club." Honours diss., School of Sport and Exercise Science, Victoria University, 2012.

Dennis, Peter, Jeffrey Grey, Ewan Morris, Robin Prior, and Jean Bou. *The Oxford Companion to Australian Military History*. 2nd ed. South Melbourne: Oxford University Press, 2008.

Harte, Chris. *The Penguin History of Australian Cricket*. Camberwell: Penguin/Viking, 2003.

Hess, Rob, Matthew Nicholson, Bob Stewart, and Gregory de Moore. *A National Game: The History of Australian Rules Football*. Camberwell: Penguin/Viking, 2008.

Main, Jim, and David Allen. *Fallen – The Ultimate Heroes: Footballers Who Never Returned from War*. Melbourne: Crown Content, 2002.

Pascoe, Robert. *The Winter Game: The Complete History of Australian Football*. Melbourne: Text Publishing, 1995.

Penglase, Joanna, and David Horner. *When the War Came to Australia*. St Leonards: Allen & Unwin, 1992.

Sandercock, Leonie, and Ian Turner. *Up Where, Cazaly? The Great Australian Game*. London: Granada, 1981.

Smith, Wayne. *A Superb Century: 100 Years of the Gabba, 1895–1995*. Sydney: Focus Publishing, 1995.

W. N. 'Bill' Carson: Double All Black, Military Cross Recipient

Lynn Charles McConnell

College of Humanities and Social Sciences, Massey University, Auckland, New Zealand

Measuring the impact of sports experience as preparation for war, and especially leadership in war, is open to debate. Accordingly, this paper is intended to highlight the role that sport played in New Zealand's effort in the Second World War and the way in which sport prepared some of those who would have positions of command in the structure of the Second New Zealand Expeditionary Force. The paper explores the realisation of the Commander of the New Zealand Division in the war, General Bernard Freyberg, that he needed to reshape his command by utilising younger, more durable, officers to cope with the more mobile methodology of the German war machine, especially after the military disasters that occurred in Greece and Crete. By concentrating on a particular soldier, W. N. 'Bill' Carson, a double New Zealand cricket-rugby representative, it is intended to show that sport was capable of providing the sort of life experiences that could prepare him for command and the need to adapt under extreme pressure by utilising the exposure to both success and failure in sport to cope with what were for him unique demands of battle.

New Zealand's small population of 1.641 million at the outbreak of the Second World War inevitably meant that in the make-up of the Second New Zealand Expeditionary Force (2nd NZEF) would be a significant number of sportsmen. In many instances these were team sportsmen, rugby and rugby league, soccer and cricket players who made the adaption from civilian life when volunteering for the military relatively seamlessly. New Zealand had little in the way of a professional Army and initially many of those chosen to lead were veterans of the First World War. Sportsmen, who were used to working for one another in a team environment, were equally able to transfer that allegiance from sport to a military sphere. As it was for the Second World War, so it had been in South Africa in the Boer War and in the First World War. Two of the greatest sportsmen produced in early New Zealand, the captain of the 1905–1906 'Originals' to tour Britain, France and North America, Dave Gallaher, and the All-England singles, and Australasian Davis Cup winning star, Anthony Wilding, were two of the most prominent casualties in First World War battles. Wilding served with the British forces and died in France in May 1915, while Gallaher, a Boer War veteran, died at Passchendaele in October 1917. His memory is honoured with the Dave Gallaher Trophy contested by New Zealand and France in rugby internationals.[1]

In highlighting the link between sport and warfare, J. D. Campbell in his paper said that the link between military sport and the spread of English games was a product of imperialism with lessons for military and social historians.[2] But there are also lessons for sports historians. The point he made, 'Cricket is an ancient and revered game with origins deeply rooted in rural England, and so was a familiar and traditional game for the upper-class officer. Football, especially rugby football, demands a high degree of fitness and agility, as well as a large amount of physical courage and teamwork, all desirable qualities for a soldier',[3] is especially pertinent in the case of Carson, who had significant careers in both sports before the war. While he was not 'an upper-class officer' in the supposedly classless New Zealand society of the day, Carson was typical of many of his ilk when he began the war as a Second Lieutenant in an artillery unit, having already been identified as officer material. By the end of his war he had attained the rank of temporary Major. A more recent example of the link between sport and leadership in warfare was seen when British military head, General Sir David Richards, put World Cup winning rugby coach Sir Clive Woodward's book *Winning* on a recommended reading list for officers to hone their leadership skills.[4] This example centres on Carson's leadership style and how he adapted himself to coping with the unorthodox fighting required, even more in Carson's situation on Crete when he was away from his artillery role, where there were no frontlines, and also the more orthodox warfare in the North African Desert and Italy. It is worth noting that Campbell also observed that 'The average officer spent the vast majority of his time occupied with sport, more so than any other single activity ...'.[5]

While this link between sport and the military was current in Britain during the First World War, it was not reflected, initially at least, by the Commander of the NZEF in that conflict, Alexander Godley. He viewed sport as a distraction and it was not until 1917 that a divisional sports co-ordinator, Lt-Col Arthur Plugge, was appointed.[6] The quality of the sporting ability of those serving during the First World War was apparent in several sports, notably rowing, where in April 1919 New Zealand's eight beat crews representing the USA and France in an inter-allied regatta, while at the Henley Peace Regatta in July 1919 Darcy Hadfield won the single sculls. At the Inter-Allied Games organised by the Americans in June–July 1918, 18 nations took part, including a team of 18 New Zealanders. Setting the scene for future middle-distance athletics success, Daniel Mason won the 800-m gold medal, and, for their feats, Mason and Hadfield were presented with gold stopwatches by France's military commander, Marshal Petain, who felt they were the outstanding athletes of the games.[7]

By contrast, General Bernard Freyberg was keen to have a sporting connection from the outset of the Second World War for the New Zealand forces. A former New Zealand swimming champion, Freyberg, in the lead-up to the Gallipoli landing on April 25, 1915, swam to light diversionary flares on the beach at Bulair while serving with the Royal Naval Division and was awarded the Distinguished Service Order for his efforts. Though he served with the British during the War, and subsequently, he always regarded himself as a New Zealander and was appointed, out of retirement, by the New Zealand Government to lead the 2nd NZEF. When he assumed command of the 2nd NZEF, it was not long before it was appreciated that his attitude to sports was much different to that of Godley. Freyberg dined with Allan Andrews, who would in time become the longest-serving Brigadier in the New Zealand Army, in Cairo on January 11, 1940, and Andrews recounted part of their conversation:

> Over a port at the end of the meal the General said: 'We must have a [rugby] tour of England after the war is over'. I thought it was a great idea and the General kept it in mind throughout the war. We talked about it many times.[8]

Andrews would manage the team that became known as 'The Kiwis' on that post-war tour.

Just how much sport was to the fore in Freyberg's approach was recounted by Andrews. Soon after the Greek and Crete campaign in 1941 and while regrouping, the remnants of the NZ Division went into the desert to do some training:

> We were 20 miles south of the South African headquarters. They [the South Africans] had been in the desert for a while and the General said he must go up and pay his respects. In the course of conversation with them he asked, 'What about a game of rugby on Saturday?' He was a real rugby enthusiast but he was dumb when he came to understanding its requirements. We hadn't played any rugby in months, we'd limped back from Greece and Crete, and they had been playing for ages. He came back and said: 'We must beat them'. I told him we had no option but to get the game put back. I said to the General: 'You can make any excuse you like, but you have to get it put back by 10 days'. I tore him apart and he reluctantly said he would get it put back.[9]

Freyberg did have the match put back and when it was played the New Zealanders managed to beat their rivals 8-0.

It was after the Cretan episode that Freyberg realised he needed to make changes. He realised he had erred in not choosing younger commanders from the outset of the war. This had been driven home to him when the failed Greek and Crete campaigns exposed flaws in the command structure. Germany's innovative warfare, especially its parachute attack on Crete, required immediate responses and trench-bound commanders from the First World War were quickly exposed:

> I should have realised that some of my Commanders, men from World War I, were too old for the hand-to-hand fighting, and were not likely to stand up to the strain of an all-out battle of the nature that eventually developed around the Maleme Airfield and its eastern approaches. I should have replaced the old age group with younger men, who as a rule, although less experienced as fighting soldiers, stood up much better to the physical and mental strain of a long and bitter series of battles.[10]

Ever since the Duke of Wellington, rightly or wrongly, made his reference to the Battle of Waterloo being won on the playing fields of Eton, there has been an appreciation of the merits of sports experience in battle.

A Second Lieutenant in the artillery during the Greek campaign, Carson had no ordnance to command on Crete. It had been discarded during the rapid evacuation from mainland Greece. He was placed in temporary leadership of other waifs and strays from Greece; petrol company men, drivers and other 'odds and sods' who had only basic infantry training. They were a composite unit known in the New Zealand Division as 10 Brigade and were called 'infantillery'. Their temporary commander was Colonel Howard Kippenberger and their assignment was to hold the strategic hilltop town of Galatas, just south-west of Canea, above the coast road leading to the aerodrome of Maleme. Carson was given only two days to work with his men before the invasion on May 20.[11]

Leadership under the circumstances was a daunting prospect. But Carson was able to call on experiences from his own life to cope with what lay ahead of him. He had an instinct that fitted perfectly what Dwight Eisenhower said of leadership:

> A platoon leader doesn't get his platoon to go by getting up and shouting and saying, 'I am smarter, I am bigger. I am stronger. I am the leader'. He gets men to go along with him because they want to do it for him and they believe in him.[12]

That also fitted J. F. C. Fuller's dictum that 'the onus was on the officer not to hide the errors of the battlefield from the soldier but to show him how they could be overcome'.[13]

Carson was a volunteer, like most in the New Zealand Division, but he had a background that prepared him ideally, and unwittingly, for command in war. In civilian life he had excelled in sports to the point he became what is known in New Zealand as a double All Black – gaining national honours in rugby and cricket. He achieved his fame in his second first-class cricket game for Auckland against Otago when sharing a world record third-wicket stand of 445 runs, his own contribution being 290 – the highest maiden century by a New Zealander, a record that stood for 67 years. Later that season he was selected to tour England with New Zealand's team of 1937 but was frustrated by a foot injury that was not attended to until the end of the tour. His highest score on the tour was 86 and he scored only 594 runs in 18 matches at an average of 20.48. This compared to his career average in 31 first-class matches of 34.88.[14]

Returning home he regained his finest touch and was among the runs again before putting on his rugby boots and being selected to tour Australia in 1938 with the All Blacks. His foot was injured once more, resulting in further frustration. However, when the trials were held in late-1939 for New Zealand's 1940 rugby tour of South Africa, Carson was regarded as a certainty to tour, although the side selected was never named due to the outbreak of war.

Carson volunteered and found himself in Egypt in late1940 and, in April 1941, after the disastrous campaign on mainland Greece, he was on Crete and in his leadership role with 10 Brigade. Carson's sergeant in his new platoon, Arthur Pope, recalled how his platoon had all looked askance at their new officer:

> At the time we regarded ourselves as the Veterans of the Div [Division], having been through the entire Wavell push in the desert prior to our going to Greece, and we didn't actually welcome an outsider. However, it was only a day or two before Bill or 'Bull' as we called him, was on Christian name terms with most of us.[15]

Campbell's comment, 'Strong character and physical prowess were then, and still are, generally accepted as essential parts of the successful combat leader's make-up',[16] summed up perfectly Carson's approach.

No one had prepared the defenders of Crete for what they found when Germany's Luftwaffe disgorged thousands of paratroopers over the defensive positions of New Zealand, Australian, English and Greek troops on the morning of May 20, 1941. It was the first parachute invasion attempted in warfare and out of the fighting that emerged, before the island was eventually secured by Germany, the reputation New Zealand would earn as the 'best soldiers in the world during the twentieth century'[17] was demonstrated again.

Carson gathered his men around him and asked: 'Is anyone scared? I know I could do with a change of underpants!'[18] Another member of the group, Arthur Lambert, said from that moment Carson had his men eating out of his hand. He had a common touch. And there was a reason for this. Having suffered his own frustrations over his poorly managed injury while in England on the cricket tour in 1937, Carson knew the value of communication. Carson's sporting experience meant he knew the bitterness of personal failure on a significant stage. He had fought back and emerged stronger. That gave him a head start on many other commanders who would take time in the aftermath of the Greek and Cretan campaigns to absorb the lessons they had endured. Again Pope described just how effective Carson was:

> When the day arrived [the invasion of Crete], we all knew Bill and he knew us. I think the time has come to say that I never heard a man question his orders, and throughout the following grim period, he was where the fighting was thickest.[19]

Carson would later describe the build-up which preceded the aerial invasion:

> They dropped bombs and machine-gunned almost every inch of our area, which was about 20 miles square. I should say there were 2000 planes above us. This went on for about an hour and a half and then at 9.30am 70 troop-carriers and 12 gliders arrived.[20]

SPORT, WAR AND SOCIETY IN AUSTRALIA AND NEW ZEALAND

Clearly it was a situation that called for clarity in command, and immediately after his underpants comment, Carson responded by shooting, with a Bren Gun, one of the first German paratroopers in the air above. Pope recounted: 'After a few minutes we accounted for around 30 of the enemy, a lot of whom were bayoneted as they hung in the trees.'[21] It is true that other officers also excelled under the unique conditions struck on Crete, where the aerial strafing and the incursion of parachutists made establishing a front line nigh on impossible. However, few operated in the free-ranging role undertaken by Carson, and certainly few had such a haphazard group under their command.

So well did Carson's men react to his left-field exhortation on that torrid May morning that by some estimates more than 100 Germans met their end at the hands of Carson's men, who would be called a guerrilla unit nowadays, and who would only be broken up when the full might of the German forces was centred on capturing Galatas on May 25. As they ranged to and fro, Carson's unit became a freelance combination, prising snipers out of trees and removing entrenched machine guns from top-storey windows in the houses in and around Galatas. They would become known for six days as Carson's Rangers, and they would form a formidable unit around and about Galatas, a strategic high point the German invaders did their best to seize for those six days. Pope said: 'Bill had discarded his revolver, for the rifle and bayonet he retained throughout, and despite the fact that he was a novice at grenade throwing, was extremely accurate'.[22]

Those operations continued until May 25, the fateful day when the Germans turned their full attention on their unrealised goal, the township of Galatas. The unit took a pounding, and when leaving his men with orders to bridge a gap in the line between Petrol Company and 18 Battalion, while he visited the command centre for orders, they were unable to execute the plan because of the onrush of Germans. H.A.R. 'Farmer' Brown related what happened when Carson came back and found them sheltering behind a tree and not having completed their assignment:

> He was wearing a brown jersey, a bandalero and carried a rifle and looked what he was –
> tough. He looked at us a second, shot out his jaw and demanded to know, 'What the hell's
> going on here! Why aren't you spreading out like I said?'[23]

He was told there were a lot of Germans in front of them. He ordered his men back to Galatas to wait for him while he informed his superiors of what had happened. 'Bill did not seem to notice all the stuff going past him', Brown said.[24] Pope recounted how Carson moved among his various groups of men throughout the strafing by the Germans in the afternoon. Carson gave Pope an order to link with a unit on his right before he moved off again. Pope said: '[I] ran into a patrol of Jerries in the act of sneaking through behind me. We didn't realise it then, but we were completely encircled'.[25] Pope was wounded but said he and another, two out of eight, managed to get back through the German line. 'Bill, I heard, when he found he was surrounded, bayoneted his way out'.[26]

Carson's unit may have been broken up, but his own appetite for the battle was not lost and he joined up with the remnants of 18 Battalion who supported the flank of C and D Companies of 23 Battalion on their famous bayonet charge into the entrenched German machine-gun positions in Galatas. Carson, when he heard of the call to action with the 18th, exclaimed: 'Thank Christ I've got my bloody bayonet'.[27] The New Zealanders were so effective in their work that they regained the town in 20 minutes of bloody carnage, much of their determination stemming from being continually on the back foot, especially while the Luftwaffe ruled the air during the daylight hours. But the charge took place at dusk and the Germans had no air cover. Their confidence without that support was not so

SPORT, WAR AND SOCIETY IN AUSTRALIA AND NEW ZEALAND

high. Those who avoided the New Zealanders' steel turned and ran. Pope was part of the main charge and said:

> In nearly six years of war, that night is the most vivid in my memory. Ammunition was scarce and that night hundreds of the Huns died with the feel of steel. Intelligence reports state the odds against us at 11 to 1 ... I never saw Bill as I said, after that afternoon, but heard from various sources that he was everywhere that night.[28]

Typical of many who were involved in the charge at Galatas, Carson said little. In a letter home, the only reference he made was to 'the big battle on Sunday night'.[29] Afterwards he wrote:

> I am certain no army has yet had to withstand what the New Zealand Division put up with. Now that I am out I can tell you that for those days of hell I never thought that I would step out of Crete and I'm sure every one of those boys thought the same.[30]

In the post-Crete mop-up, the NZ Division underwent a significant policy change in relation to appointing front-line officers. The older hands from the First World War were phased out. The remainder of Carson's war was fought with his artillery unit, as a battery captain, and while that required more orthodox methodology it proved no less fearsome. During the battle of Mareth, his actions in supporting an English armoured car unit from the King's Dragoon Guards saw him awarded a Military Cross, something his gunners said had been a long time coming. Earlier, at Sidi Rezegh, and at Alamein, his units played significant roles in the Battles, especially in their work against German tanks.

But throughout it all there was a regard for the men he went to war with. Colin Sinclair, a sergeant of Carson's 4th Field Artillery Regiment, said:

> Bill Carson had a wonderful, almost unbelievable, influence on men during times of stress. Merely to see him standing quietly behind the guns, or chatting to the men, was enough to put new spirit and determination into battle-weary soldiers ... He was a splendid example and a real inspiration.[31]

Away from the action he encouraged his men in their pursuit of sport and he took part in athletics, basketball, baseball or swimming with his men, while also pursuing cricket when he could, including leading the New Zealand 2nd NZEF team in 1943 in six major games, including three against the South Africans which New Zealand won 2–1. Sinclair said:

> When his troop took part in the chase from Bardia to Tripoli, part of the equipment that jolted across the desert on a truck were two basketball posts. War or no war, Bill was not going to be caught without facilities for sport.[32]

It was in the Italy campaign that Carson's war came to its end. He was in a jeep going onto a bridge when a German mortar bomb landed on a bank above the jeep. He sustained liver damage and was treated in field hospitals before being put on a hospital ship returning to New Zealand. While on the ship he wrote to his sister:

> I have made a wonderful recovery. Several times during the last few weeks the medical officers have said they didn't know why I was so well. I'm sure one reason was because I was so fit. However, I have had the very best of medical brains and attention since I was hit. By the time I reach NZ, I shall be as fit as ever again, but I'm being sent because there is the remotest chance that in these cases the liver or lung may go wrong.'[33]

Sadly, his liver did 'go wrong' and Major W. N. 'Bill' Carson died at sea, on October 8, 1944. Carson's experiences in sport, not only on the field, but also off it, especially in the England he toured in 1937, where cricket was still of the 'Gentlemen and the Players' structure, exposed him to social circumstances that were out of the ordinary for most New Zealanders and to a level of class beyond the comprehension of many. As a warehouseman from Auckland, he met and dined with the English owners of the company he worked for, none of which would have been possible without his sporting prowess. The resulting worldliness undoubtedly contributed to his military leadership style. Campbell has noted:

> An active, fit officer who revels in outdoor pursuits, one who can properly function as a member of a team, and one who is willing to sublimate personal success and fame for the greater glory of the team are highly desirable attributes for a military leader, attributes that armies still search for and try to inculcate in their leaders today.[34]

Carson had played on the great sports grounds of the world, and had suffered success and failure. He had witnessed greatness at first hand, he had observed leaders in sport, he had coped with Kipling's imposters of 'triumph and disaster'[35] and he had overcome the disappointments of failure to rise again. That could only have made him stronger. Carson was not only Campbell's ideal in the New Zealand sense, but he was also the epitome of the modern military leader his General, Freyberg, sought as New Zealand's Division also recovered from the calamities that were Greece and Crete.

Notes

1. For further information on the careers of Wilding and Gallaher, see Richardson, *Anthony Wilding*, and Elliott, *Dave Gallaher, the Original All Black Captain*.
2. Campbell, "'Training for Sport'."
3. Ibid., 23.
4. *Sunday Times*, April 21, 2013.
5. Campbell, "'Training for Sport'," 23.
6. McGibbon, "Military and Sport."
7. Ibid.
8. Cited in McConnell, "After the War, a Rugby Invasion."
9. Ibid.
10. Cited in Freyberg, *Bernard Freyberg VC*, 304.
11. Kippenberger, *Infantry Brigadier*.
12. "Eisenhower" in Bradley, *The International Dictionary of Thoughts*, 432.
13. Cited in Strachan, "Training, Morale and Modern War," 211.
14. Carman, *W.N. Carson, Footballer and Cricketer*.
15. Letter from Arthur Pope to Carson family, April 30, 1948.
16. Campbell, "'Training for Sport'," 25.
17. Keegan, *The First World War*, 242.
18. Lambert, *From Greece to Crete 1941*, 48.
19. Letter from Arthur Pope to Carson family, April 30, 1948.
20. Cited in *New Zealand Free Lance*, July 2, 1941.
21. Letter from Arthur Pope to Carson family, April 30, 1948.
22. Ibid.
23. Letter from H.A.R. "Farmer" Brown to Jim Henderson, Jim Henderson Papers, NZ National Archives, WA II 1 DA 70/15/8.
24. Ibid.
25. Letter from Arthur Pope to Carson family, April 30, 1948.
26. Ibid.
27. Cited in Brian Bassett Papers, NZ Archives, WA II 1 DA 50.1/10/2.
28. Letter from Arthur Pope to Carson family, April 30, 1948.
29. Cited in *New Zealand Free Lance*, July 2, 1941.

SPORT, WAR AND SOCIETY IN AUSTRALIA AND NEW ZEALAND

30. Ibid.
31. Cited in *Auckland Star*, October 21, 1944.
32. Ibid.
33. Letter from Bill Carson to his sister Alison, September 21, 1944.
34. Campbell, "'Training for Sport'," 25.
35. Cited in Campbell, "'Training for Sport'."

References

Bradley, John. P. *The International Dictionary of Thoughts*. Chicago, IL: J.G. Ferguson, 1969.

Campbell, J. D. "'Training for Sport is Training for War': Sport and the Transformation of the British Army, 1860–1914." *The International Journal of the History of Sport* 17, no. 4 (2000): 21–58.

Carman, Arthur. *W.N. Carson, Footballer and Cricketer*. Wellington: Sporting Publications, 1947.

Elliott, Matt. *Dave Gallaher, the Original All Black Captain*. Auckland: HarperCollins, 2012.

Freyberg, Paul. *Bernard Freyberg VC, Soldier of Two Nations*. London: Hodder and Stoughton, 1991.

Keegan, John. *The First World War*. New York: Vintage, 2000.

Kippenberger, Howard K. *Infantry Brigadier*. London: Oxford University Press, 1949.

Lambert, Arthur. *From Greece to Crete 1941*. Whangarei: Arthur Lambert, 2001.

McConnell, Lynn. "After the War, a Rugby Invasion." *Evening Post*, June 19, 1998.

McGibbon, Ian. "Military and Sport – South African and First World Wars." In *Te Ara Encyclopedia of New Zealand*. http://www.TeAra.govt.nz/en/military-and-sport/page-2

Richards, Sir David. *The Sunday Times*, April 21, 2013. London. http://www.thesundaytimes.co.uk/sto/news/uk_news/Defence/article1248808.ece

Richardson, Len. *Anthony Wilding: A Sporting Life*. Christchurch: Canterbury University Press, 1999.

Strachan, Hew. "Training, Morale and Modern War." *Journal of Contemporary History* 41, no. 2 (2006): 211–227.

The Controversial Cec Pepper and the Australian Services Cricket Team: The Test Career That Never Was

Peter Crossing

Independent Scholar, Canberra, Australia

The Australian Services cricket teams of both WWI and WWII played an important role in the immediate post-war period. A number of the players involved went on to forge successful Test cricket careers. This paper mentions the exploits of some of the players involved in these matches with particular focus on Cecil (Cec) Pepper. Cec Pepper represented the WWII Australian Services Team with distinction during the exhausting schedule of matches played in England, India and Australia from June 1945. However, in the match between the Australian Services Team and South Australia played at the Adelaide Oval over the Christmas–New Year period of 1945/1946, Pepper was involved in a controversial incident with the South Australian captain Donald Bradman and umpire Jack Scott. The incident and its subsequent ramifications were to have a huge impact on Pepper's cricket career. Pepper should have been in contention as a future Australian Test player. Instead, his career took another direction completely. This paper discusses Pepper's career and traces further links between the three Adelaide protagonists, Bradman, Scott and Pepper. A comparison is also made between Cec Pepper and other Australian spin bowlers of the era.

Introduction

Cecil (Cec) Pepper was a very good batsman and leg-spin/googly bowler. He was a committed team player who was uncompromising in his on-field interactions with opponents and umpires. He was loud, and while at times he could be uncouth, he was also capable of the hilarious comment. Over the years, anecdotes involving Cec Pepper have enlivened many a cricket dinner. A brochure from the Tour of India by the Services XI team in 1945 stated that Pepper was 'generally regarded as a Test class all-rounder'.[1] This paper proposes the case that Pepper should have played Test cricket for Australia.

Over the New Year period in 1945–1946 the Australian Services XI team played a match against the South Australian team at the Adelaide Oval. It was here, on December 31, 1945, that a significant incident related to Pepper's career occurred. The batsman concerned, Donald Bradman, was playing for South Australia (SA) in his second first-class match since cessation of the competition in 1940/1941. The bowler was Pepper, a member of the Services XI returning to Australia at the end of an eight-month post-war cricket tour consisting of 58 matches. The umpire was John (Jack) Drake Scott. Bradman's role in the history of Australian cricket is well known. Not so, the other two.

An earlier version of this paper was delivered at 'Sporting Traditions XIX', a conference held in Canberra in July 2013.

SPORT, WAR AND SOCIETY IN AUSTRALIA AND NEW ZEALAND

The Australian Services Cricket Team during World War I

In 1919, at the conclusion of the Great War, the Australian Imperial Force (AIF) Services cricket team played matches in England, South Africa and Australia. In his excellent paper 'Forgotten Heroes: The 1945 Australian Services Cricket Team', Ed Jaggard quotes British author Richard Holt who stated that after WWI 'there was a special need for reassurance, to know that the essence of England had survived'.[2] Cricket's revival was at the core of this, because, according to Holt, 'more than any other game [it] was bound up with the ruralism of an England overburdened with great cities'.[3] As Jaggard explains, cricket was a sport that

> ... evoked the pastoral in English life, and in 1919 the [AIF] ... team helped provide the necessary reassurance by playing first-class matches around Britain, before crowds far exceeding expectations.[4]

Following the matches in England, the team also played matches in South Africa and then back in Australia. The AIF team was first captained by Charles Kelleway. Kelleway had made a century at Lords in a neutral Test against South Africa in 1912. However, after scoring 505 runs in nine innings at the start of the tour, Kelleway left the team and returned to Australia in somewhat controversial circumstances.[5] The new captain, Herbert Collins, was the only other player with prior first-class cricket experience. Collins was a Lance Corporal in charge of a team containing seven commissioned officers. Collins along with fellow team members Jack Gregory, Johnny Taylor, William 'Bert' Oldfield and Nip Pellew subsequently played Test cricket for Australia. The best known of these are Gregory and Oldfield. Jack Gregory formed a formidable fast bowling partnership with Ted McDonald. Oldfield, who before the war had been a 3rd Grade District wicketkeeper in the Sydney competition, became wicketkeeper for the AIF XI and eventually one of Australia's great Test wicketkeepers, playing 54 Tests and effecting 130 dismissals.[6]

In his book, *The Ashes Captains*, Gerry Cotter states:

> If Armstrong takes the credit for captaining his great team [of 1920–1921] the man who must take much of the credit for putting it together is Herbie Collins ... [who] was able to nurture the likes of Jack Gregory and Bert Oldfield, helping them become the outstanding players they were.[7]

Following the retirement of Armstrong, Collins captained Australia in 11 Tests, winning five and losing only two. Cotter continues:

> His success as a captain was founded on an ability to observe closely the temperament of each of his team and to treat them accordingly. Quietly spoken, thoughtful and a good friend to his players, he was a shrewd and knowledgeable cricketer who studied the opposition thoroughly.[8]

In earlier times Collins had been a bookmaker and apparently his ability to win the toss was legendary. Collins also had a sense of humour. Cotter relates the story of a Sydney grade match where a slow bowler who had been hit for several sixes in few overs asked his captain, Collins, to be taken off. 'No fear', said Collins, 'I haven't enjoyed anything like this for years'.[9]

John Scott and Donald Bradman

Collins was captain of the New South Wales (NSW) Shield team from 1919 to 1926 and led them to four Sheffield Shield wins. One of the fast bowlers in the 1925 team was John Drake Scott. According to author Johnny Moyes, 'Scott was a fast bowler – really fast – and something of a rival to Tibby Cotter ... He had the extra few yards of pace which matter [and] ... could make the ball fly shoulder high'.[10] Scott had apparently bowled a form of bodyline in a state match for NSW, but his captain Collins disliked the technique and would not let him use it.[11] Scott moved to SA to continue his career and in 1927 he dismissed a young Donald Bradman who was playing in his first Shield match for NSW. Bradman had made 118 at the time. It is not recorded whether or not Scott was bowling a form of bodyline. Bradman was fortunate to be playing in the match. The NSW selectors had intended that he would be 12th man but Archie Jackson developed a boil on his knee and had to be replaced. In an exciting finish to the match, SA won by one wicket. Scott was involved in a ninth wicket partnership that took the side to within four runs of victory.[12]

While Donald Bradman continued his extraordinary cricket career through the 1930s, Jack Scott was contributing at the local level. In the Annual Report of the Prospect District Cricket Club (SA) for the 1934/1935 season, Club Secretary G.C. Paterson stated:

> Our Club was most fortunate in securing the services of such a well-versed and experienced Coach as Mr J. D. Scott, who ... has had a vast experience in International and Interstate cricket matches, as a player, and is now one of our Interstate umpires. Jack was most assiduous at practice, taking a very keen interest in all players, particularly the Juniors, being ever ready at all times to help any player in difficulties, and also watching most closely all minor points, which are so easily overlooked, yet so important.[13]

Scott went on to become a Sheffield Shield and Test umpire, officiating in 10 Tests. As an umpire, he earned a reputation for disciplining fast bowlers for bowling short rising deliveries – the type of bowling for which he had been known as a player.[14]

Cec Pepper

Cecil George Pepper was born in Forbes in 1916, 160 kilometres from Cootamundra, where Bradman had been born eight years earlier. As a young man Pepper was employed as a blacksmith's striker in Parkes, where he played cricket. In his first match in the Grinstead Cup competition at age 16, he was described as a 'promising colt'. In the six years before he moved to Sydney, Pepper became the most outstanding cricketer in the Forbes/Parkes district. His innings of 258 not out stands to this day as a batting record for most runs scored in an innings of a Parkes competition match. In *The Grinstead Cup*, Michael Greenwood records that Pepper is credited with 'one of the biggest sixes ever hit on Woodward Park in Parkes – the ball apparently landed alongside the Showground gates in Victoria Street'.[15] Former Canberra Comets player and Australian Capital Territory cricket selector Darryle Macdonald, who hails from Parkes, says that, on the evidence, it was a monster hit that would have 'easily cleared the grandstand at Manuka Oval, Canberra, and then some ... the ball would have travelled close to 120 metres, cleared the oval fence, then three tennis courts and a wide street – and it's up-hill'.[16] Pepper also played a key role in the shortest Grinstead match ever conducted. The opposing side was dismissed for 21 runs. Pepper opened the innings and hit four sixes from the first four balls bowled.[17]

In 1937, at the age of 21, Pepper moved to Sydney to play club cricket for Petersham. He was first selected for the NSW Sheffield Shield team in 1938/1939 but it was in the next season that he really began to make his mark. Of significance is the Shield match NSW versus Queensland in 1939/1940. Pepper made 81 in 61 minutes (74 in boundaries; seven sixes and eight fours) including 40 (18 and 22) taken from consecutive overs by W. Tallon. And apparently most of the sixes did not just go over the boundary fence, they soared out of the ground. The *Sydney Morning Herald* reported:

The outstanding feature of the NSW innings was the magnificent effort of the young Petersham all-rounder … He gave a glorious display of scientific hitting … a grand display of faultless hitting … nothing finer of the kind has been seen in Brisbane. He made a length of the bowling to suit himself … lifting those pitched up, with perfect timing, out of the ground.[18]

The innings is also significant for the fact that Pepper's teammates, Test batsmen Stan McCabe and Jack Fingleton, were both dismissed without scoring. On the following weekend, Pepper made 107 in 114 minutes for Petersham against Waverley in the Sydney Grade Cricket competition.[19] Pepper was also a useful bowler. He bowled leg spinners and googlies and developed his own form of flipper, a ball bowled with backspin out the front of the hand that keeps low and slides or skids towards the batsman. Against Victoria in December 1939, Pepper captured his first five-wicket haul in only his seventh Shield match. He took 5/114 from 31 overs and eight wickets for the match. In the same match, Bill O'Reilly took 5/72 from 27 overs.[20] Tables 1 and 2 show the first-class bowling figures from 1939 to 1941 for the relevant players and indicate that, during this time, Pepper's performances were as good as any other Australian spin bowler – apart from the great O'Reilly.[21]

Table 1. Sheffield Shield performances 1939/1940.

1939/1940	State	First-class matches	Wickets	Runs scored
Bill O'Reilly	NSW	7	55	26
Doug Ring	Vic	7	34	243
Cec Pepper	NSW	7	31	253
Dick Fleetwood-Smith	Vic	6	17	24
Ian Johnson	Vic	7	13	313
Colin McCool	NSW	1	1	34

Table 2. Sheffield Shield performances 1940/1941.

1940/1941	State	First-class matches	Wickets	Runs scored
Bill O'Reilly	NSW	8	55	132
Doug Ring	Vic	6	18	215
Cec Pepper	NSW	6	26	286
Ian Johnson	Vic	5	25	296
Colin McCool	NSW	6	24	416

The Australian Services Cricket Team during World War II

Pepper enlisted in the Australian Army in March 1941 and travelled to the Middle East in September of that year. He returned to Australia in March 1942 and then served in New Guinea in 1943 and 1944. From late 1944, he was a member of the Second AIF Reception Group in the UK.[22] During the war years, organised cricket was played, albeit in a curtailed format, and Prime Minister Robert Menzies urged the Australian Cricket Board to continue the Sheffield Shield Competition in 1939/1940 'for the morale of the people'.[23] Eventually, official competition was suspended but other matches continued in various forms. Shield matches continued in 1940/1941 and Pepper played some grade cricket when in Australia during the war years. Just like the rest of society, war had a dramatic effect on cricket and cricketers, as the following examples illustrate. In 1941 English Test cricketer Bill Edrich flew a morning mission over Europe in a Blenheim bomber. His squadron lost two aircraft with all the crew. During the afternoon, Edrich played for a squadron cricket team against a local village XI in Norfolk. Edrich says it was a good game but he had trouble concentrating and his mind kept turning to the pal he had shared a joke with in the morning who was now dead.[24] Charlie Walker, the Australian wicketkeeper, who toured England in 1938 as a member of the Australian Ashes squad, was a bomber pilot killed when shot down over Germany in 1942.[25] Ken Farnes, the English fast bowler, also a pilot, was killed in a night flying exercise in Oxfordshire in 1943. Farnes had played 15 Tests and toured Australia with Allen's side in 1936/1937.[26] Keith 'Nugget' Miller was a fighter pilot deployed with the Royal Air Force (RAF) at Bournemouth. One weekend in 1943, while Miller was away in London playing in a cricket match for an Royal Australian Air Force (RAAF) team captained by Keith Carmody, the pub where he usually ate lunch on Sundays was hit by a German air strike. His lunch mates were all killed.[27] Miller was a law unto himself. Once, flying over Germany, he broke off from the main formation and flew down the Rhine till he reached the city of Bonn. He then circled it a couple of times before flying back. Miller's reason for doing this was because Bonn was where Beethoven was born and classical music was a particular passion.[28]

At the end of the war, an Australian Services cricket team was formed in England. The team played matches against a number of English cricket teams, including a series of Victory Tests. The team then played matches in India, Ceylon and back in Australia. The story of the Services team, of which Pepper was a member, has been well documented by Ian Woodward and Jaggard.[29] Marylebone Cricket Club (MCC) Secretary Sir Pelham Warner conceived the idea for the matches after watching Miller and Carmody batting for an RAAF team against the British Services Side at Lords in 1944. The plan began to take shape when Warner met Australian Prime Minister John Curtin and Australia's highest-ranking officer, Field Marshal Sir Thomas Blamey. Blamey had created sides led by Gunner Lindsay Hassett in Egypt in 1941. These teams had beaten sides drawn from British (including English Test player Freddie Brown), South African and New Zealand forces.[30] So, in late 1944, members of the Second AIF Reception Group, including Hassett, Pepper and Albert Cheetham, found themselves on *SS Bloemfontein* which embarked to England, via the USA. Not considered were Arthur Morris, Ray Lindwall, Doug Ring and Colin McCool who were with the Army in New Guinea. Ian Johnson and Bill Brown, serving in the Pacific were also unable to join the group.[31] The non-availability of these cricketers of significance for the Services team may be one of the reasons that the Services players did not ever receive Australian caps. Unlike the AIF team in WWI, where all the players were serving in Europe, Pepper, Hassett and Cheetham had been sent from Australia. The matches involving the Services team were extremely popular and large crowds attended. Over 350,000 people attended the five so-called Victory Tests, and at Lords a new record of 93,000 for a three-day match was set.[32] As with the AIF team of WWI, the captain Lindsay Hassett, the only player with Test cricket experience, was again outranked by many other members of his team. Of the others, Miller, Pepper, Keith Carmody, Bob Cristofani, Ross Stanford, Reg Ellis, Richard (Dick) Whitington, Graham Williams and Stan Sismey had played Sheffield Shield cricket. There are fascinating stories about them all. The team acquitted itself well and drew the Test series 2-2 against an England team that boasted Test players Edrich, Len Hutton, Cyril Washbrook, Wally Hammond and Denis Compton. Many players on both sides would later say it was the happiest cricket of their life. The reason for this was the attitude of captains Lindsay Hassett and Wally Hammond, who had a 'common resolve ... to play "differently"'.[33]

As Knox states, at that moment 'Cricket had the chance to be what it had not been – a ritualization of warlike behavior – but war's antidote'.[34] Moreover, as he explains:

> The cricketers of the Victory Tests were uniquely placed to put the importance of the game into perspective. They wanted something played in better spirit. The warlike temper of 1930s Ashes cricket seemed stupid, almost obscene.[35]

Miller's reflections concerning the crowd reaction when the recently released prisoner of war Graham Williams walked onto the field for the opening match at Lords are enough to give the reader goose bumps.[36] Williams had played for SA before the war and had earned high praise for his stamina and accurate bowling. The Services tour was something of a coming of age for Miller and the Lords Test was Miller's match. He made 105 in his debut first-class innings at the ground, hitting seven sixes which crashed high into the grandstand. *The Times* reported that the innings was 'as good a century as has been seen at Lord's in many a long day'.[37] Pepper, nicknamed 'The Ox' because of his 'massive physique ... (and) ... [the fact that] "Oxen" are not easily overawed',[38] featured in an important partnership with Miller. His innings included a six hit onto the top tier of the Grandstand from a straight ball of 'excellent length' bowled by Lieut-Col Stephenson.[39]

In the match at Bramhall Lane, English fieldsman Errol Holmes allowed a stroke from Pepper to run through his fingers for four. The following banter was heard from a spectator:

> Yorkshire patriot 'Whaat's thaat tha haast abaat neck, Guvner – a cravaat?'
> Holmes ... sadly nodded his handsome head.
> 'Well toighten if Guvner, toighten it'.[40]

Services Team member, Whitington, later a journalist and author,[41] wrote:

> Pepper was a superb all round cricketer and an inveterate trier. He had a great duel with Wally Hammond at Bramhall Lane. Hammond made a century which Pelham Warner described as 'one of the best innings he has ever played'. This caused Hammond to say 'Pepper's was some of the finest spin bowling I have ever faced'.[42]

Whitington continued:

> ... that Pepper maintained an impeccable line and length with his leg break and 'flipped front of hand off break' bowling. As a batsman he had a sound defence and was one of the most powerful strikers of the ball of any era. As a cover, slip or close to the wicket fieldsman he was of the highest class.[43]

The team was not totally reliant on Miller, Hassett or Pepper, and every member put in a good performance at some stage. Pepper was the most consistent. As Jaggard notes:

> While the legendary all-rounder Keith Miller was a natural crowd pleaser, especially with his flamboyant batting, Cec Pepper was not far behind. Hitter of prodigious sixes, and a far more penetrating bowler than Miller, Pepper was a potential match winner in all conditions, yet who remembers him now?[44]

He then adds elsewhere 'it seems astonishing that his [Pepper's] talents were lost to the relative backwater of Lancashire League cricket'.[45]

Pepper made 168 against H.D.G. Leveson-Gowers' XI at Scarborough including what Bill Edrich says was one of the biggest sixes he had ever seen when Pepper hit Eric Hollies 'out of the ground and clean over some boarding houses five stories high, into Trafalgar Square ... I saw the ball go over the top myself'.[46] Pepper would gladly confirm that the ball sailed past 'the third chimney to the left of the gap',[47] and using a bat weighing no more than 2lb 4oz.

SPORT, WAR AND SOCIETY IN AUSTRALIA AND NEW ZEALAND

Following the matches in England, the team then toured India where things did not go as well. There were long train journeys, sickness, biased umpiring and an Indian team full of individuals intent on proving themselves against the Australians.[48] It was then back home to Australia and the end of two very long campaigns – the individual contributions each team member had made to the war effort followed by an arduous, gruelling tour of 58 cricket matches in England and India in the eight months from May to December 1945. As Woodward describes:

> Most had been away for three years, some five, and were dismayed to learn that instead of being allowed to return to their homes and families ... they were to be sent off on a six week tour of the States in order 'to help put cricket back on its feet in Australia'.[49]

Services Team manager Keith Johnson protested that the players were being asked to do too much. Illness had taken its toll – 16 of the 19 players had become incapacitated at some stage and 'thus would not be able to produce their best'.[49] Indeed, while in India, wicketkeeper Stan Sismey had been sent to a military hospital to have several shrapnel particles removed from his back. Captain Lindsay Hassett said 'members of the team were suffering from exhaustion'.[49] The Australian Board of Control refused to shorten the program stating that: 'Due consideration had been given the players and their criticism was not warranted'.[49] It was a tour too far. In Australia, the Services team did not produce their best and were comprehensively beaten, and this resulted in some derision of the team from certain members of the press.[50]

The Incident

In some ways, much of the above is background to a controversial incident in Adelaide which took place in the match between the Services team and SA over the Christmas–New Year period of 1945. Bradman was captain of a South Australian team that contained some notable cricketers from that state: F.C. 'Chester' Bennett, a schoolteacher who later became coach and mentor to Test players Ian and Greg Chappell and Ashley Woodcock; Ron Hamence toured England with Bradman's team in 1948; while Geff Noblet represented Australia against South Africa (1949/1950, 1952/1953) and the West Indies (1951/1952). The team also included Bruce Dooland, the young leg spinner and would-be rival to Pepper. One of the umpires was Jack Scott. SA batted first and Pepper, who had achieved early success, later became very frustrated.

> Pepper bowled Hamence ... with a ball which appeared to make pace and keep low ... When Pepper, at slip, held the ball chest high and Cheetham (silly mid-on) and Pepper appealed for a catch from Craig off Ellis's bowling, the position would have been desperate had Umpire L A Smith upheld the appeal. He did not, to the obvious consternation of Pepper and Cheetham ... Craig had a 'life' when Sismey (keeper) failed to take the ball cleanly ... off Pepper's bowling.[51]

Then the fateful incident occurred. The *Advertiser* reported that 'When Bradman was on 53, Umpire J D Scott turned down a leg before appeal by the wicketkeeper, Sismey and the bowler, Cec Pepper'.[51] Quoting Miller:

> At that time, Cec Pepper was, in my opinion, the best all-rounder in the world. Pepper deceived Bradman with his flipper, a kind of leg break which scarcely turned but made a lot of pace off the pitch. Most of the players on the field believed that Bradman had failed to spot the flipper and was plumb leg before. Stan Sismey, the wicketkeeper, as fair a man as you could wish to meet said there was no doubt. There was a terrific appeal but Umpire Jack Scott failed to grant it. In the heat of the moment, Pepper turned to Scott and said something ... Scott reported him.[52]

In *Inside Story*, Gideon Haigh and David Frith quote Pepper's fellow Services XI player, Whitington:

> ... when Scott refused the appeal. Pepper put his hands on his huge forehead and exclaimed 'What do you have to do, Jack?' On his way back to bowl the next ball Pepper shook his head several times and mumbled some words into what, had he been WG Grace, would have been his beard. From the last ball of the over Bradman took a characteristic single and as he completed the run called to Scott 'Do we have to put up with this sort of thing'?[53]

Umpire Scott, a South Australian Cricket Association employee, informed Pepper that in view of Bradman's complaint he had no alternative but to report the incident. Whitington wrote that the report went to the South Australian Cricket Association and was forwarded on to the Australian Cricket Board of Control. Haigh and Frith relate that the Board discussed the report which also stated that Pepper 'during practically the whole time he was bowling, continuously used filthy language and had questioned his [Umpire Scott's] decisions'. And there was the fact that Pepper had almost got himself into trouble with the Services Team in India with the vehemence of his appealing. And to add insult to injury, Pepper himself had been dismissed LBW during the Services XI innings. Pepper wrote a letter of apology and it was handed to Services Team Manager Keith Johnson. Haigh and Frith write that Scott accepted Pepper's apology but they also report Whitington's version of the story that the letter had been sent but in 'some way it had become lost in transit'. Board officials said that the letter had never arrived and requested another. Pepper reasoned that if his word was not good enough to be accepted, he would not send another apology.[54] Shortly after this, the team for the forthcoming 1946 tour of New Zealand was selected (Bradman was a selector) and Pepper was not among those chosen.

Keith Johnson said that the Adelaide complaint was a matter of great regret and that even though he believed there had been other offences of a similar nature, none of them had been reported. Johnson asked the Chairman of the Board if the report had affected Pepper's chances of selection for New Zealand Tour. He was told that no instruction had been given to the selection committee.[55]

However, the damage had been done. Not selected for the New Zealand Tour, Pepper, who had been offered a contract with Lancashire League club Rochdale, decided that he had no future in Australian cricket. Miller wrote:

> I saw the report and it finished Pepper. He should have been a cast iron certainty for the tour of New Zealand ... Pepper realized he had 'had his chips' ... I hold no brief for Pepper making the remark he is supposed to have made, but it would be a poor look-out for all of us if our careers were held in forfeit of one remark said in temper. I think Bradman should have realized that and intervened on Pepper's behalf. He could have done so very easily. Surely he had the power to save Pepper. As it was, a potentially great player was lost to Australia.[56]

Like Miller, Clarrie Grimmett had also suggested that Pepper be selected for the New Zealand tour. Grimmett, the grand old 'fox' of Australian cricket, named six certainties for Australia's 1946/1947 touring team to New Zealand – Bradman, Hassett, Brown, Tallon, Barnes and O'Reilly. He also suggested places for Bill Alley and Pepper. Grimmett observed:

> Cec Pepper is another batsman who can hit. He belts the ball hard because he naturally swings his 14-odd stone behind the bat, easily, and without striving. Cec Pepper is the most improved cricketer I've seen. Before the war he was a good Shield man. Now he is a personality all-rounder. He bowls a lot of rubbish at times, but when he strikes the spot he will bowl any batsman in the world. There have not been many other big men as smart and keen in the field as Pepper.[57]

No effort appears to have been made to confront Pepper in order that he explain his behaviour in Adelaide. Nor were there were any efforts made to counsel him. The Australian Cricket Board appears to have simply washed their hands of him. Pepper's reaction to the refusal of the appeal was unacceptable. However, it was understandable given that Pepper, a somewhat volatile character, was at the end of an arduous tour of matches that had most recently included some 'appallingly biased umpiring' in India. There was also the fact that, after their significant commitments to the war effort, Pepper and the other members of the Services team had immediately been involved in such a whirlwind of cricket matches that 'tempers were bound to fray after such a journey'.[58] As Miller suggests, the situation was not irretrievable.[59] In view of the gamesmanship and disputing of decisions that has occurred in cricket at the highest level over the years, it would certainly seem that Pepper was hard done by. In any case, the tour of New Zealand would have done little to advance any claims Pepper may have had to a regular spot in the Australian Test team. The team selected, captained by Bill Brown rather than Services Team captain Hassett, was bristling with bowling talent – Miller, Lindwall, O'Reilly, Ernie Toshack, Ian Johnson, McCool and Dooland. In the only test match, played at Wellington, 'New Zealand won the toss and batted on a rain-affected pitch. Brown's toughest task was deciding who should be given the ball to do the destruction'.[60] A very much under-strength New Zealand were routed. The scorecards in the four lead-up matches and the Test match indicate that the aging O'Reilly was given the bulk of the slow bowling duties, with a modicum of support from the younger brigade. In the Test match, O'Reilly took 5/14 in the first innings and 3/19 in the second innings of what became his final test.[61] In the second innings, Brown tossed a coin to decide whether McCool or Johnson would be given the ball to finish off the match.[62]

Aftermath

After the series of Services matches, Hassett wrote that 'This is cricket as it should be … let's have no more talk of "war" in cricket'.[63] This was not exactly the situation when England toured Australia in 1946/1947. Known as the 'Goodwill Tour', it was a concession from Lords to Bradman and Australia so that Bradman would tour England with Australia in 1948. England needed Bradman to tour. He was the essential financial ingredient to help the counties and the MCC to get back on their feet again in the post-war environment. However, in contrast with the cricketers of the Victory Tests who were 'uniquely placed to put the importance of the game into perspective',[64] the war seemed to have left Bradman's uncompromising approach to cricket untouched and the 'Goodwill' tour was so-called in name only.

Controversy began in the First Test in Brisbane. Jack Ikin, fielding in the gully, appeared to catch Bradman off the bowling of Bill Voce. Bradman did not walk from the wicket, saying later that in his opinion 'The ball touched the bottom of my bat just before hitting the ground and therefore it was not a catch'.[65] The Englishmen did not appeal, apparently because the catch seemed so obvious. Umpire George Borwick gave Bradman not out and did not consult square leg umpire Jack Scott, the same umpire who had refused Pepper's appeals the previous summer. Scott later said that he agreed with Borwick's decision.[66] From his position at the bowler's end, Hassett thought it was a bump ball.[67] Whitington wrote that 'Bradman deserved great credit for the way he accepted his dismissals. I have never known him to show displeasure or dissent when umpires ruled against him'.[68] Other opinions varied:

There was consternation in the British media contingent, and among those Australian pressmen, such as O'Reilly and ... Jack Fingleton, who disliked Bradman ... Keith Miller, sitting in the dressing room waiting to bat, thought it was out too.[69]

Australian player McCool remarked 'as (Miller) at the time was sitting next to me in the pavilion, that's the biggest mystery of the lot'.[70] English captain Wally Hammond was livid, evidenced by his exclamation that 'This is a bloody fine way to start'.[71] Bradman's refusal to walk was within the rules, and even the spirit of the game. But it 'snuffed out all hope of a new ... spirit'.[72] And the antagonism did not stop there:

Keith Miller was deeply affected by the Second World War. In the first post-war Ashes Test in Brisbane ... England were caught on a sticky ... [and] Bill Edrich came in. He'd had a serious war and he survived and Miller thought, 'He's my old Services mate. The last thing he wants after five years' war is to be flattened by a cricket ball, so I eased up. Bradman came up to me and said, "Don't slow down, Keith. Bowl quicker". That remark put me off Test cricket. Never felt the same way about it after that'.[73]

During the second Test in Sydney, Bill Edrich said he 'withdrew my subscription from the Bradman fan club' over Bradman's appealing for an LBW from point.[74] However, Haigh and Frith present a fair summary of Bradman's overall contribution at this time:

Bradman's contribution to the continuity of personnel and keeping peace after the war, in fact, cannot be underestimated ... Bradman was not quite the unimpeachable figure he became; as captain, selector and board member as well as a player, a combination unprecedented in history, he presented an inviting target. He was criticised in 1946-47 for being too aggressive, too defensive, too tactful and too tough.[75]

Bradman went on to lead the Australians on 'The Invincibles' tour of 1948. Scott retired from Test umpiring at the end of what he called the nastiest and most acrimonious season he had ever experienced, adding that his decision had been prompted by unfair press criticism of his decisions during the series.[76] Two years later Scott was involved in a verbal slanging match with Jack Fingleton in the letters pages of the *Argus*. Fingleton had criticised both Bradman and the initial non-selection of Miller for the South African Tour.[77]

Comparison of Pepper with McCool, Tribe, Johnson and Other Australian Slow Bowlers

At the time of WWII, a new generation of promising young spinners arrived on the Australian cricket scene – Bruce Dooland (SA), Ian Johnson, Doug Ring and George Tribe (Victoria), Colin McCool (NSW and then Queensland) and Pepper (NSW). The intervening war meant five lost years in their careers and most were in their mid- to late-20s at the end of the war. From these players would come the replacements for Grimmett (retired 1941) and O'Reilly (retired 1946). There was conjecture as to who would be picked for the Australian tour of New Zealand (as discussed above) and the subsequent Ashes Tests against England in Australia in 1946/1947. Pepper was playing in Lancashire and there seemed little prospect of his return. The off-spinner Johnson, whose bowling had bewildered the Services batsmen in the match against Victoria at the St Kilda Cricket Ground in 1946, had toured New Zealand.[78] Would McCool be selected? O'Reilly provided his thoughts on the spin-bowling department:

The slow bowlers available are G. Tribe, B. Dooland, Ian Johnson, C. V. McCool and D. R. Cristofani. Tribe bowls left arm and turns well, either way, possessing a good googly. Dooland, a right hand spinner, has a handy knack of making the ball lift ... Johnson, a slow off-spinner can bowl well to his set field, spins the ball a lot and he thrives on plenty of hard work. McCool, who bowls really well on his day, is a handy all-rounder. In his first season with Queensland, when he shouldered full responsibility of the slow bowling department, he did remarkably well. Toshack, the medium-paced left arm stock bowler who can spin the ball either way is sure to be an asset to the final team.[79]

O'Reilly mentions Bob Cristofani, also a member of the Services team:

Cristofani bowls the leg-break and top-spinner well. He too, needs plenty of work … His experience in England with the Services team against many of this touring MCC team should be of great value if he gains selection in an Australian side.[80]

This latter statement could well have been made of Pepper, as a very valid reason for him to have been selected for the New Zealand tour and later, if he had been in contention, the Ashes team in 1946/1947. Table 3 shows the 1945/1946 statistics (wickets taken, runs scored) for the leg spin bowlers who would eventually replace O'Reilly. O'Reilly's figures are included for comparison as are those of Johnson, an off-spin bowler.[81]

Table 3. 1945/1946 batting and bowling figures.

Season 1945/1946	Team	Age in 1945	First-class matches team 1945/1946	Wickets	Runs scored
Bill O'Reilly	Australia, NSW	40	10	61	43
Doug Ring	Vic	27	-	–	–
Cec Pepper (1945)	Services XI	29	19	78	1039
Ian Johnson	Australia, Vic	28	10	31	370
Colin McCool	Australia, Qld	29	11	42	668
George Tribe	Vic	25	7	40	210
Bruce Dooland	Australia, SA	22	9	36	133
Bob Cristofani	Services XI, NSW	25	15	39	648

The Australian team for the Ashes Tour of 1953 included the promising young leg spinner Richie Benaud, but there was some criticism of Benaud's bowling from Bill O'Reilly.[82] Whitington also compared the merits of Pepper and Benaud:

Some who have watched Pepper and Richie Benaud at their best class Pepper as the more gifted and formidable … He turned his leg break further and more sharply than Benaud. His 'flipped' wrong-un was better disguised and came more swiftly from the pitch. His batting technique was far more correct … He was exactly the type of player whom Hassett needed in England in 1953, whom Ian Johnson would have welcomed in 1956. His loss to Australia was immeasurable and the manner of his virtual banishment was thoughtlessly and ruthlessly executed.[83]

While Whitington suggests that Pepper was 'the type of player Johnson would have welcomed', it is another matter to suggest that this may actually have been Pepper. By 1956 Pepper had reached the age of 40 and his career in the Lancashire League was on the decline. Ian Johnson himself was 39 and his cricket performances for the season were such that Sid Barnes wrote that Johnson was the 'non-playing captain'.[84] Johnson himself has written that he considered himself over the hill.[85] Jim Laker was a sprightly 34 when he produced his stellar performances in 1956. On the other hand, Richie Benaud was aged 26 and Tony Lock 27.

Postscript

The post-war period in Lancashire was a time when cricket loomed large in the social fabric. Mill workers and their families gained great pleasure from observing the exploits of the cricket professionals in the leagues every weekend. Pepper made a new home in

Lancashire in the gritty north of England, and he became an inspiration in Lancashire League cricket. In a sense, Pepper was continuing the work begun by the Services team. The real pity is that he was not doing it for Australia. In an obituary in the *Independent*, Derek Hodgson wrote:

> Pepper was welcomed joyfully into league cricket in northern England where his phenomenal rate of scoring runs and taking wickets, his tactical acumen and his ability to inspire his amateur colleagues made him a legendary performer.[86]

Hodgson also wrote of Pepper's 'bewildering variety of spinners' and his

> ... awareness that knowledge of the technique was reinforced by physical prowess, physique, an intuitive awareness of a batsman's weaknesses and an overpowering confidence. Even when a batsman got the better of him on the field, and there were not many of those, he would have beat them with his tongue, for no cricketer, ever, has had a sharper sense of humour.[87]

Pepper played for Rochdale in the Central Lancashire League (1946–1948) and for Burnley in the Lancashire League (1949–1953). He did the double twice, scoring 100 runs and taking 100 wickets in both of his first two seasons. In 1950 he took all 10 wickets in an innings twice within a fortnight.[88] At a time when there was something of a revolving door in the spin bowling department of the Australian cricket team, Pepper was taking wickets and making runs consistently in League cricket in Lancashire. While there is certainly a difference in standard between the Test arena and League cricket, Pepper's achievements with bat and ball at this time are the equivalent or better than those of Dooland and McCool when they played in the Leagues and compare favourably with Test players such as Vinoo Mankad, Everton Weekes and Clyde Walcott.[89] However, it was more than just runs and wickets – it was the way Pepper went about his cricket, as indicated by Joe Hamilton, the Rochdale secretary of the time:

> People would roll down to our ground in Dane St to see Cec Pepper hit the ball out of sight. He was magnificent to watch. We broke our gate receipts records every year for the three years he played for us, 1946-48. It was the tradition to take up a collection in a blanket if a player scored fifty or took five wickets and Pep did that on plenty of occasions. But after the game he was always the first to get to the bar and buy drinks all round.[90]

On the cricket field Pepper could be described as forthright and he was certainly less than politically correct, particularly in his approach to Indian and West Indian players. However, he did become a great friend of cricketers such as Frank Worrell and Garry Sobers. He brought Worrell a £1000 car during his Manchester University days, and Worrell paid him back later. And Pepper regularly paid off Sobers' gambling debts. The West Indian cricketer Collie Smith was also a great friend, and Pepper was present at Smith's bedside on the night of the fateful car accident.[91] Former Lancashire Schools Cricket coach Colin Dunkerley remembers:

> Cec was a very loud and unforgiving player on the cricket field but he was a respected chap who would help anyone. He delighted in accepting invitations to play in testimonial games for teammates or even cricketing opponents.[92]

In *The Slow Men*, David Frith wrote of Pepper:

> Never one to think twice before making a comment, such as at Commonwealth Tour of India in 1949 which he abandoned in disgust over umpiring standards before the scheduled end. He then set about carving a name for himself as an entertainer and draw card for various northern league clubs, belting fast fifties and hundreds for fat cash collections and zipping through his googlies and flippers to the mortification of inept batsman who tried to play him off the pitch.[93]

A verbal slanging match with the volatile Roy Gilchrist also confirmed that Pepper was never one for taking a backward step on the field.[94] Pepper was invariably a member of

'Best of' teams selected from ranks of professional cricketers in the Lancashire League.[95] Following his long career as a player, Pepper became a first-class umpire in 1964 and remained on the list until 1979. Typically, he would air his opinions on such matters as the selection of Test umpires and the throwing (chucking) controversy involving West Indian fast bowler Charlie Griffith.[96] Woodward states that:

> ... in 1965 he [Pepper] was thrust back into the limelight ... over the alleged reluctance of the MCC – which had led a campaign to stamp out 'chucking' – to challenge paceman Charlie Griffith during the tour by the West Indies two years earlier. A British newspaper published letters which showed that Pepper would have had no hesitation in no-balling Griffith, but that he had been encouraged to go easy.[97]

Conclusion

There is no doubting of Pepper's outstanding all-round abilities as a cricketer. On the evidence of his on-field performances with NSW and in particular with the Australian Services Team, the case is strong that he should have played Test cricket for Australia. Pepper died in Littleborough, Lancashire, in 1993, a larger than life character whose tumultuous cricket journey made him an unforgettable teammate and opponent. His *Wisden* obituary noted that 'no match involving Pepper ever pursued a peaceful course' but there was 'usually more humour than anger' and that 'many of the stories concerning Pepper mentioned his generosity'.[98] In 2010, in Keast Park in Parkes, a plaque and memorial bench were unveiled as permanent commemorations of Pepper's cricketing achievements.[99] In the words of Bradman: 'Another who showed every sign of being a great player was Cecil Pepper'.[100]

Acknowledgements

Sincere thanks to Deborah Crossing (Canberra, ACT), Bruce Coe (Australian Society for Sports History, ACT) and Robert Messenger (Australian Society for Sports History, ACT). Thanks also to Colin Clowes (NSW Cricket Association Library), Michael Greenwood (Parkes, NSW), Darryle Macdonald (Canberra, ACT), Tom Lowrey (Adelaide SA) and Colin Dunkerley (Lancashire, UK) who have provided information, and to the staff of the National Library of Australia and the State Library of NSW.

Notes

1. Tour programme, India, Australian Services X1, 1945, State Library of New South Wales.
2. Cited in Jaggard, "Forgotten Heroes," 62.
3. Ibid.
4. Ibid.
5. Pollard, *The Bradman Years*, 10.
6. Martin-Jenkins, *The Complete Who's Who*, 218.
7. Cotter, *The Ashes Captains*, 123.
8. Ibid., 124.
9. Ibid.
10. Moyes, *Australian Cricket*, 288.
11. Douglas, *Douglas Jardine*, 75.

SPORT, WAR AND SOCIETY IN AUSTRALIA AND NEW ZEALAND

12. Bradman, *The Bradman Albums*, 23; and *Adelaide Advertiser*, December 22, 1927, 13.
13. Prospect District Cricket Club, *Annual Report, 1934/35*. Private communication with club historian.
14. http://en.wikipedia.org/wiki/John_Scott_%28cricketer%29, accessed April 2013.
15. Greenwood, *The Grinstead Cup*, 23.
16. Email communication with Darryle Macdonald, April 2013.
17. Tindall, *Parkes*, 272.
18. *Sydney Morning Herald*, November 20, 1939, 13.
19. Email communication with NSW Cricket Association Library, April 17, 2013.
20. http://cricketarchive.com/Archive/Scorecards/17/17234.html, accessed April, 2013.
21. See the range of documents at http://cricketarchive.com/, accessed April 2013.
22. National Archives of Australia, "Records Search," http://recordsearch.naa.gov.au/NameSearch/Interface/ItemDetail.aspx?Barcode=4659481, accessed April 2013.
23. Cited in Harte and Whimpress, *A History of Australian Cricket*, 382.
24. Knox, *Bradman's War*, 11–2.
25. http://en.wikipedia.org/wiki/Charlie_Walker_%28cricketer,_born_1909%29, accessed April 2013.
26. *Wisden Cricketers' Almanack*, http://www.espncricinfo.com/england/content/player/12812.html, accessed April 2013.
27. Perry, *Miller's Luck*, 62.
28. Ibid., 102.
29. See Woodward, *Cricket, Not War*; and Jaggard, "Forgotten Heroes."
30. Ibid., 68–9.
31. http://en.wikipedia.org/wiki/Australian_Services_cricket_team
32. Perry, *Miller's Luck*, 128.
33. Knox, *Bradman's War*, 13.
34. Ibid., xiv.
35. Ibid., 11.
36. Cited in Fitzsimons, "Keith Miller," 524.
37. Perry, *Miller's Luck*, 108.
38. Whitington, *Keith Miller*, 73.
39. Ibid., 74.
40. Ibid., 76.
41. On several occasions Whitington was a co-author with his close friend Miller.
42. Cited in Whitington, *Keith Miller*, 103.
43. Ibid.
44. Cited in Jaggard, "Review of Ian Woodward," 157.
45. Jaggard, "Forgotten Heroes," 67.
46. Edrich, *Cricket Heritage*, 46.
47. http://www.espncricinfo.com/england/content/player/7104.html, accessed April 2013.
48. Woodward, *Cricket, Not War*, 77, and also described in some detail in Chapter 9 of Miller and Whitington, *Cricket Caravan*.
49. Woodward, *Cricket, Not War*, 83.
50. Whitington, *Keith Miller*, 104.
51. *Adelaide Advertiser*, January 1, 1946, 3.
52. Miller, *Cricket Crossfire*, 25.
53. Cited in Haigh and Frith, *Inside Story*, 97–9.
54. Ibid., 99.
55. Ibid.
56. Miller, *Cricket Crossfire*, 25–6.
57. *Adelaide Mail*, January 19, 1946, 3.
58. Haigh and Frith, *Inside Story*, 99.
59. Miller, *Cricket Crossfire*, 26.
60. Perry, *Bradman's Invincibles*, 318.
61. http://cricketarchive.com/Archive/Events/1/Australia_in_New_Zealand_1945-46.html, accessed April 2013.
62. Robinson and Haigh, *On Top Down Under*, 218.
63. Cited in Perry, *Miller's Luck*, 132.

SPORT, WAR AND SOCIETY IN AUSTRALIA AND NEW ZEALAND

64. Knox, *Bradman's War*, 11.
65. Bradman, *Farewell to Cricket*, 120.
66. Cited in Ibid.
67. Cited in Whitington, *Keith Miller*, 111.
68. Ibid.
69. Ibid.
70. Knox, *Bradman's War*, 40.
71. Ibid.
72. Ibid., 41.
73. Quoted in *Wisden*, 2003, 1671.
74. Cited in Knox, *Bradman's War*, 48.
75. Haigh and Frith, *Inside Story*, 100.
76. *Barrier Miner*, March 7, 1947, 1.
77. *Argus*, October 24, 1949, 1, and also *Argus*, October 27, 1949, 2.
78. Woodward, *Cricket, Not War*, 86.
79. *Sydney Morning Herald*, September 28, 1946, 9.
80. Ibid.
81. See the range of documents at http://cricketarchive.com/, accessed April 2013.
82. *Sydney Morning Herald*, July 2, 1953, 9, and also *Sydney Morning Herald*, July 30, 1953, 9.
83. Whitington, *Keith Miller*, 104.
84. Smith, *Cricket's Enigma*, 187.
85. Haigh, *The Summer Game*, 99.
86. http://www.independent.co.uk/news/people/obituary-cecil-pepper-1456497.html, accessed April 2013.
87. Ibid.
88. Woodward, *Cricket, Not War*, 96.
89. http://cricketarchive.com/Archive/Events/8/Lancashire_League_1953/, accessed April 2013.
90. *Sunday Telegraph*, May 18, 1986.
91. Stephen Thorpe, *Wisden Cricket Monthly*, 1989, http://www.espncricinfo.com/wcm/content/story/70793.html.
92. Colin Dunkerley, personal email communication.
93. Frith, *The Slow Men*, 124.
94. http://www.manchestereveningnews.co.uk/news/nostalgia/crickets-original-bad-boy–927037, accessed April 2013.
95. *Manchester Evening News*, August 13, 2007.
96. Stephen Thorpe, *Wisden Cricket Monthly*, 1989, http://www.espncricinfo.com/wcm/content/story/70793.html.
97. Woodward, *Cricket, Not War*, 125.
98. *Wisden*, 1994, 1350.
99. http://www.nswalp.com/getattachment/d8e8bd3d-1416-489d-b1e1-16201137eb89/country/, accessed April 2013.
100. Bradman, *Farewell to Cricket*, 117.

References

Bradman, Donald. *The Bradman Albums: Selections from Sir Donald Bradman's Official Collection. Vol. 1 (1925–1934)*. Sydney: Rigby, 1987.
Bradman, Don. *Farewell to Cricket*. London: Hodder & Stoughton, 1950.
Cotter, Gerry. *The Ashes Captains*. Sydney: Hutchinson, 1989.
Douglas, Christopher. *Douglas Jardine: Spartan Cricketer*. London: Allen & Unwin, 1984.
Edrich, W. J. *Cricket Heritage*. London: Stanley Paul, 1948.
Fitzsimons, Peter. "Keith Miller." In *The Best Ever Australian Sports Writing*, edited by Dave Headon, 523–526. Melbourne: Black, 2001.
Frith, David. *The Slow Men*. London: Allen & Unwin, 1984.
Greenwood, Michael J. *The Grinstead Cup*. Dubbo: Masterprint, 1985.
Haigh, Gideon. *The Summer Game: Cricket in Australia in the 50s and 60s*. Sydney: Australian Broadcasting Corporation, 2006.

Haigh, Gideon, and David Frith. *Inside Story: Unlocking Australian Cricket's Archives*. Melbourne: News Custom, 2007.

Harte, Chris, and Bernard Whimpress. *A History of Australian Cricket*. London: Andre Deutsch, 1993.

Jaggard, Ed. "Forgotten Heroes: The 1945 Australian Services Cricket Team." *Sporting Traditions* 12, no. 2 (May 1996): 61–79.

Jaggard, Ed. "Review of Ian Woodward, *Cricket, Not War: The Australian Services XI and the "Victory Tests" of 1945*." *Sporting Traditions* 12, no. 2 (May 1996): 156–158.

Knox, Malcolm. *Bradman's War*. Melbourne: Viking, 2012.

Martin-Jenkins, Christopher. *The Complete Who's Who of Test Cricketers*. Sydney: Rigby, 1980.

Miller, Keith. *Cricket Crossfire*. London: Oldbourne Press, 1956.

Miller, Keith, and R. S. Whitington. *Cricket Caravan*. London: Latimer House, 1950.

Moyes, A. G. *Australian Cricket: A History*. Sydney: Angus and Robertson, 1959.

Perry, Roland. *Bradman's Invincibles*. Sydney: Hatchett Australia, 2008.

Perry, Roland. *Miller's Luck: The Life and Loves of Keith Miller, Australia's Greatest All-Rounder*. Sydney: Random House, 2005.

Pollard, Jack. *The Bradman Years: Australian Cricket, 1918–48*. North Ryde: HarperCollins, 1988.

Robinson, Ray, and Gideon Haigh. *On Top Down Under*. Kent Town: Wakefield, 1975.

Smith, Rick. *Cricket's Enigma: The Sid Barnes Story*. Sydney: Australian Broadcasting Corporation, 1999.

Tindall, Ron, ed. *Parkes: 100 Years of Local Government*. Netley: Griffin Press, 1982.

Whitington, R. S. *Keith Miller: The Golden Nugget*. Sydney: Rigby, 1981.

Woodward, Ian. *Cricket, Not War: The Australian Services XI and the "Victory Tests" of 1945*. Melbourne: SMK Enterprises, 1994.

Index

Note:
Page numbers in **bold** type refer to figures
Page numbers in *italic* type refer to tables
Page numbers followed by 'n' refer to notes

Adam-Smith, P. 32
Addington railway workshops (NZ) 82
Adelaide Oval 106
Adie, K. 33
Advertiser (Adelaide) 44, 125
Afghan cameleers 75
Afyon POW camp 72–3
Alderson, Lt Col E.A.H. 8
Aldrich, R.J.F. 86–7
All Blacks rugby team: allowed defaulters to
    play 88–9; and Bill Carson 111–18; double
    (rugby and cricket) 114
Allen, James 84
American Expeditionary Forces 27
American forces 4
Amos, H. 59
Anderson, Bob 57
Andrews, Allan 112; manager of The Kiwis
    112–13
Andrews, E.M. 58
angling 8
anti-militarism 81; strands 82
Anti-Militarist League 82
Antwerp Olympic Games (1920) 28
Anzac Day 33, 45n, 53, 64n, 84
Anzac Illusion (Andrews) 58
Anzac Muster, An (Smart and Wood) 32
Anzac significance to POWs 68–9
Anzac troops 38, 42
archives 35
Argus (Melbourne) 25, 60, 128; soccer
    resumption (1919) 60; Wilding-Fairbairn
    heroes enlistment call 25, 29n
Argyllshire Volunteers 11
Ariotti, K.: and Crotty, M. 68–80
Armstrong, Warwick 120
Army Council 8
Army Football Association 7; annual Cup 12
Army Gymnastics 12

Arnold, Frank 55
Arras Flying Services Memorial 24
Artillery Regiment (22nd) 103
Ashes 61, 70, 107, 129
Ashes Captains, The (Cotter) 120
Ashes (Gibb-Campbell cigars) 61–2
athleticism 5–7, 10–13; cult 9; games
    fanaticism 6–7; ideology and influence 10;
    and masculinity 10; and militarism link 5–7;
    practical 11
*Athleticism in the Victorian and Edwardian
    Public School* (Mangan) 5
athletics 19, 68; carnivals 69; 100-yard dash 68;
    long jump 68; New Zealand Amateur
    Association 87; Olympic team 20; shot put
    68; track 19
Auckland 84
Australasian Davis Cup 111
Australian Comforts Fund 34
Australian Flying Corps 73
Australian Imperial Force (AIF) 1, 27, 52–4,
    57–8, 70, 120; Ballarat citizen tree planting 37;
    as deeply racist 75; Field Artillery Brigade (1st
    Div) 24; 19th Battalion (2nd Div, Sportsmen's
    Unit) 24–6, 34, 53; Second Reception Group
    122; Sports Control Board 26–7
Australian and New Zealand Army Corps
    (Anzacs) 1, 32, 58; Anzac Day 33, 45n, 53,
    64n, 84; and Anzac legend 32, 45n, 53;
    British-born percentage 58; studies 33
Australian Research Council: Anzac studies/
    projects 33
Australian Services Team (cricket): and Cec
    Pepper 119–33; during WWI 120; during
    WWII 122–5; India tour 125; members 120,
    123; and New Zealand tour 126–7
Australian Society for Sports History (ASSH)
    1–2; Sporting Traditions XIX 1
Australian War Memorial (AWM) 1, 54, 61

INDEX

Australia's War 1914-18, Gender and War (Damousi and Lake) 33

Baden-Powell, Robert 8
badminton: *burfu* played at Afyon camp 72
Bailes, Tich 55
Baker, Reginald 20
Balsdon, J.W. 59
Barassi line 54, 65n
Barnard, L. 39
Barnes, Sid 129
baseball 101
basketball 4, 70
Baxter, A. 83
Bean, C.E.W. 58
Beaumont, J. 32, 69, 78n
Belemedik POW camp 72, 76
Bell, H.A. 59
Bellenden Road Board School 11
Bell's Life 8
Benaud, Richie 129
Bennett, F.C. (Chester) 125
Bennett, Gordon 70
Berlin Olympic Games (1916) 25, 28
Berlin-Baghdad Railway project 72
Best, G. 5–8
Beyond the Metaphor (Blair) 53
Bing Girls 41
Blackburn, K. 69–71, 78n
Blair, D. 53–4
Blamey, Field Marshal Sir Thomas 123
Blunt, H. 40
Boan, Harry 36–8; elected as Member of Parliament 37; store and women's football team 35–8, **36**
Boardman, Leslie 22
Borwick, George 127
boxing 12, 20, 27–8, 55, 69, 72
Bradman, Donald 119–21, 125–8, 131; and Invincibles Tour (1948) 128; refusal to walk 127–8
Briggs, M. 83
British Commonwealth 96
British Empire 23, 97
British Football Association 61–2
British forces 3
British National Archives 33, 46n
British prisoners-of-war 75–6
Broken Nation (Beaumont) 32
Brown, Bill 123, 127
Brown, H.A.R (Farmer) 115
Brown, Jack 55
Brown, James 72
Buck, H. 86
Burdekin, Beaufort 21, 26
Burke, P. 34–5, 39
Burma-Thai Railway 70
Burra Record 40

Caffyn, Marshall 55
Caledonians Club 59, 63
Cambridge University 27
Campbell, George 62
Campbell, J.D. 12, 111, 114, 117
Campbell, Maj R.B. 12
Camperdown Chronicle 54
camps in Turkey 71–6
Canberra Comets 121
Canterbury Rugby Football Union 85
Carlton Football Ground 96, 103–5; and Recreation Committee 108
Carlyon, L. 32
Carmody, Keith 70, 123
carnivals: athletics 69
Carpenter, Stanley F.: Victoria Cross recommendation 54
Cashman, R. 62
Cavalry Division (2nd) 103
Cecil Healy: In Memoriam 25; profits invested in War Loan Bonds 25
Champion, Malcolm 22
Changi prison 69–74; Australianness 71; Brownlow Medal 71; inmates moved to labour camps 70
Chappell, Greg 125
Chappell, Ian 125
Charles Moore and Company (women's football) 44, 47n
Cheetham, Albert 123
Chemical Warfare Service (US) 107
Christadelphians 83
Christchurch Magistrates Court 86
Christmas/New Year activities 73
Church of Christ 37
civil rights deprivation 86–7
Cliffe, C. 72
Cliffe, W. 72
Cliverd, R. 9
Coe, B. 19–31
Colditz Castle (POW camp) 73
Collingwood Football Club 103–4, 105
Collins, Herbert 120–1
Commonwealth Clothing Factory 37–9; Bugle Band 39; as fund raisers 39; Khaki Girls football team 37–9, 44; Physical Culture Squad 39; Rifle Squad 39
Compton, Denis 123
compulsory military training (CMT) 82–7, 90; register failure and convictions 82; reinstated after war 86; resister terms 84
conduct and fair play 5
Cook, Joseph 24
Coombes, D. 76
Corio Oval (Geelong) 103
Cotter, Albert (Tibby) 25–6; killed at Beersheba 26

INDEX

Cotter, G. 120
Cousens, Syd 62
Crapp, Harry 36
Creedon, D. 73
cricket 4–7, 19, 25–6, 85–6, 112; Ashes 61, 70, 107; Australian Board of Control 96; and double All Black Bill Carson 111–18; New Zealand Council 87; and prisoners-of-war 69–72; Sheffield Shield 96; Stalag Luft III Sagan team 70; venues used for troop training/accommodation 104–8
Crimean War (1853–6) 74
Cristofani, Bob 123, 128–9
Crossing, P. 119–34
Crotty, M.: and Ariotti, K. 68–80
cultural memory 51–4
cultural superiority/identity 69–71, 74–7
Curtin, J. 97, 98, 100–2, 108–9, 123
cycling 56

Daily Herald (Adelaide) 43
Daily News 58; and soccer team volunteers 58–9
Daily News (Perth) 19
Damousi, J.: and Lake, M. 33
Davus Cup 111
Dedman, J. 98; *List of Reserved Occupations* Directorate 98
defaulters camps 82
Delpratt, M. 68–9, 76, 79n
Derwentside 52, 63, 64n
Dexter, Jack 27
Dinkum Aussie 52, 64n
Disher, H.C. 27
diving 20
Dockerty, Harry 60
dog racing 100
Dooland, Bruce 125–30; and Cec Pepper comparison 128–9
Dundasch, A. 62
Dunkerley, Colin 130
Dunstan, A. 98
Durack, Sarah (Fanny) 20–3
Durant, H. 9

E. Lucas and Company 37–9; founder 37–8; women's football team 37–9, **38**, 45
East Newcastle Club (soccer) 54
Easter festivity events 68, 76
Edinburgh University 7
Edrich, Bill 122–4, 128
egg-and-spoon race 68
Egypt 1, 32, 59, 73, 123
Eisenhower, Pres Dwight 113
elementary schools 10–11
Ellis, Reg 123
Emerald Hill Record 55–6, 60

enlistment: for military service 98; and soccer teams 58–61
equestrianism 8
equipment supplies 70–2
Essendon Football Club 96, 104
Etherington-Smith, Raymond 20
Eton College 8
Euroa Advertiser 57
Euroa Magpies Australian Rules FC 57
Evans, H.L. 88
Excelsiors 41
exhibition games: women's football 37–8, 44

fair play 5, 10–11
Fairbrother, D.G. 89–90
Farnes, Ken 123
fencing 8–9, 12
Field Artillery Regiment (4th) 116
Fielding Star 85
Fingleton, Jack 122, 128
Fitzhardinge, Roger 26
foot beagling 8
football 3–4, 7, 10, 19, 72–4, 85; Association (FA) cup 7; Christmas day match (1914) 3–4; elementary school 10–11; matches 7; New Zealand Association 87; Patriotic League 40; policies during WWII 98–102; and regimental identity 12; as security risk 99; Third Lanark FC 11; Wellington Association 90; women's 32–48
football, Australian Rules 32–48, 47n, 53–6, 69; League 53; mobbing 53; prisoner-of-war league (Hohenfels) 70; Roll of Honour 55; and women 32–48
football grounds access 51–2
Football Record 56
Footscray Football Ground 96, 103–4, 107–8; Harriers 105
forfeit of sporting rights to compete 81, 84–90
Forgotten Heroes (Jaggard) 120
Foy and Gibson team 35–7
Frances, R. 38; and Scates, B. 38–9
Free Lance 86
Freedom League 82
French, D. 12
French prisoners-of-war 75–6
Freyberg, Gen Bernard 111–13, 117; Distinguished Service Order 112
Frith, D. 130; and Haigh, G. 126–8
Front: reports/letters from 54–8
Fry, Charles Burgess 19
Fuller, J.F.C. 13, 113
fund-raisers 37–41, 44

Gallagher, Dave 89,111; Trophy (rugby) 111
Gallipoli (1915) 1, 23–8, 32–4, 58, 82, 112; letters from the Front 55; soccer players/ volunteers 59–62

INDEX

Galway, Lady Marie 43
gambling 81, 100
Games Cult 5–7
games fanaticism 6–7
Gammage, W. 32
Gates of Memory (Lucking) 32
George V, King of England 27
Geraldton: soccer resumption (1919) 59–60
Geraldton Association 59–60
Geraldton Guardian 57
Germany 23, 69; Catspaw (Turkey) 74; forces
   3; and prisoners-of-war 69–70, 74–7
Gibb, Alec 62
Gilchrist, Roy 130
Gill, F.M. 59
Girls' Carnival 42–3, 48n
Godfree, D. 9
Godley, A. 112
golf 69
Grace, W.G. 126
Grand Challenge Cup (rowing) 20–1
Great War (First World War, 1914–18) 1,
   12–13, 111; Australasia's Olympians (1912)
   19–31; and Australian soccer 51–66; declared
   (Aug 4) 23; enlistment rate 23–4; prisoners
   and sport 68–79; and sporting myths 3–16
Greece 74, 113, 117
Greenwood, M. 121
Gregory, Jack 120
Grey River Argus 86–8
Greymouth 88
Griffith, Charlie 131
Grimmett, Clarrie 126
Grinstead Cup (Greenwood) 121
Groom, C. 62–3
gymnastics 4, 12

Hadfield, Darcy 112
Hague Conventions (1907) 72
Haig, Field-Marshall Douglas 12
Haigh, G.: and Frith, D. 126–8
Hamence, Ron 125
Hamilton, Joe 130
Hammond, Wally 123, 128
Handsley, G. 73
Hardwick, Harold 19, 22–3, 27–8; and boxing
   23; as Ideal Sportsman of the Empire 27
Hassett, Lindsay 123–7
Hauenstein, Harry 26–7; Military Medal 26–8
Hawthorn Football Club/Ground 102–4
Healy, Cecil 19; killed in battle (Mont St
   Quentin) 25–6; 19th Battalion 25; Olympic
   and Great War swimmer 22–6; *Peace of
   Europe* article 23–5; photo album and
   inscription 26; Royal Army Medical Corps
   Lieutenant 26; as volunteer 25
Healy, Leo 61
Heck, S. 9

Helms World Trophies 30n
Heritage, Keith 21, 24, 25; Military Cross 24–5,
   28
Hess, R. 32–50
Hickey, C. 11; and Mangan, J.A. 10–11
Hiskins, Poddy 55
Hiskins, Stan 56
HMAS: *Australia* 57; *Kuttabul* 106; *Sydney* 97
HMS: *Hunter* 61; *Prince of Wales* 97; *Repulse*
   97; *Swiftsure* 57
100-yard dash 68
Hobson, E. 76
hockey 70–2, 85
Hodgson, Derek 130
Hohenfels POW camp 70
Hollies, Eric 124
Holmes, Errol 124
Holmes, R. 13
Holt, R. 120
horse racing 81, 85, 100
Howlett, Miss G. 36
hunting 8
Huszagh, Kenneth 22
Hutt Club 86
Hutton, Len 123

identity 34
Ikin, Jack 127
imprisonment 90, 92n
Independent 130
Indian prisoners-of-war 75–6
Inside Story 126
Inter-Allied Games 27, 112
International Journal of the History of Sport 1
International Olympic Committee (IOC) 21
Ireland 24; Easter Uprising (1916) 24
Islam 74–5; and Australia's contact with
   Muslim world 75
Italy 112, 116

Jack, J.F. 59
Jackson, L. 11
Jaggard, Ed 120, 123–4
James Marshall and Company (women's
   football) 44
Japan 68–72, 103; advances halted/codes
   cracked 106; Australian mainland bombings
   (1942–3) 97; impact on war 97–8; Pearl
   Harbor attack (1941) 97; and prisoners-of-
   war sports 69–70, 74, 77; victory in
   Southeast Asia 71
Jeans, C. 59
Jennings, A.R. 103
Jess, Brigadier-General Carl 26
John, S. 4
Johnson, Ian 123, 127; and Cec Pepper
   comparison 128–9
Johnson, Keith 125–6

INDEX

Johnson, R.S. 86
Jones, E.H. 72
Jones, T. 57

Kahanamoku, Duke Paoa 22
Kane, Father Paul 88
Kardinia Park 103
Kay, J.: and Vamplew, W. 8
Kedos officer's camp 73–4
Kelleway, Charles 120
Kelly, Frederick Septimus 20; Distinguished
    Service Cross 24
Kelly, William 24
Kennedy, B. 94–110
Kerr, G. 73
Kerrigan, C. 10–11
Khaki Girls (Commonwealth Clothing Factory)
    37–9
Kipling, Rudyard 117
Kippenberger, Col Howard 113
Kitchener, Lord Herbert 82
Klein, Y. 33
Knox, Maj Gen Alfred 8, 124
Kormoran (German cruiser) 97

Laidlaw, Wal 55–6
Lake, M. 76; and Damousi, J. 33; and
    Reynolds, H. 33
Laker, Jim 129
Landis, K.M. 101
Le Journal 25
Leander Club (rowing) 20
Leveson-Gowers, H.D.G. 124
life skills 6
Lindwall, Ray 123, 127
Liston, J.J. 108
Littlejohn, Charles 21, 26, 29n; Military Cross
    26
Lock, Tony 129
London Hospital Medical College 21–2
Lone Hand 22
long jump 68
Longworth, Billy 19, 22–3; and AIF Sports
    Control Board 27
Lowerson, J. 8
Lowrey, Joe 55
Lucas Girls (E. Lucas and Company) 37–9, **38**
Lucking, T. 32

MacArthur, Gen Douglas 98, 106
McBrien, Likely 100–4
McCabe, Stan 122
McCartney, Miss N. 41
McConnell, L.C. 111–18
McCool, Colin 123, 127–30; and Cec Pepper
    comparison 128–9
Macdonald, Darryle 121
McDonald, Ted 120

McKane, A.H. 88
McKernan, M. 32
McManns, J. 63
McVilly, Cecil 21–3, 28
Malaysia 70, 74
Maleme Airfield 113
Manawatu Rugby Union 85–6
Mangan, J.A. 5–9, 13; and Hickey, C. 10–11
Mankad, Vinoo 130
Mannix, Dr Daniel 99
Manuka Oval Ground (Canberra) 121
Mareth Battle (1943) 116
Marks, E.S. 22–3, 28
Marlborough College 6
Marylebone Cricket Club (MCC) 123, 127
masculinity 10
Mason, Daniel 112
Mason, T.: and Riedi, E. 4, 9, 12–13
Melbourne 106–7
Melbourne Cricket Ground (MCG) 104, 107–8;
    as Camp Murphy (US Air Force) 104–5
Melbourne Cup 71
Melbourne Football Clubs 96, 102–4
Menzies, Prime Minister Robert 96, 122
Mercier, Cardinal 28
Mercury (Hobart) 52, 60
Merrick, James 21
Mesopotamia 73
Mettam, George 27
Middleton, Sydney 20, 23–7; Distinguished
    Service Order 26–8; 19th Battalion 26;
    Officer of the Most Excellent Order of the
    British Empire 27; as organising secretary of
    AIF Sports Control Board 26–7; rank and
    Mentioned in Dispatches 26
Mildura: two-team soccer competition 63
militant mining communities 83
militarism 5–7, 23; drill 10; king and country
    principles 12; poetry as promotion 4–6;
    training and sport 10–13
Miller, Keith (Nugget) 123–8
Miller, Lt Col E.D. 8
Mills, Bert 55
Monteath, P. 69–70
Moran, Paddy 23–4
Morris, Arthur 123
Mosley, E.D. 89
Moyes, J. 120
multi-national sporting competition 68
Munro Ferguson, Gov Gen Ronald 43
Munro Ferguson, Lady Helen 43
Murray, William 21, 27

national curriculum 10
Naval and Military Expeditionary Forces 24
Neale, J.S. 59
Nelson, Dr B. 1
Nelson, H. 69–71, 78n

INDEX

New British Cemetery (Assevillers) 25
New History of Soccer (Reynolds) 58
New York Times 25
New Zealand 81–92; Amateur Athletics
 Association 87; Athletic and Cycling Union
 87; Boxing Council 86; and compulsory
 military training (CMT) 82–4; conscientious
 objectors (1916–23) 81–92; Defence Act
 (1909) 82; Defence Amendment Act 86;
 defence capability 82; Expeditionary Force
 Reserve 82; Farmers' Union 84; Labour party
 82, 88; Military Service Act (1916) 82–3;
 Military Service Amendment Act (1920) 84;
 National Register (volunteers) 82; Peace
 Council 82; Returned Soldier's Association
 (RSA) 81–90; Rugby Football Union 85;
 sporting associations support for RSA 87–9;
 10th Division (infantillery) 113
Newbolt, H. 4–5, 9, 15n
Ngakawau Miners Union: politics and no place
 in sport (dissenters) 88–90
Noblet, Geff 125
non-volunteers 24
North Africa 74
North Port Oval 103
North *vs.* South Adelaide game 42–3
novelty/fancy dress matches 41
Nunn, H. 86

officer sports 7
Old Wykehamists 7
Oldfield, William 120
Oldridge Road Board School (Balham) 11
Olympians 19–31; at War 22–6; post-war sport
 26–8
Olympic Games 8–9
Oppenheimer, Melanie 43
O'Reilly, Bill 122, 127–9
Otago Rugby Football Union 86
Ottoman Empire 74
Oxford University: rowers 21

Palmerston North 84
Passive Resisters' Union 82
Paterson, G.C. 121
Patriotic Fund 36, 101; and football income
 surpluses 95
patriotism 38–9; and women's football 38–9, 42
Pellew, Nip 120
pentathlon 8–9
Perry, R. 71
Pershing, Gen John 27
Perth team volunteers 58–9
Petain, Marshal Philippe 112
Pfeiffer, W. 90
Phillips, Murray 34, 53
pig-sticking 8
Playford, T. 100

Plugge, Lt-Col Arthur 112
polo 8
Pommy schoolteachers 52, 64n
Pope, Arthur 114–16
Port Melbourne Football Club 103
Potter, Col H.R. 83
Pozieres British Cemetery 25
Press, The 85
Prospect District Cricket Club (SA) 121

Quakers 83

RAAF *vs.* British Services (Lords 1944) 123
racial inferiority: to POW captives 74–7
racism 74–7
Randall, W. 74
Red Cross Society 33–4, 70–2; Australian 43,
 46n, 72; Ballarat East 37; German and
 Samaritan 43; women's football games 42–4
Red Federation 82
Referee (Sydney) 21
Register (Adelaide) 44, 54; *Feminine Football*
 article 44
rehabilitation schemes 83–4
Reid, Pat: escape from Colditz 73
religious issues 74
Returned Soldier's Association (RSA): and
 Anzac Day 84
Reynolds, H.: and Lake, M. 33
Reynolds, P.S. 58
Richardson, J. 57
Riedi, E.: and Mason, T. 4, 9, 12–13
Ring, Doug 123; and Cec Pepper comparison
 128–9
Rīpapa Island defaulters' camp (Christchurch)
 82
RMS *Osterley* 19, 28, 30n; Olympic team
 19–20
Robinson, W.: dissenter who played for All
 Blacks 89–90
Robson, L.L. 32
Roosevelt, Pres Theodore 101; Green Light
 Letter 101, 109
Rosendale Road Board School (Lambeth) 11
Ross, Claude Murray 24
Ross, Roderick 24
Ross-Soden, Harry 27
rowing 19–28; Council of New Zealand
 Association 87; King's Cup 27; Olympic
 team 20; Oxford-Cambridge Boat Race
 (1914) 26; and war 23–6
Royal Air Force (RAF) 123
Royal Artillery (RA) 13
Royal Australian Air Force (RAAF) 24, 107,
 123
Royal Australian Army Medical Corps
 (RAAMC) 26, 72
Royal Engineers (RE) 7

INDEX

Royal Flying Corps (RFC) 24
Royal Henley Regatta 20–1, 24; Diamond
  Challenge Sculls 21–3; Grand Challenge Cup
  24; Peace 26, 112
Royal London Hospital Archives 26; photo
  album of Stockholm (1912) 26
Royal Marines (RM) 25
Royal Naval Division (RND) 24; Hood
  Battalion 24
Rue-des-Berceaux Cemetery (Richebourg
  L'Avoue) 25
rugby 5, 22–3, 55–6, 107; All Blacks (NZ)
  88–9, 111–18; codes 54; and conscientious
  objectors 85–6; Dave Gallagher Trophy 111;
  Hawksbay and Auckland 90; National
  League 24, 53; New South Wales 54; New
  Zealand RFU 85, 89; and prisoners-of-war
  69–71; Union 27, 88; Wellington (NZ) 88
Rugby School 8
running 8–9; cross-country 12
Russell, Maj Gen Andrew 83
Russian prisoners-of-war 75–6
Ryan, Edward J. 56–7
Ryan, G. 81–93

sacred playing field 5
Saddleworth Total Abstinence Society 40;
  picnic and ladies football game 40, 47n
Sage, A. 59
St Kilda: Cricket Ground 128; Football Ground
  96, 103–4, 107–8
Salt, J. 74
Samoa 82
Scates, B.: and Frances, R. 38–9
Schryver, Frank 28; Distinguished Conduct
  Medal and MM 28
Scott, J.G. 59–60
Scott, John (Jack) 119–21, 125–7
Second New Zealand Expeditionary Force (2nd
  NZEF) 111, 116; games and sports 116;
  sportsmen members 111
Seventh Day Adventists 83
Sherbourne School 5
shooting 7–9; public schools tournament
  (Ashburton Shield) 7
shot put 68
Shrewsbury School 7
Sick Man of Europe 74
Simpson, Mrs A.A. 43
Sinclair, Colin 116
Singapore 70, 74; fall of (1942) 71
Sismey, Stan 123–5
skiing 73
skills: transferability 7–9
Sloss, Bruce 55
Slow Men, The (Frith) 130
Smart, J.: and Wood, T. 32
Smedley, Albert 27

Smith, Collie 130
Smith, J. 86
Smith-Dorran, Gen H. 5; Harrow speech (1917)
  5
Sobers, Garry 130
Sobocinska, A. 71
Soccer Anzacs (Williamson) 58, 63
social engineering 5
Soldiers' Fund 41
Soldiers and Sportsmen (AIF) 26
South African War (1899–1902) 10, 82
South Australia: women's football 39–44, **42**,
  47n
South Australian Cricket Association 126
South Australian National Football League 40
South Barwon Shire 103
South Melbourne Football Ground 55, 104–8
Southland 84
Sport newspaper 26
sport and war 3–18; Australian government and
  professionals 101; evidence and actuality 13;
  facts, myths and conventional wisdom 3–4;
  opposing views on participation during
  wartime 96–9; and other ranks 9–13; public
  school preparation 4–7; sporting skills
  transferability 7–9
sporting competitions: POW 69–74
sporting shirkers 81
SS *Bloemfontein* 123
Stalag Luft III Sagan 70
Stanford, Ross 123
Stanley, P. 75
State Library of South Australia, Searcy
  Collection 43–4
Stedman, Ivan 27
steeplechasing 8
Stephen, M. 43
Stephenson, P. 75
Stevens, C. 75
Stewart, William Allan 21–3, 26; medical
  student and athlete 22–3; rugby player 22–3
stigma 87
Stipendiary Magistrate V.G. Day 86
Stubbs, S. 59
Sun-Herald (Sydney) 62
Sunday Times (Sydney) 23–5
Sunshine Advocate (Melbourne) 52
surf life-saving 70
Sutherland Highlanders (93rd) 7
swimming 8–9, 12, 19–23, 27, 74; controversy
  22; freestyle 22; International Jury 22; New
  Zealand Council 88, 91n; Olympic team
  20–2
Sydney Cricket Ground (SCG) 106
Sydney Morning Herald 61–2, 74; report on
  Cecil Pepper 121–2
Sydney Rowing Club 20
Syson, I. 51–67

INDEX

Talbot, W.G. 87
Tallon, W. 121
Taranaki Regimental District 86
Tartakover, Theo 20–3; New South Wales Agent-General 21
Tasmania 60
Taylor, Johnny 120
team games 10–11; moral values 10; and prisoners-of-war 69
tennis 21, 70; Wimbledon 21
Third Lanarkshire Rifle Volunteers 11
Thompson, W.D. (Tillie) 37
Times, The 124
Timms, J.G. 10–11
tobogganing 73
Toowoomba British Football Association 62–3
Toshack, Ernie 127–9
training colleges 10
Trentham Military Camp 83
Tribe, George 128
Turner, Les 56
Twomey, C. 69

University Oval (Adelaide) 41
Unomi (Perth soccer journalist) 59, 62

Vamplew, W. 1, 3–18; and Kay, J. 8
Victorian British Football Association 60
Victorian Football Association (VFA) 94
Viewless Winds (Moran) 23–4
Vitai Lampada (Newbolt) 4–7; Abu Klea Battle (Sudan 1885) 6; jammed Gatling 4–6
Voce, Bill 127
Volunteer Rifle Corps 11
volunteers 10; enlistment call 25; National Register (NZ) 82; organizations 33; rifle brigades 11

Waitemata (troopship) 83
Walcott, Clyde 130
Walker, Charlie 123
walking 21
Wallabies (rowing) 20, 23–4
war employment planning 98; impact on sports and competitions 98–109; *Schedule of Reserved Occupations and Industrial Priorities* 98
War Pennant and War Services Cup 101

Ward, Hugh 20–1, 24; Boat Race (1913) 23; Military Cross 28; Olympic rower 20–1; Rhodes Scholar 21; studied at Oxford 21–3
Ward, Sir Joseph 82
Warner, Sir Pelham 123
Warwick Examiner and Times 54
Washbrook, Cyril 123
Webb, Paddy (Labour MP NZ) 83
Webb, R.C. 60
Weekes, Everton 130
Wellington 84–6
Wellington, Arthur Wellesley (Duke of) 113
Wellington Cricket Association (NZ) 86
West Coast Rugby Union (NZ) 88
Western Australia and Victoria women's football 33–9
Western Mail 36
What's Wrong with Anzac? (Lake and Reynolds) 33
White, T. 73
Whitington, Richard 123–9
Wilding, Anthony 21, 24–5, 29n, 111; killed in action Neuve Chappelle 25
Williams, Graham 123–4
Williamson, J. 58, 63
Williamstown: women's football 37, 47n
Wilson, W.J. 10
Winchester College 7
Winning (Woodward) 112
Winter, Jay 32
Wood, T.: and Smart, J. 32
Woodcock, Ashley 125
Woodward, Ian 123–4, 131
Woodward, Sir Clive 112
Woolley, C. 73
Woolloongabba Cricket Ground (Brisbane) 106–7
Workers' Memorial Fund 32
workplace: women's football matches 35–9, 44
World War I *see* Great War
World War II (1939–45) 1; prisoners-of-war 69, 73; propaganda posters 71; role of sport 69
Worrell, Frank 130
Wrightson, P. 59
Wylie, Mina 20–3

Young Men's Christian Association (YMCA) 41, 57, 70; Perth 58–9
Ypres 26